B
4/09

THE AMERICAN BAR ASSOCIATION

You

Your AND

Aging

Parents

Walla Walla
County Libraries

OTHER TITLES BY THE AMERICAN BAR ASSOCIATION

The American Bar Association Complete Personal Legal Guide:
The Essential Reference for Every Household

The American Bar Association Guide to Wills and Estates,
Third Edition

The American Bar Association Legal Guide for Americans Over 50

The American Bar Association Guide to Credit and Bankruptcy

The American Bar Association Guide to Marriage,
Divorce, and Families

The American Bar Association Guide to Home Renovation

The American Bar Association Guide for Women

The American Bar Association Guide to Workplace Law,
Second Edition

The American Bar Association Guide to Starting a Small Business

The American Bar Association Guide to Resolving Legal Disputes:
Inside and Outside the Courtroom

646.7
You AND
2009

YOU AND YOUR AGING PARENTS

THE AMERICAN BAR ASSOCIATION

GUIDE TO LEGAL, FINANCIAL, AND HEALTH CARE ISSUES

RANDOM HOUSE REFERENCE
NEW YORK   TORONTO   LONDON   SYDNEY   AUCKLAND

Points of view or opinions in this publication do not necessarily represent the official policies or positions of the American Bar Association.

This book is not a substitute for an attorney, nor does it attempt to answer all questions about all situations you may encounter.

Copyright © 2009 by The American Bar Association

All rights reserved. Published in the United States by Random House Reference, an imprint of The Random House Information Group, a division of Random House, Inc., New York, and simultaneously in Canada by Random House of Canada Limited, Toronto.

RANDOM HOUSE is a registered trademark of Random House, Inc.

Please address inquiries about electronic licensing of any products for use on a network, in software, or on CD-ROM to the Subsidiary Rights Department, Random House Information Group, fax 212–572–6003.

This book is available at special discounts for bulk purchases for sales promotions or premiums. Special editions, including personalized covers, excerpts of existing books, and corporate imprints, can be created in large quantities for special needs. For more information, write to Random House, Inc., Special Markets/Premium Sales, 1745 Broadway, MD 6–2, New York, NY 10019 or e-mail specialmarkets@randomhouse.com.

Visit the Random House Reference Web site: www.randomhouse.com

Printed in the United States of America

10   9   8   7   6   5   4   3   2   1

Library of Congress Cataloging in Publication Data
You and your aging parents : guide to legal, financial, and health care issues / American Bar Association.
        p.   cm.
Includes index.
ISBN 978-0-375-72301-8
1. Older people—Legal status, laws, etc.—United States.
I. American Bar Association.
KF390.A4Y675 2009
646.7'9—dc22   2008050964

First Edition

AMERICAN BAR ASSOCIATION

Henry F. White Jr.
Executive Director

Sarina A. Butler
Associate Executive Director, Communications Group

Mabel C. McKinney-Browning
Director, Division for Public Education

Catherine Hawke
Series Editor

Marguerite Angelari, J.D.
Marcia Spira, Ph.D
Authors

REVIEWERS

MEMBERS OF THE ABA SENIOR LAWYERS DIVISION

Margadette Demet
Milwaukee, Wisconsin

Bryan Liang
San Diego, CA

Allan Hikoyeda
San Jose, CA

Stephen Maskaleris
Florham Park, NJ

John Huffaker
Berwyn, PA

Carolyn L. Rosenblatt, R.N.
San Rafael, CA

Michael A. Kirtland
Colorado Springs, CO

Catherine Seal
Colorado Springs, CO

STANDING COMMITTEE ON PUBLIC EDUCATION

Chair
Dwight L. Smith
Tulsa, OK

Chair, Law Day
Allan J. Tanenbaum
Atlanta, GA

Board of Governor's Liaison
Paulette Brown
Short Hills, NJ

Cory M. Amron
Washington, DC

William E. Brown
Gordonsville, VA

Karen Marie B. Edwards
Memphis, TN

Gary T. Johnson
Chicago, IL

Allen W. Kimbrough
Phoenix, AZ

Jill S. Miller
Durham, NC

Harry Truman Moore
Paragould, AR

Marty N. Olsen
Midvale, UT

Gary Slaiman
Washington, DC

Alan S. Kopit
Cleveland, OH

William J. Woodward, Jr.
Philadelphia, PA

ADVISORY COMMISSION TO THE
STANDING COMMITTEE ON PUBLIC EDUCATION

Lee Arbetman
Silver Spring, MD

AnnMaura Connolly
Washington, DC

Timothy Davis
Alexandria, VA

Valerie Hans
Ithaca, NY

Mary Hubbard
Birmingham, AL

Marguerite Kondracke
Alexandria, VA

Peter Levine
College Park, MD

Orlando Lucero
Albuquerque, NM

Harriet S. Mosatche, PhD
New Rochelle, NY

Robert M. Paolini
Montpelier, VT

Gayle Y. Thieman
Washougal, WA

Christopher L. Tomlins
Chicago, IL

Deborah Williamson
Frankfort, KY

Young Lawyers Division Liaison
Renata Biernat, Esq.
Chicago, IL

CONTENTS

Foreword ix
Introduction xi

1. Making the Transition 1
How and When to Become a Caregiver for Your Aging Parent

2. Care Plans 21
Developing and Implementing the Steps to Support Your Aging Parent

3. Planning for Incapacity 31
The Steps to Legal Preparedness

4. Legal Interventions 56
When There is No Power of Attorney

5. Money Matters 73
Identifying and Accessing Income and Assets

6. Health-Care Help 101
Becoming Involved in Health-Care Decisions

7. Paying For Health Care 108
Understanding Insurance, Government Benefits, and More

8. In-Home Assistance 148
Service Options

9. Supportive Housing Options 172
Assisted-Living Facilities, Nursing Homes, and More

10. Transportation 207
When Driving Becomes Dangerous

11. Protecting Your Parent 215
What You Need to Know About Elder Abuse and Neglect, Financial Exploitation, and Consumer Fraud

12. Mental Health Issues   248
Helping Your Parent Deal with a Changing Lifestyle

13. Taking Time for Yourself   259
The Physical and Emotional Impact of Caring for Your Aging Parent

APPENDIX A Where to Go for More Information   267

APPENDIX B Health-Care Advance Directive   276

FOREWORD

Executive Director Henry F. White, *American Bar Association*

As Americans live longer and the population of older Americans increases, a new area of the law called elder law is evolving. Professionals in this area focus on the unique legal needs of our aging population. We hope that this book gives you insight into this important and growing area of the law.

You and Your Aging Parents allows you to access the expertise of the ABA's nationwide network of lawyers in your own home. This book was developed with the guidance of the ABA's Standing Committee on Public Education and written with the aid of ABA members with expertise in elder law. ABA members have reviewed draft chapters, providing clarifications and suggesting additional topics that, based on their experience, would be helpful to you, and polished the manuscript to ensure that every reader will be able to understand these legal concepts. These reviewers brought to this project their experience and hands-on knowledge of these issues; they include professors of law and specialists in the legal problems of the elderly. Thanks to all of the volunteers who worked on this book, you can be sure that the information within is even-handed, current, and reader-friendly.

The American Bar Association is the nation's premier source of legal information. With over 400,000 members, the work of the ABA touches every specialty and every type of legal practice across the country. The ABA is thus uniquely positioned to deliver comprehensive, up-to-date, and unbiased legal information—not only to lawyers, but also to the general public. The ABA is the largest voluntary association in the world. Through its extensive network of legal practitioners and experts, the ABA is able to educate Americans about the legal system in general and, more specifically, about the impact of the legal system on their everyday lives. The ABA's Division for Public Education offers a variety of programs and publications that promote public understanding of the law and its rule in society, including this book.

Besides its commitment to public education, the ABA provides programs to assist lawyers and judges in their work and initiatives to improve the legal system for the public. These include promoting fast, affordable alternatives to lawsuits, such as mediation, arbitration, conciliation, and small claims courts. Through ABA support for lawyer referral programs and *pro bono* services (where lawyers donate their time), people like you have been able to find the best lawyer for their particular situation and have received quality legal help within their budgets.

Henry F. White Jr. is the executive director of the American Bar Association. He was formerly president of the Institute of International Container Lessors, the trade association for the worldwide container and chassis leasing industry, and is a retired rear admiral in the U.S. Navy.

INTRODUCTION

Dwight L. Smith, *Chair,*
ABA Standing Committee on Public Education

Today, more and more adults—often referred to as the "sandwich generation"—are faced with caring for their aging parents as well as their own children. If you are caring for an aging parent, you are likely confronting a host of hurdles and situations that no other generation of Americans has confronted in quite the same way.

You and Your Aging Parents is designed to help you and your parents prepare for the future. By outlining the steps required for adequate planning, explaining the various government and private support options, and providing tips for dealing with the unexpected, this book serves as a guide to caring for your parents at this stage in your relationship. *You and Your Aging Parents* walks you through the legal pitfalls and hurdles many families face as their parents age, including: powers of attorneys, privacy laws, health-care insurance, and competency issues, as well as the social and personal concerns that come hand-in-hand with elder law. Not only will this book explain the legal options for your family, it will also help you understand what your parents are experiencing and guide you through the conversations you will likely find necessary to have.

One of the best aspects of this area of law, from a family's perspective, is that there are options. For example, there are a number of possible answers to each of these questions:

- What health-care options are available?
- Where will my parent's income come from as he or she ages?

- How can my family best prepare for the possibility of my parent becoming incapacitated?
- What should we know about nursing homes?

How to Use This Book

We've structured this book based on the major changes to your parent's, and your, life. It's clearly organized so that you can easily find the help you need at every stage. This book is not intended to replace qualified legal advice. Rather, it should help you understand the important issues, decide when you need to seek the advice of an attorney, and, when you do, make you a more educated client. By focusing on explaining the basics of planning for incompetency or the various levels of supportive housing, this book can serve as your guide to the aging process, and, with the help of an attorney, should ensure that your family is fully prepared to face any bumps along the road.

Each chapter addresses a unique issue related to the aging process today. *You and Your Aging Parents* starts by examining the aging process and its diverse impacts on parents and adult children. Next, we review the various tools your family can use to ensure that you are fully prepared with a plan of action in case the unexpected happens; this includes care plans, powers of attorney, living wills, health-care surrogacy laws, and guardianships. The next chapters deal with the two most pressing issues for most aging Americans: money and health care. These discussions are further enriched by looking at the more day-to-day concerns for families, including in-home assistance, alternative housing options, and transportation. Lastly, we turn to some important topics that are often ignored: elder abuse, your parents' mental health, and your own personal stress and mental health issues.

Finally, *You and Your Aging Parents* concludes with a variety of appendices that are intended to provide you with the resources and examples needed for you to effectively implement these tools.

Written With You in Mind

We've made a special effort to make this book practical by using situations and problems you are likely to encounter. Each chapter is laid out clearly, using questions and answers to address issues similar to those that you may actually be facing. Within each chapter, special sidebars alert you to important points. These include practical tips; clear, plain-English definitions of important terms; additional information resources; and warnings about pitfalls. Each chapter concludes with a "Remember This" section highlighting the most important points that chapter has covered.

With this book, you and your family will be able to make informed decisions about a wide range of problems and opportunities. Armed with the knowledge and insight provided in the following pages, you can be confident that the decisions you make will be in your parents' and your best interest.

Dwight L. Smith is chair of the ABA's Standing Committee on Public Education and is an attorney in private practice in Tulsa, Oklahoma. His practice focuses on the areas of general business, commercial litigation, dispute resolution, banking, and probate.

CHAPTER 1

Making the Transition

*How and When to
Become a Caregiver
for Your Aging Parent*

*Rich has noticed that things aren't the same with his mom any-
more: she has started to forget his kids' names and is missing due
dates for the utility bills. Rich's father passed away seven years
ago and he is worried about his mom living alone. What if she
continues to miss payments and loses the house? At what point
can he, or should he, step in and help her?*

In a perfect world, each of us would retain our full mental capacity as we age. No one would ever have to face the frightening realities associated with the loss of intellectual or cognitive
function. However, for many, such a perfect world is far from reality. In all likelihood, as your parent ages, he or she will experience some physical or mental changes that will force your role,
and that of your family, to change. Other parts of this book will explore in detail the legal and planning tools that can be used to address cognitive decline in your parents. In this chapter, we discuss
when it is time to assess your role, and how to talk to your parent
about needed changes and steps—both when your parent still has
cognitive ability, and if his or her abilities have started to decline.

UNDERSTANDING AGING

**Q. My parents are starting to show signs of cognitive
decline, and their doctor has said that some sort
of assessment may be helpful. Exactly what do
these assessments entail?**

A. Assessments of your parents' mental capacity and ability can cover any number of skills and factors. A common type of assessment includes an evaluation of your parent's ability to perform routine daily activities. These skills, referred to as the **activities of daily living (ADLs),** include dressing, bathing, eating, toileting, and walking. It may also be helpful to assess your parent's ability to perform other more complex activities. Such activities, called **instrumental activities of daily living (IADLs),** can include:

- using a telephone;
- balancing a checkbook or securing money orders to pay bills;
- keeping track of money and assets;
- preparing food;
- cleaning house;
- obtaining transportation such as by driving, calling a taxi, or using a bus independently; and
- accurately using medication.

Assessments of the activities of daily living can be completed by geriatric case management services that are often provided by private or public agencies. Check your local department on aging website to determine the availability of such services.

If your parent requires help with one or more activities of daily living, additional assessments may be recommended and supportive services such as cleaning services, meal services, and medicine management may be required in order to allow your parent to live independently. Other assessment tools are used to evaluate mental capacity. A common test that may be given to your parent is the Folstein Mini Mental State Examination. This thirty-point short exam screens for problems with cognitive function.

Q. What are signs that my parent is experiencing a change in mental capacity?

A. Cognitive decline involves deterioration of memory and slowing of other mental functions. Your parent may struggle with language skills, learning and memory, thinking clearly, or paying attention. It may be harder for your parent to remember a word or telephone number, or where he or she has put the keys. Occasional and mild forgetfulness is experienced by almost everyone. It is sometimes referred to as absent-mindedness, "brain burps," or senior moments. Although these experiences may initially be annoying and frustrating, they are not serious, nor do they necessarily signal the presence of dementia. However, these signs should, at the very least, put you on alert for other signs or signals.

Q. Are there specific signs that may indicate a need to assess my parent's mental capacity?

A. Yes. Although your parent's mental capacity will change over time, there are certain signs that indicate something could be going on. These include:

- impairment of daily life activities;
- persistent and consistent short-term memory loss;
- repeated and increasingly frequent losing of items;
- becoming disoriented and confused (for example, not being able to find the way home from the store);
- missing appointments;
- poor concentration and attention to details;
- losing the ability for abstract thought;
- trouble with daily activities, including cooking, driving, paying bills, and balancing a checking account;
- difficulty comprehending stories, including media broadcasts;
- difficulty turning attention from one task to another;
- difficulty with language and reasoning;
- inability to follow simple instructions;
- compensating for difficulty with language by finding alternatives to common words and substituting empty phrases (for example, "that thing");
- confusing one person with another;
- exhibiting inappropriate behavior;
- showing impulsive behavior; or
- loss of the "social filter" (for example, making socially inappropriate or thoughtless comments).

If your parent displays these symptoms, consider consulting a physician. By no means should you try to diagnose your parent on your own. Many conditions share common symptoms, and accurate assessment is important for treatment. A physician may verify these symptoms by taking a history from you or a close relative of the observed changes in your parent. In addition, the physician will also need to examine your parent to assess his or her physical and mental status.

Q. I think my mom's mental capacity is declining, but she doesn't always show it. Is this normal?

A. It can be. Healthy older adults often find methods to compensate for behavior such as slips in memory. However, for some adults, problems with memory go beyond "normal." If more serious deficits occur, compensatory methods may not work to cover the loss. These coping mechanisms, combined with a family's failure to talk about changing cognitive abilities, can result in such decline becoming a "family secret" until the symptoms become impossible to ignore. At the early stages of decline, patients may be well aware of their deficiencies. Family members often respond initially by accepting the noticed forgetfulness as random blips in memory that are insignificant. Often, family members have difficulty acknowledging an older person's confusion and lack of recognition. Family members may mistakenly personalize the older person's lack of responsiveness, especially lapses in recognition. It can be very hurtful when a loved one does not recognize you, and your initial reaction may be simply to ignore such changes.

Additional strain between family members can be caused by differing views of the parent's decline. For example, family members often argue with one another as to the extent of a parent's impairment. Some feel a great sense of obligation, and may make decisions for their parents too quickly.

Q. My mom slipped and fell on the bathroom floor last month and broke her hip. Does this indicate a need to begin to assess her ability to care for herself?

A. Physical injury can cause disorientation and other changes in your parent's mental status. But don't panic: these changes may not be permanent. Once your mom's injuries begin to heal, she may resume a higher level of function than she experienced during her hospitalization or treatment.

The hip fracture itself may trigger further evaluation by members of her medical team. Due to her injuries, your mom may require time in a rehabilitation unit and, during this time, her functional abilities will naturally be assessed.

If her fall is part of a pattern of increasing accidents or other physical problems, this may be an indicator that the time has come to assess her physical and mental abilities. At the very least, you can use the accident as a reason to begin having these discussions and as justification to begin planning.

Q. What are some other physical changes in my parent that may indicate a need to assess his or her need for assistance?

A. If your parent has started to have more difficulty moving about, or has any other physical infirmities that impair his or her ability to provide self-care, these may be signs that it is time to assess whether he or she needs assistance. Some conditions such as severe arthritis, macular degeneration, or diabetes may create specific needs for help. If your parent has been asking for more help with daily activities, or is complaining more about being unable to do certain things, these should all be signs that an assessment may be appropriate.

UNDERSTANDING YOUR NEW ROLE

Q. If my parent shows a decline in mental capacity, what are my responsibilities?

A. The role of the son or daughter as caregiver changes over time and will depend on you, your circumstances, your parents, and their abilities. For example, if you have historically lived close to your aging parent and then move across the country, your role will obviously change.

Additionally, the caregiving role often evolves over time. Some caregivers take on more and more responsibilities, without realizing how involved they have become. For others, caregiving comes in a time of crisis, unplanned and unexpected. Overnight, a sudden illness can turn an independent older person into someone who needs daily assistance. You must be alert to changes in your role. At first the process may be seamless, allowing you to maintain the relationship as it has always been. However, if you don't recognize the changing nature of your role as a caregiver, stress can increase. Problems may ensue for you, your parent, and your relationship if either of you fails to acknowledge these changes.

Q. How will my role change if one of my parents has started to decline, but the other is still fully functioning?

A. There are several possible scenarios, each raising its own unique concerns. The changes to your relationship and role will depend on your family's dynamics before the decline. For instance, if your more functional parent was very dependent on your declining parent for daily tasks such as bill paying or bank account management, he or she may try to enlist you as a substitute for the declining spouse. In some cases the more functional parent may try to exclude you in order to demonstrate his or her independence and control. He or she may try to engage another member of the family or a friend to "fill in" for your declining parent.

In any case, you must try to understand that there will likely be some shifting of responsibilities and roles. These transitions are normal and require a lot of reflection, patience, and understanding of what is different and what is the same within the family. If the rebalancing feels uncomfortable, don't be afraid to consult a clinical social worker or other mental health professional to review the situation and gain some perspective.

Q. Am I legally responsible for providing personal care to my eighty-four-year-old father, such as helping him clean his house, go grocery shopping, or do his laundry?

A. Depending on the law in your state, you may be legally responsible for caring for your father or for procuring care for him if any of the following apply:

- you are your father's court-appointed guardian;
- you are your father's agent under a power of attorney, and have acted as such on his behalf;
- your state has a filial responsibility law and enforces it; or
- you are your father's caregiver and your state's elder abuse and neglect statute provides that anyone providing care to an elderly person (whether by contract or agreement) can be held liable for neglect if the elderly person becomes dependent on that care and the caregiver ceases to provide or provides inadequate care.

Q. If I have been appointed by a court to act on behalf of my father (for example, if I am the guardian of his estate or his agent under a power of attorney for property), am I required to use my own funds to pay for his care?

A. No. Guardians of estates and agents under powers of attorney for property are not required to use their *own* funds to care for their parents (these legal relationships are discussed further in chapters 3 and 4). Rather, such individuals must ensure that the *parents'* funds are used to provide for the parents' care.

Note that performing this role requires that due care be exercised. If a guardian or agent acts negligently or misuses a parent's funds, a court can find him or her liable and require reimbursement to the parent's estate. Chapter 11 provides more information on how to protect yourself should you have financial responsibility for your parents.

Q. My dad is thinking about moving into an expensive nursing home. I am really worried about having to pay for his housing. Are there any circumstances under which I could be required to pay for my parents' care out of my own funds?

A. There are two such circumstances. The first involves a filial responsibility law. The second involves a Medicaid estate recovery program and/or fraudulent conveyance laws. Filial responsibility laws are discussed in the next section, and Medicaid recovery programs and fraudulent conveyance laws are discussed in chapter 7.

Filial Responsibility Laws

Q. What are filial responsibility laws?

A. Filial responsibility laws (also called **family responsibility laws**) are state laws that require adult children to pay for their parents' care in certain circumstances. This financial obligation can extend to both the parents' present care needs as well as to expenses for past care. At least half of the states have such laws.

Q. Are these laws actually enforced and, if so, by whom?

A. While these laws have been on the books for many years, historically they have rarely been enforced. Depending on state law, filial responsibility laws may be enforced by the elderly person himself or by the state when an elderly person becomes a **public charge.** This usually means that the person has become dependent on a state need-based program such as Medicaid. In the past few years, a few states have begun enforcing filial responsibility laws; check with an attorney in your state if you have any questions about your responsibilities under the law.

▶ **ONCE YOU START, DON'T STOP**

The general rule is that, regardless of whether you have a legal responsibility to provide care in the first place, once you start caring for your parent if your parent becomes dependent on your help, then you may not be able to stop without first making alternative arrangements for care. Consequently, it is important to take stock of your other long-term obligations and responsibilities before volunteering to help care for your parents. If you don't think you will be able to help in the future, you should look into other options and services.

Talking to Your Parents

Q. Everything my mom and I have read about the aging process mentions the importance of prior planning. Why is this so important?

A. Without proper planning, you may not be able to access information about your mother or make decisions on her behalf should she no longer be capable of making or communicating such decisions on her own. Planning can help your mother decide how she wishes to be cared for and how she will fund that care, and will give her the peace of mind that comes with knowing her wishes and desires will be carried out. These are very personal decisions that require an understanding of both the law and your mother's values. For instance, your mother may want to stay in her home as long as possible, regardless of the expense. She also may assume that her children will be able to assist her as she herself assisted her aging parents. Or, on the contrary, your mother's primary concern may be that she not burden her children and that they inherit as much of her nest egg as possible. However, without planning, there is a chance you may not ever know your mother's desires.

When planning for incapacity, a frequently used tool is the **durable power of attorney** (discussed in chapter 3). Most states recognize two kinds of powers of attorney: the **power of attorney for health care** and the **power of attorney for property.** By drafting these documents while she still has the capacity to make decisions, your mother can ensure that a loved one will be authorized to help her. Other tools that can help plan for incapacity include living wills and various types of trusts, all of which are discussed in more detail in later chapters.

Q. What is the best way to raise this topic with my aging parents?

A. It's best if you bring up the topic while your parents are still able to participate in the decision making. Often the following events can serve as jumping-off points for such conversations:
- the illness or death of a relative or neighbor;
- one of your parents' friends moving to an alternative living situation;
- a transition in your own life that prompts discussion about changes;
- the recent or impending retirement of one or both parents;
- the changing of your parents' neighborhood as old friends leave and younger families arrive (in which case you may want to discuss your parents' wishes to stay or move);
- changes in your parents' health status, which may prompt conversations about powers of attorney and decisions for care; or
- the need to make decisions about health insurance, including Medicare coverage and supplemental coverage, which may present the opportunity to discuss more difficult types of decisions.

Q. What topics do I need to discuss with my parents?

A. All of your concerns are important. Most conversations include issues of living options, driving, caregiving, and health. Additional concerns may be related to finances and housing. You

▶ **PLANNING BEFORE A CRISIS**

Crisis-driven decisions often exclude your parent's input. Even when your parent would ordinarily have been able to participate in decision making, plans may be hurriedly made during a crisis that prove unacceptable to your parent—for example, caregivers whom your parents do not like may be hired at the last minute. Whenever possible, let your parent meet and interview potential service people. And whenever possible, plan before any crisis arises.

may also have concerns about your role and responsibilities. You need to determine your parents' expectations of you, and what kind of help you can or cannot provide. Consider talking to your parents about the need to allow service providers into their home when necessary.

If your parent is already having some difficulty, suggest possible solutions. For example, if you are concerned about your parent's balance and the possibility of falls, you might suggest hiring an occupational therapist. Your parent may be able to continue to live independently at home with a few accommodations, such as grab bars. Below we present tips for raising topics that are commonly discussed in this context.

Living Options

If you need to have a conversation with your parent about living options, first establish the goals that are important to your parent in his or her living situation. Ask your parent where he or she sees him or herself in the next several years. You can then use these goals as a starting point for your discussion, and work to determine the pros and cons of satisfying your parents' wishes.

You can also help your parent reflect on the personal consequences of staying at home or moving. This may be easier after you have established what is most important to him or her. In many families, independence, safety, and financial security are the three most important factors in considering where to live. For instance, your parent may be surprised to learn that his or her independence might be increased by moving to a place that provides transportation and meal services.

Don't forget to talk about your own sense of comfort and well-being regarding your parent's living situation. Once the issues are out on the table, options can be discussed that might serve everyone's stated needs. Housing options are discussed further in chapter 9.

Driving

If your parent drives, you may want to have a general discussion about when an individual should give up driving. Many older adults are reluctant to give up driving and the independence it affords them. Again, conversations are more productive when goals are established at the beginning. For example, your goal might be to find ways to maintain your parent's independence. If that is the case, you will want to focus the conversation on alternatives to driving rather than on reasons why your parent must stop driving. (See chapter 10 for more information on driving-related issues.)

Health Care, Advance Directives, and End-of-Life Issues

It is essential that you discuss the idea of advance directives (see chapters 3 and 4 for details about how these legal tools work), because it is important to know who will make medical decisions for your parents when they cannot make such decisions for themselves. You must learn what your parents' wishes will be for medical treatment, as well as for interventions at the end of life. It is also important to talk about the kind of care they may need or want in their home.

Reading examples of powers of attorney and living wills that are valid in your parents' state will help you prepare them for the decisions they will need to make. Examples of the decisions your parents must make include:

- naming a health-care agent;
- selecting the kind of medical treatment they want or don't want;
- discussing what steps to take regarding life support;
- deciding what they want in terms of comfort care (or palliative care); and
- discussing how and where (i.e., at home vs. residential hospice) they wish to be treated in the event of coma or terminal illness.

Legal

It is never too early to discuss the importance of consulting an elder law attorney for planning purposes. Perhaps your parent has never heard the term "elder law attorney." If this is the case, it may help to explain that an elder law attorney helps people use all available legal tools to ensure that their lifestyle choices are honored as they age. Talking about the legal issues associated with aging can also be done in the same context you would discuss estate planning with your parent (though your family should be aware that, for legal purposes, there is a difference between an elder law attorney and an estate planning attorney).

Money Matters

If there comes a time when your parent's mental capacity declines to a point at which they need your help, you will need to be familiar with their sources of income, their assets, and any and all legal documents that have been drafted on their behalf.

A loss of mental capacity can occur suddenly, as in the case of a stroke. For this reason, it is important that you know the location of all documents pertaining to your parents' finances. You may want to frame any discussions with your parents about money and finances in these terms: that you are trying to gather the necessary information so you can step in seamlessly when (and if) you are needed. These issues are discussed further in chapter 5.

Q. Who should be present at these conversations?

A. This depends on your family dynamics and on the personality, marital status, and health of your parent. If possible, talk with your siblings or other family members before talking with your parent. Give them an opportunity to share any concerns regarding your parent's situation. This will preclude conflicts over the outcome of your discussions with your parent. If questions arise regarding your parent's care, you also may want to meet with an elder law attorney, or geriatric social worker or geriatrician (a doctor who specializes in the needs of older adults) beforehand. These professionals can be helpful both during pre-conversation preparations and, depending on the topics you plan to address, even during your actual conversations with your parents. They can provide a good foundation of information, and help steer you toward the topics you need to discuss.

▶ **ONLINE PLANNING RESOURCES**

There are many resources online to help you and your parents prepare for the aging process. Having a resource to guide your conversations can be helpful, especially if you or your parent finds these discussions uncomfortable. AARP provides an excellent guide for many discussion ideas and additional resources on their website (www.aarp.org).

Your Parent's Reactions

Q. Is my parent likely to resist these discussions?

A. You may be surprised to learn that your parent may actually be relieved to have these conversations. In many families, it turns out that such conversations are actually much harder for the adult children than for the parents. Sometimes older people are reluctant to talk about their fears and concerns simply because they are worried about burdening their children, or because they fear their children will do something they don't want. By initiating the discussion, you may be providing an outlet that your parents have sought for some time.

Of course, it is important to recognize that your parents may not want to have discussions about aging. This may be particularly true if your parents have had negative experiences with aging, perhaps with their own parents or with other relatives.

Q. My parent refuses to talk to me about anything related to aging. What creates such barriers?

A. Barriers to communication may arise due to a number of factors. Most often, a parent's reluctance to discuss these issues is the result of miscommunication. For a successful discussion to take place, your parent must be—and must feel like—the principle decision maker. Be aware that other parties to these discussions may have different goals than you do, and may create other barriers to effective communication with your parent. For example, well-intentioned family members with different points of view may try to influence you or your parent. In addition, sometimes you (or even a physician or social service agency) may suggest services that your parent does not need or want, which may create further barriers to communication.

Q. How can I avoid these barriers?

A. Don't wait for a crisis before dealing with your parent's needs or helping them make decisions about advance directives.

The more you can learn about your parent's beliefs and wishes before a crisis, the easier your conversations with him or her will be. One easy way to increase the chances of a successful conversation is to do your homework. Make sure you understand your parent's wishes, needs, and the options available in your parent's hometown. If you are uncertain, the resulting conversation may prove difficult and unfocused. You may need to contact a professional to assess your parent's needs, or your local area agency on aging (AAA) to find out what local assessment programs and services are available. Whenever possible, your parents should be given choices and asked to assess their own needs and desires.

Sometimes, despite your best efforts, conversations may not go as planned. When this happens, don't blame yourself. Try again later.

Q. Should I conduct any follow-up after the conversation ends?

A. Yes. Remember that, while your parents' wishes may remain stable, their needs will inevitably change. Be willing to revisit old topics and any forms or care agreements that your parents have previously completed. Most important, listen carefully to what your parents tell you. For as long as possible, your parent should be the primary decision maker regarding his or her own care. Let your parents know that they have your support, and that you can work together now and in the future.

Q. What if my parent just doesn't want to talk about it?

A. This is certainly your parent's prerogative. Ask him or her if it would be easier to talk to someone other than you. If the answer is yes, suggest that your parent instead talk to a social worker or even to another family member or friend who has been through the process. In the end, as long as your parent still has the capacity to make his or her own decisions, choosing not to discuss these issues is completely within his or her rights. Sometimes dropping the subject and returning to it at another time is helpful. Recognize that part of your goal is to ensure that your parents have the opportunity to make decisions about their future while they still can. Ultimately, if they refuse that opportunity, you must respect that decision.

Q. Is there anything I can do to prepare for my parents' possible decline in mental capacity, even if my parent refuses to talk to me about these issues?

A. Yes. You can familiarize yourself with the options for care in your parents' community. You can also familiarize yourself with the laws governing surrogate decision making in your state. These laws are discussed further in chapters 3 and 4.

FIRST STEPS AND CONVERSATIONS WHEN YOUR PARENTS SHOW SIGNS OF COGNITIVE DECLINE

Q. My mom has started to show signs of cognitive decline; for example, she is not always able to carry on conversations with me. How should I talk to her about aging and planning?

A. As noted earlier, conversations about advance planning are sometimes more difficult for the adult children than for the parent, and the situation can be even more difficult if your parent has already begun to show signs of decline. However, in the early stages of cognitive decline, it is more than likely that your parent has the capacity to participate in these conversations. Capacity for decision making is rarely all or nothing, and some days may be are better than others. You should try to find a good day and a good time of day to have the conversation. Watch your parent, and talk to his or her caregivers in order to determine which day may be best.

Capacity can also be situational. Thus, your parent may be more willing and able to participate in the conversation if he or she is in a comfortable and familiar place.

Often the best way to begin these conversations is to tell your parent you have been considering the issue of advance directives for yourself. Ask if he or she has thought about the same issues, or knows anything about advance directives. Make it a personal discussion that includes some opportunities for both of you to learn about the options together. Perhaps be prepared with some educational materials, or even a sample of the advance directives used in your parent's state. In addition, you may want to offer the opportunity to talk to an elder law attorney about the details of these documents.

Q. How much do I need to tell my parent? Can I just make decisions? I feel like that will be so much easier on everyone.

A. Simple answer: NO! This is your parent's life and, although he or she is aging, you cannot simply step in and start making decisions for your parent and telling him or her how to live.

For as long as possible, your parent must play the leadership role when it comes to making decisions or planning. As the adult child, your role is not to step in whenever you feel like your parent needs your help. Instead, alert your parent about what to watch for, and help your parent determine when and from whom to seek help. Your parent should feel empowered to ask for help when:

- his or her health profile changes;
- he or she needs help with daily tasks;
- financial resources change;
- he or she becomes confused and unable to care for him or herself;
- his or her decision making is questionable;
- legal issues arise;

- there is conflict over his or her care;
- he or she is alone most of the time;
- his or her social network diminishes;
- his or her residence is no longer adequate for his or her needs;
- he or she is depressed or anxious; or
- he or she becomes unreasonably suspicious of mistreatment by others.

Q. What is the first step my family should take after my mom has started to show signs of cognitive decline?

A. Don't panic. The best first step is to contact a doctor, prefer ably a geriatrician, and have a medical evaluation to make sure the symptoms are not due to the presence of other medical is sues. It is not imperative that you contact a geriatric case man ager immediately. However, when further home services or a change of residence seems necessary, it will be useful to know the resources that are available. If your parent has started to show signs of cognitive decline but is still functional, work with him or her immediately to draft any necessary advanced direc tives while he or she is still capable.

Q. Can anything be done to stop cognitive decline?

A. Early intervention is the best bet when it comes to lessening the effects of cognitive decline. Current drug treatment efforts are geared to slow or stop progression of mental diseases and de clines. However, to date, attempts to retrieve lost functions have been less successful. Early intervention is key to providing the best opportunity to create a care plan and positive drug therapy for your parent.

REMEMBER THIS

- Signs that your parent is experiencing some cognitive decline may include: disorientation and confusion, short-term memory loss, losing items, and having trouble with daily activities, such as cooking, driving, paying bills, and balancing a checking account. If these symptoms are present in your parent, consider consulting a physician. Early intervention and diagnosis can increase the chances that your parent will have a favorable response to medical involvement, and will help you understand what your parent is going through and properly plan for the coming years.

- If your parent has started to show signs of cognitive decline, a medical assessment may help identify the appropriate services and agencies that can help you and your family.

- You are likely not legally responsible for your parent's care and services, unless you have begun to provide these services and then fail to make necessary arrangements, or unless your parent's state has a filial responsibility law and is seeking payment from you under that law.

- Advance planning is incredibly important to ensure that you and your parent experience an easy transition as your parent ages. Without proper planning, you and your family may not be able to access information about your parent or make decisions on his or her behalf should your parent reach a point where he or she can no longer make or communicate such decisions.

CHAPTER 2

Care Plans

Developing and Implementing the Steps to Support Your Aging Parent

Sara lives across the country from her mom. She has gone to great lengths to help her mom, and to find qualified caregivers in her mom's city, including a homemaker, an in-home nurse, and a physical therapist. Sara thought that everything was set. But last week, her mom's neighbor called and told Sara that there were no groceries in her mom's home. Sara is in a panic at the thought of her mom being without food. Whose responsibility was this? A well-drafted care plan could have saved Sara the worry, and ensured that Sara, her mom, and her mom's caregivers were all on the same page.

As your parents age and others take on more responsibilities for their day-to-day care, it is important to make sure that everyone is on the same page and knows who is taking care of what. A care plan, if developed correctly and routinely updated, will save everyone a lot of worry and headache. This chapter will help you assess whether your family needs such a plan—and, if so, how to develop one. It also explores the special considerations that come with caring for a parent across distances, as well as the role played by **geriatric care managers**—professionals who specialize in caring for older Americans.

DETERMINING THE NEED FOR A CARE PLAN

Q. What exactly is a care plan?

A. A **care plan** is a comprehensive document outlining the areas in which your parent may need help, as well as the tasks he or she can accomplish without assistance. A care plan contains information about your parent's current health, both physical and mental. It also inventories other important information, such as his or her contact and health insurance information. A plan like this ensures that all individuals helping with your parent's care are in agreement about what needs (and possible solutions) have been identified. If you are working with a geriatric care manager, this is the individual who will actually draft the document; otherwise, it may be a more informal document drafted by you or another loved one.

Q. How do I know if my parent would benefit from a plan?

A. First of all, listen to your parent. Has he or she started to ask for more help, or begun complaining about not being able to complete daily chores? Has your parent recently suffered a health crisis or a change in mental status? If your parent is no longer able to manage daily tasks, it is likely time to develop a plan for his or her care.

A thorough assessment by professionals should be conducted to determine the need for any such assistance. This assessment should evaluate your parent's physical, mental, psychological, social, and health status.

Q. What does such an assessment entail?

A. At the very least, it should evaluate your parent's ability to perform the activities of daily living, and the adequacy (including safety) of his or her living arrangements and social supports. Usually such an assessment will also include a preliminary evaluation of your parent's mental status, cognitive function, and ability to make decisions.

Any assessment should also take into account your parent's lifestyle and routines. What have his or her daily routines been like? What would enable your parent to continue these routines? Disruptions to your parent's routines may cause additional stress, so it is important to understand the schedule your parent likes to keep, and to maintain it as much as possible.

Q. Who is the best person to conduct such an assessment?

A. A team of professionals is best qualified to complete an assessment. This team should include:

- geriatricians (physicians who specialize in the issues of older adults);
- geropsychologists (psychologists who specialize in the issues of older adults);
- clinical social workers;
- physical, occupational, and speech therapists;
- dieticians; and
- geriatric nurse practitioners.

Appendix A includes contact information for various agencies and organizations that can help you identify professionals who are qualified and available in your parent's area. Not all of these potential team members are required for every assessment, but the services of each should be available to the person coordinating the assessment.

The result of the assessment will likely be a geriatric care plan. This plan will provide a current evaluation and recommendation for services.

Q. My mom has been showing some signs of confusion. For instance, when I last visited, she had food in the cabinet that should have been refrigerated. Also, she was very anxious about paying a bill for some plumbing work, even though the invoice clearly indicated that the bill had been paid a long time ago. Should we develop a care plan for her?

A. Yes. If your parent's ability to make reasonable decisions seems to be changing, it is time for an assessment and a care plan. If your parent is engaging in behaviors that carry a high risk of harm, immediate help is likely needed. Such help may range from supportive services in one specific area of daily life to a more comprehensive geriatric care plan providing for round-the-clock support.

Q. What role will my parent play in developing a care plan?

A. At one end of the help spectrum, your parent may be able to choose what kinds of services he or she requires. At the other end of the spectrum, you may need to act pursuant to a power of attorney or petition for guardianship in order to make decisions on your parent's behalf. If your parent has begun to require your help in making decisions and accessing services, and if he or she has not yet drafted powers of attorney but can still articulate whom he or she would like to serve as an agent, your parent should *immediately* draft a power of attorney appointing a surrogate decision maker (an agent) before there is any further decline. Having your parent appoint surrogate decision makers is an important part of developing and implementing a care plan. Chapters 3 and 4 describe the legal options that are available when appointing such decision makers.

Q. How do we find the service providers my parent needs?

A. A variety of agencies and service providers can help your parent with everything from laundry and cooking meals to managing medications and home health services. Chapter 8 outlines in detail some of the more common services that are available.

▶ **COMPETENCE VS. CAPACITY**

It is important to recognize that competence and capacity are not the same thing. **Competence** is a legal concept, and is based on a judicial determination. **Capacity** is a medical and social concept, and involves the ability to understand information and circumstances and make decisions based on informed consent. A decision that an elderly person lacks capacity should be based on an assessment from multiple professionals who work with older adults.

In addition, your local agency on aging can help you identify established service providers in your area. A geriatric care manager (discussed later in this chapter) can also be a key resource in identifying the agencies appropriate for your parent.

Q. Once we have developed a care plan and identified the caregivers, how do we implement everything?

A. There are several important issues to address with those who will be caring for your parents:

- **Make sure your parents are included.** Your parent should play an important part in any discussions about his or her care plans. Make sure that any plan reflects your parent's perceptions and wishes: What kind of help does your parent want? What kind of help will he or she accept? With whom will your parent be most comfortable?
- **Be realistic when dividing the labor.** Be clear and realistic about who will perform which caregiving tasks. When deciding how tasks will be divided, it is important to take into consideration the desires and abilities of each caregiver. For instance, your sister might be willing to contribute money toward hiring a housekeeper to clean your parents' home, but may not want to provide such help herself. Another person might currently be willing to drive your parent to every doctor's appointment, but everyone should recognize that this person may not always remain available for this task.

  It can be useful to give each person specialized tasks that match his or her skills and abilities. For example, if your parent's neighbor is an accountant, it may make sense for that person to take care of your parent's bills, and for your uncle who is a doctor to accompany your parent to medical appointments.
- **Make sure everyone is on the same page.** Each person who is providing care, whether a local sibling or a hired caregiver, may have differing views of his or her responsibilities.

▶ **DON'T PROCRASTINATE!**

Many people put off planning until there is a crisis. However, this is one of the most avoidable errors you can make. Some people may just hope (and even assume) that situations will change for the better, and that planning therefore will not be needed. But caregiving situations rarely become simpler on their own or over time; most situations just get more difficult as new crises and issues emerge. The more planning you can do with your parents now, when everyone is relatively healthy and has the ability to make decisions, the better off you will be in the long run.

Therefore, it is important to make sure that everyone knows his or her own role, as well as that of the other parties. To address this, you may want to create a chart outlining each person's activities.

- **Create a process that allows for periodic assessments and updates.** Make sure that you and your parent regularly assess his or her needs and abilities. These may change over time, and it is important to modify the care plan regularly and accordingly.
- **Give validation to all of the caregivers.** It will be important for all caregivers to know their work is valued and that they are an important part of the team. If you don't provide this type of feedback, over time the caregivers may begin to criticize one another for not spending enough time on assigned tasks.

Don't be afraid to ask for help in addressing conflict among your parent's caregivers. Social workers can help facilitate discussions between siblings and other caregivers to determine needs, resources, and a workable division of labor.

CARING FOR YOUR PARENTS
LONG-DISTANCE

Q. I live and work in Ann Arbor, Michigan and my dad lives in Portland, Oregon. I can't be there every day to check on him, but he is starting to need daily care and support. How can I provide care long-distance?

A. Caring for a parent long-distance is a complex matter. To deal with the practical concerns involved, you must develop good communication with people who live close to your parent, be they relatives, family friends, or hired caregivers. It is important that you and your parent stay in touch with someone you both trust and with whom you are both comfortable. If you are not comfortable with the role of long-distance caregiver, it is essential that you let your parent know. For many families, the best solution may be to hire a geriatric care agency. (These agencies are discussed in further detail later in this chapter.)

You may have to accept that the people who are geographically closest to your parent may not carry out plans exactly as you would if you were there yourself. This can sometimes result in feelings of guilt and even resentment toward the person who is helping your parent on a daily basis. Good planning and open, regular communication between all involved parties can alleviate some of this tension. Try to bring all interested parties— including your siblings, other family members, and any geriatric care providers—into any planning discussions.

Q. What if there are problems with my parent's caregivers?

A. If you live long-distance, even small issues like personality conflicts and scheduling problems can cause great distress to you and your parent. Again, open communication can help alleviate these concerns.

▶ **WELLNESS CHECKS**

If you live far away from your parent and haven't yet had the chance to establish a workable care plan, look into local agencies that offer "wellness checks." During wellness checks, agency staff members visit older community members, especially during times of severe weather such as a heat wave or blizzard. This type of care may provide you with much-needed peace of mind. Your parent will likely have to register for such a program. Check with your parent's local area agency on aging for more information about available services.

Most qualified geriatric care agencies will have backup plans in case personality or scheduling problems render the original caregiver unacceptable or unavailable. Try to identify a contact at the agency who can be reached on a twenty-four-hour basis. Additionally, having your parent participate in the selection of the caregiver and the services to be provided can help to avoid problems in advance. Issues of abuse and neglect are discussed in more detail in chapter 11.

GERIATRIC CARE MANAGERS

Q. What is a geriatric care manager?

A. A **geriatric care manager** is a specialist with training in gerontology, psychology, social work, or other issues related to aging. These people have specialized expertise in issues affecting older adults. They coordinate assessments and services for their clients, and often suggest appropriate programs and services. Geriatric care managers are also frequently employed when there is a family conflict or when family members have difficulty making tough decisions.

Geriatric care managers can help you address any mental health or social needs your parent may have. The geriatric care manager can also act as a liaison between you and other professionals or service providers, including:

- attorneys;
- social workers;
- hospital personnel;
- nursing home administrators;
- residential facilities; and
- home health-care agencies.

Geriatric care managers can be especially helpful if you live far away from your parent.

Q. My dad doesn't need someone to help with everything. Can a geriatric care manager help him with just one aspect of daily life, but not others?

A. Yes. The care provided by a geriatric care manager can be limited to the one aspect of care for which you and your parent need assistance or advice. For instance, you may enlist the help of a geriatric care manager if your parent needs to change housing due to a health crisis, current inadequate housing, a mental health concern, or money management problems. A geriatric care manager may also help with appointments, interviews, or paperwork—in short, anything in your parent's life that he or she is unable to accomplish alone. This type of support may help your parent to live independently in his or her own home, and to retain decision-making abilities without the appointment of a guardian or agent.

Q. How will we pay for a geriatric care manager?

A. Geriatric care managers are most often paid with private funds. Each manager sets his or her own fees, depending on the services provided, and some may have a sliding scale of fees that depends on ability to pay. Generally, services provided by a geriatric care manager are not reimbursed by insurance, Medicare, or Medicaid. However, long-term-care insurance likely will cover these services, and some states offer programs that provide geriatric care assessments on a sliding-fee scale or for no fee at all. If your parent is on a fixed income and you think he or she needs such an assessment, check with your local area agency on aging to learn what is available in his or her community.

Some health insurance companies are starting to subsidize the services provided by geriatric care managers. Check with your parent's insurer to learn whether such services are covered.

Q. How can I find a geriatric care manager?

A. Contact your local area agency on aging (call 1–800–677–1116 to find the AAA in your area). Your local AAA may help you locate low-cost or no-cost geriatric care planning through community agencies. Additionally, AARP (*www.aarp.org*; search their website for "geriatric care manager") can provide you with tips for finding a geriatric care manager who will best fit your family's needs. The National Association of Professional Geriatric Care Managers (*www.caremanager.org*) and the National Academy of Certified Care Managers (*www.naccm.net*) can also provide information on finding a professional in your parent's community.

REMEMBER THIS

- A care plan is a detailed outline of your parent's daily needs, his or her current health status, and the responsibilities of your parent's caregivers.

- An assessment of your parent by an interdisciplinary team may provide valuable help in the development of a care plan.

- If your parent still has decision-making capacity, he or she must be a part of any discussions about a care plan or caregivers.

- A geriatric care manager is a professional who can help you and your parents coordinate services, and who may be able to suggest programs and services that you may not have known about.

CHAPTER 3

Planning for Incapacity

The Steps to Legal Preparedness

Melanie has started having conversations with her parents (both aged sixty-five) about their futures. Her parents are ready and willing to start planning, but none of them knows where to start. Who can help them with these discussions? How should they proceed? What must her parents do to ensure that Melanie has access to their information if she needs it?

Planning for incapacity is an important step for any family, but for many, it can be a difficult and long process, fraught with tough questions and frightening answers. Luckily, there are a number of legal tools that can simplify the process. Whenever possible, it must be your parents who determine who will serve as their surrogate decision maker, as well as who will have specific caregiving responsibilities. This chapter examines the process of working with an attorney to plan for your parent's incapacity, the advantages and disadvantages of legal tools such as powers of attorney, and the legal concerns associated with caring for someone other than your parent.

WORKING WITH AN ATTORNEY

Q. My family has started discussions and planning for my mother's aging. Should my mother consult an attorney?

A. Consulting an attorney is strongly recommended. Ideally, the attorney will have a practice either dedicated to or concentrating in elder law. He or she *must* be licensed to practice in the state where your mother lives.

Among the topics that an elder law attorney will cover include the Medicare and Medicaid programs, private health insurance options, housing options, Social Security and private pensions, long-term-care insurance, trusts, and annuities.

In addition, an attorney will draft durable powers of attorney to ensure that a decision maker will be in place should your mother no longer be able to make her own decisions. Many people complete a power of attorney for health care without the assistance of an attorney. However, the power of attorney for property is a much more complex document, and most people require the assistance of an attorney to complete it accurately. As part of a comprehensive estate plan that may also include a will, the attorney will likely work with your mother to draft the documents needed for creating each of these relationships. These documents and tools are discussed in further detail later in this chapter and in chapter 4.

Q. What is a good way to find an elder law attorney?

A. There are many ways to find a reliable lawyer. One of the best is to ask for recommendations from a trusted friend, relative, or business associate. However, be aware that each family's situation is different, and that a lawyer who is right for someone else may not necessarily be right for your parent. Bar associations in most communities make referrals according to specific areas of law, and can help you find a lawyer with expertise in elder law issues. Many referral services also have competency requirements for lawyers who wish to receive referrals in a particular area of law. You can find your local bar association in the phone book's white pages, either under your community's name ("Centerville Bar Association") or under your county's name ("Cass County Bar Association"). You can also find your bar association's website through your favorite search engine, or through the ABA's website at *www.abanet.org*.

Planning for incapacity will require your parent to identify his or her values and discuss very personal issues. Your parent will want to feel comfortable enough to tell the lawyer, honestly and completely, all the facts necessary to plan for his or her future. Therefore, when selecting a lawyer, your parents shouldn't rely only on what they have heard or read about the attorney. Before hiring him or her, your parents should meet and evaluate the lawyer for themselves—only your parents can determine which lawyer is best for their situation. Your parents also may want to find an attorney who works closely with a social worker or other mental health professional. For more information on how to locate an elder law attorney, see Appendix A.

Q. If both of my parents are still alive, do they each need their own attorneys?

A. Most married couples work together with the same attorney to plan for incapacity. However, this may not be appropriate if your parents have different views about where and how they want to live. Whether your parents will need two attorneys will depend on their circumstances. If your parents have questions as to whether they should hire separate attorneys, each should consult an attorney individually to get a professional opinion on that issue.

Q. What is the difference between an elder law attorney and an estate planning attorney?

A. While elder law and estate planning attorneys use many of the same legal tools, they use them with different ends in mind. Broadly speaking, elder law attorneys help people plan for incapacity. They focus on maximizing the value of the person's income and assets to ensure that the older person will be able to live the lifestyle of their choosing. While elder law attorneys may draft wills and trusts that benefit third parties, their primary focus is on the older person's needs during his or her lifetime. Elder law attorneys are knowledgeable about the laws and practices regarding public benefits for older people in their state.

In contrast, estate planning attorneys generally focus on assisting wealthier clients with the management and disposition of assets to family and charities during their lifetime and after their death. Estate planning attorneys often focus on more complex estates with values that exceed the federal estate and gift tax exemption ($3.5 million in 2009) and state tax exemptions (which may be lower). Estate planning focuses more on what happens after death, although some aspects of estate planning will include creating trusts for use during a person's lifetime.

ADVANCE DIRECTIVES

Q. What tools or legal documents will my mother need to plan for her incapacity?

A. The specific documents needed will vary depending on your parent's circumstances and the state where your parent lives. Likely, your parent should draft a living will, a power of attorney for health care and a power of attorney for property. Of course, it can also be very useful to draft various estate planning documents, such as a will or trust, while your parent still has the capacity to do so.

Q. What is an advance directive?

A. Advance directive is a general term that refers to any statement (written or oral) of a person's wishes for the future. Living wills and do-not-resuscitate orders (DNRs) are two types of advance directives. Federal law and many states consider powers of attorney a type of advance directive. Such documents can play an important role in planning for incapacity and carrying out an individual's wishes.

Q. What is a power of attorney?

A. In general, a **power of attorney (POA)** is a document that allows one person, the **principal**, to designate another person, the **agent** (or **attorney in fact**), to obtain private information and make decisions on the principal's behalf. For instance, you might give your accountant or lawyer power of attorney to obtain documents and take certain actions on your behalf. Or you might give your child-care provider the power of attorney to make medical decisions for your child when you are not available. The agent does not actually have to be an attorney.

Q. What are "durable" powers of attorney for health care and property?

A. Historically, powers of attorney (POAs) have been used to give an agent authority to take specific acts and did not "survive" incapacity—that is, a POA was not valid if the principal no longer had decision making capacity. For example, if you were your mother's health-care POA and she lost cognitive ability, you could not step in and make a decision on her behalf. In contrast, durable POAs are designed to allow agents to act when the principal has lost decision making capacity. While most states recognize durable powers of attorney for health care and property, state law varies on the specific requirements for each. For this reason, it is not advisable to use generic forms that you find on the Internet or in books. Your local agency on aging or state department on aging can provide you with information about your state's specific requirements.

Q. What is a "statutory form" power of attorney?

A. Many states offer **statutory form powers of attorney**. In these states, a power of attorney can be created using a specific form that contains words defined in the law. The theory behind these statutory forms is that they reduce the possibility of disagreement over the meanings of particular words in the document. However, it is important to realize that, when delegating power to make property decisions, the statutory forms for POAs for property may not address the specific issues that are important to the principal. In these cases, statutory forms may actually increase the likelihood of future disagreements. Consequently, if you or a family member are considering a POA for property, it is advisable that you work with an elder law attorney who can make sure that the document is drafted in order to carry out the principal's desires.

> ### POWERS OF ATTORNEY:
> ### TERMINOLOGY AND PROCEDURE
>
> When it comes to the terminology used in powers of attorney, there are significant variations among the states. The information provided in this chapter is designed to give you a general idea of how things work in some states. Keep in mind that things may be very different in your state. What follows is a general list of what you should know before drafting a power of attorney or agreeing to serve as an agent.

Q. What powers can be covered by a power of attorney?

A. This answer depends on the type of durable POA being used.

Health-Care Power of Attorney

In general, health-care powers of attorney can be used to delegate the power to:

- review medical records;
- make medical decisions, including end-of-life treatment decisions (although many states allow an agent to make such decisions only if the document creating the POA contains specific language authorizing it);
- authorize organ donation;
- authorize an autopsy; and
- dispose of remains.

Power of Attorney for Property

Depending on state law, a power of attorney for property can be used to delegate the power to:

- buy and sell real property, personal property, and stocks and bonds;

- invest assets;
- purchase or cash out insurance and annuities;
- handle tax and legal matters;
- borrow money;
- make gifts of money and property;
- name or change beneficiaries of trusts or wills (though this power may vary by state, so if you plan to take such an action, consult with an attorney first);
- operate a business;
- delegate responsibilities and hire people to assist; and
- be compensated for services rendered under the power of attorney.

Some states require that the document specifically indicate which powers have been delegated to the agent. Therefore, if you have been named an agent under a power of attorney for property, it is best to seek the advice of an attorney to determine your exact powers over the principal's property.

Q. Who can serve as an agent under a power of attorney for health care or property?

A. An agent can be a family member, friend, neighbor, coworker—pretty much anyone the principal trusts to act on his or her behalf. Note that in order to be an agent, you must be an adult. In some states, the law specifically states that certain people—such as the treating physician or an employee of the facility where the principal lives—cannot serve as agents. It is also important to select an agent who is qualified to handle the duties given to him or her. For example, an agent who is designated to handle financial matters should have some understanding of how to balance a checkbook.

Q. I am not sure I want total responsibility for all of my parents' decisions. Is it possible to have more than one agent?

A. In some states it is possible to have co-agents. To ensure that any document appointing co-agents is legally valid, it is very important to make sure that your parent's state permits them. Even where co-agents are permitted, this approach is not recommended if there is any potential for disagreement. The co-agents will have equal decision-making power and would likely have to go to court to resolve any disagreements, which would defeat the purpose of the POA. In most states, it is possible to have one person serve as agent under a power of attorney for health care and another person serve as agent under a power of attorney for property. However, even in this type of situation, conflict is still possible. Although you and the other agent will each have your own powers, some coordination will be necessary.

Q. Should I help my parent decide who should be the agent under a POA?

A. If your parent asks you for guidance on whom to appoint, you can certainly discuss the matter with him or her. It is very important, however, not to give unsolicited advice or pressure your parent to appoint you (or someone else) as an agent, as this could be perceived as "undue influence" and result in the invalidation of the document.

You may want to provide your parent with a copy of the Values History Form, which was created by the University of New Mexico Health Sciences Center Institute for Ethics and is available online at *http://hscwebdev.unm.edu/SOM/ethics/adVdir/vhform_eng.shtml*. This tool will help your parent to articulate his or her desires for his or her medical future.

Q. My mom wants help picking an agent. What factors should we consider?

A. When both spouses are still alive, it is common for each to name the other as agent, and to name another person (such as an adult child) as successor agent. The successor agent takes over when the agent is unwilling or unable to act on behalf of the principal.

Other factors that should be considered include:

- **Geographic proximity.** For you to be your parent's agent, it is generally not required that you live in the same state. However, in order to properly care for your parent, geographic proximity is ideal. Frequent contact and close monitoring of your parent is critical, as an older person can decline rapidly. It is important to note that unless the POA contains language to the contrary, an agent usually not permitted to delegate legal duties to someone else. It is possible for an agent to hire a geriatric care manager, accountant, or financial institution to assist him or her in carrying out responsibilities. In this scenario, however, the agent may be legally responsible for any neglect or malfeasance on the part of the person or institution hired.

- **Special skills or training.** For instance, putting other factors aside, it would probably make sense for a daughter who is a doctor to serve as the health-care agent, and a daughter who is an accountant to serve as the agent for property.
- **Other commitments.** As an agent, you must be available to assist his or her parent day to day, as well as in emergency situations. If the agent has a particularly demanding job or young children, he or she may need to decline when asked to serve as your parent's agent.
- **Ability to understand the principal's values and wishes, and the ability to act according to them.** Chances are that an agent will be asked to make value-laden decisions for his or her parent. If you do not share the same values as your parent, you will need to put your own values aside and act as your parent would have wanted.

  For instance, if you are your father's agent and he does not wish to be kept alive artificially, and if he then becomes terminally ill, you may have to decide that your dad will not be placed on a ventilator. This decision could result in your dad's death. If you do not believe that you would be willing or able to make such a decision when the time comes, then you probably should not serve as your parent's agent.
- **The ability and willingness to interact with other agents.** If your mother asks you to act as a POA for health care and your brother to act as a POA for property, then you need to

be able to work together. So, for example, if you and your brother have not spoken in twenty years because of a major falling-out, it probably is not a good idea for the two of you to serve as agents.

Q. What if I disagree with my mother's choice of agent?

A. At the end of the day, it is your mom's decision, not yours. It is important to recognize that choosing an agent is a very personal and, in some cases, difficult decision. Many people never complete these important documents because they are unwilling or unable to make this decision. Children who disapprove of their parent's choice of agent should carefully consider the basis of their disapproval. If there is concrete evidence that the proposed agent is likely to neglect or financially exploit the principal, then you should speak up. Without such concerns, however, it may be best to keep your thoughts to yourself.

Q. What if my mom has started to demonstrate some cognitive decline? Do I still have to go along with her selection of an agent?

A. Even if your mom is experiencing some level of cognitive impairment, she can still make decisions about whom she wants to serve as her agent. The essential question is whether your parent understands the purpose of the appointment of the agent and the expected role the agent will play, and whether your parent drafted the document without undue influence or coercion, or while under duress. If you have questions about your parent's capacity to choose an agent, you should consult with your parent's doctor or attorney—they will be able to make a professional judgment as to your parent's ability to make such an appointment, and can help you and your parent decide upon your next steps.

Q. Years ago, my dad drafted a POA appointing his brother as agent. My dad and his brother then had a major falling-out, and they haven't spoken

in years. Now my dad wants to appoint me as his agent instead. Can a POA be modified?

A. Powers of attorney may be modified at any point, as long as the principal (in this case, your dad) has the necessary decision-making capacity. States vary as to the exact level of capacity they require for modification. In order to avoid any confusion, it is likely best for your parent to revoke the first power of attorney, then draft a new one appointing you as an agent.

Q. I found two powers of attorney for my mom. Which one dictates?

A. If two powers of attorney exist, a court will look at the precise language of the documents to determine which power to follow. In some jurisdictions, the more recent POA will control. If you are attempting to act as your parent's agent and are faced with two POA documents, talk to an attorney experienced with such issues to determine how this situation is handled in your state.

Q. Can a POA be revoked?

A. Powers of attorney can be revoked at any time. Interestingly, some states do not require that the principal have decision-making capacity in order to revoke the document. Moreover, simply stating that he or she no longer wants a particular agent—or any agent at all—may be sufficient for the principal to revoke a power of attorney. However, in order to ensure that there is no confusion, the better practice is to revoke a POA in writing.

If a POA has been revoked and a new one has not been drafted, health-care providers may turn to health-care surrogate laws, or the family may go to court to obtain guardianship (See chapter 4, "Legal Interventions: When There Is No Power of Attorney" for an explanation of health-care surrogate laws and guardianships.)

Q. I am my mother's agent under her powers of attorney. What should I consider when making decisions on her behalf?

A. Most states require agents to use **substituted judgment** when deciding how to act under a POA. This means that the agent should act as he or she believes the principal would have acted. If the state does not require substituted judgment, or if the agent does not know what the principal would have wanted, then the agent must apply the **best-interest standard**, meaning that the agent must make decisions based on what he or she believes is in the best interest of the principal. For more information on these two standards, see chapter 4, "Legal Interventions: When There is No Power of Attorney."

Q. If I am appointed as my mother's agent, will anyone monitor me? Do I need to report to anyone?

A. Agents are required to keep records and receipts of all expenditures and transactions made or undertaken on behalf of the principal. However, there is no court or government agency that automatically monitors the actions of agents under powers of attorney. It is possible for your parent to include a clause in a power of attorney for property that requires the agent to provide periodic reports to your parent or to a third party, but this is not common. In some states, the government's elder abuse agency can require the agent to provide an accounting when there has been a report of financial exploitation. Depending on what the agent has done wrong, the principal can also bring a court action against an agent who has abused a POA. If your parent no longer has the capacity to bring such an action, or has since passed away, your parent's guardian or any interested party, such as the administrator of his or her estate, can also bring such a court action.

Q. What are the penalties for violating the terms of a power of attorney for property?

A. Penalties may include removal of the agent, an order requiring the agent to repay the principal any funds lost as a result of his or her improper action, and even possible criminal prosecution.

It is important to note that an agent is also a fiduciary. A **fiduciary** is defined as a person who must act for the benefit of another person to whom he or she owes a duty of good faith, trust, confidence, and honesty. Therefore, if an agent misuses funds or acts in any other way that is either harmful to the principal or against the prior wishes of the principal, the agent is guilty of violating both the power of attorney act and state laws regulating fiduciaries, which could warrant criminal penalties.

Q. What are the penalties for violating the terms of a power of attorney for health care?

A. If a family member (or any other interested person) believes that the agent under a power of attorney for health care is violating express terms in the document or is not acting in a way the principal would have wanted (or using the best-interest standard where it applies), and if the principal lacks decision-making capacity, then the family member can petition for guardianship and ask that the power of attorney be revoked. State law may provide for additional remedies. An experienced elder law attorney will be able to outline your options under state law.

Q. What if I feel my parent is being exploited by someone else through a power of attorney? What can I do?

A. If the principal lacks decision-making capacity, any interested party can petition to have a power of attorney revoked due to misuse of funds or self-dealing. In this instance, **guardianship** (referred to in some states as **conservatorship**) must be initiated in order for you to assume some or all of the responsibilities of an agent. You can ask to have yourself appointed as guardian (or conservator), or you may nominate a third party or agency. Courts are reluctant to terminate powers of attorney because they express the principal's choice of surrogate decision maker. However, courts will remove an agent or limit his or her powers where there is evidence that the agent:

- is not acting in accordance with the terms of the document;
- is financially exploiting the principal; or
- is failing to act or is neglecting the principal.

Q. I am my mom's agent. Can I pay myself for all the work that I'm doing?

A. In some cases, yes. Look carefully at the document creating the POA for property to see whether it specifically states that you can get paid and specifies a pay rate. Then contact an attorney to advise you on the law and practice in your state. Some POAs provide only for reimbursement of expenses, so don't assume you will be paid without checking first.

Q. When does the power of attorney go into effect?

A. A power of attorney may go into effect immediately upon signing, or the document may include a **springing clause**, which means that it becomes effective upon the occurrence of some specified triggering event. Some attorneys believe that it is best for the power of attorney to go into effect immediately. This way, the principal can monitor the actions of the agent while he or she still has decision-making capacity. Any plan to appoint an agent in this manner should be implemented carefully and, in most cases, only after talking to an experienced elder law attorney. An important point to remember is that just because the agent has been given powers, such as the ability to review medical records or spend the principal's funds, the agent does not need to act on those powers if the principal retains decision-making capacity.

A POA with a springing clause will require an "extra step" before the agent can step in—that is, there must be some determination that the principal no longer has capacity. The procedures required for making this determination should be spelled out in the POA. For example, a springing clause might use language such as "when a physician states in writing that I no longer have decision-making capacity." The agent may then have to prove to banks, hospitals, and other institutions that the requirements of the springing clause have been met.

Q. My father does not remember whether he drafted any POAs. Will someone else know?

A. Unfortunately, this can be difficult to determine. A principal under a power of attorney for health care or property is not required to ask an agent whether he or she wishes to serve as agent, or to notify an agent that he or she has been so named. Most states do not require that powers of attorney be filed with any kind of state agency. Form documents for powers of attorney for both health care and property are widely available on the Internet, in bookstores, and in senior centers. While it is advisable to consult an attorney, especially with a power of attorney for property, this is not required. As long as a document has been drafted and witnessed in a manner that conforms with state law and any other specific state requirements, it is a valid legal document.

Many people draft powers of attorney for health care when they enter hospitals or nursing homes. Under the federal Patient Self-Determination Act, health-care providers and nursing homes are required to provide patients with a copy of the state's power of attorney for health documents. These documents can be completed in waiting rooms, put into medical files—and sometimes forgotten.

▶ CHECKLIST: FINDING A POWER OF ATTORNEY

Common places where you might be likely to find a forgotten POA include:

- with any attorney who provided legal services for your parents;
- with any health-care provider (e.g., a physician or hospital) where your parents received treatment;
- wherever your parents keep important documents such as the title to their home, copies of insurance policies, etc.;
- in your parents' safe-deposit box at their bank;
- with other relatives or close friends; and
- in your parent's wallet (which may contain a card indicating where a POA is located).

If you believe your father has drafted POAs, contact any doctors or attorneys with whom he has had a relationship. On the previous page, we provide a checklist of other places to look if you find yourself in this situation.

Q. My dad says he wants to appoint me as his agent under a POA, and I think this is a good idea. What is our first step?

A. Any discussion with a parent about planning should begin with an effort to determine whether powers of attorney have already been completed—and, if so, who has copies of the relevant documents. As stated above, your dad is not required to talk to his proposed agents before drafting any POAs. However, in order to prevent possible confusion and to ensure that the agents are both willing to serve and able to follow your father's wishes, it is always wise to talk to the agents beforehand. After that, your father will want to identify his values and wishes for the future, as these will dictate what should be included in the document creating the POA.

The agent or agents should have copies of the original documents. A copy of the health-care power of attorney should go to your father's primary care physicians and any other health-care providers he sees. A copy of the power of attorney for property should be given to his bank, and to any other institutions or individuals that manage his assets. Your father's bank may require both your father and his agent to sign the bank's own POA forms in order to allow the agent to access your dad's accounts and safe-deposit boxes.

Q. I just learned that my father named me as his agent under a power of attorney, and I do not want this responsibility. He no longer has the capacity to name another agent. Is there anything I can do?

A. You are not legally obligated to act as your father's agent just because he appointed you. However, once you begin acting as his agent, you are legally obligated to continue to act as required

▶ **WHAT TO KNOW BEFORE DRAFTING A POWER OF ATTORNEY OR AGREEING TO SERVE AS AN AGENT**

As this chapter demonstrates, states have varying requirements when it comes to POAs. If your parent is drafting a power of attorney, or if someone has asked you to serve as an agent, there are a variety of questions to ask about the specific requirements in his or her state. These include:

- Does the state distinguish between powers of attorney for health care and property, or are both covered in one document?
- Does the state have a statutory form? Do attorneys in the state advise using this form?
- What, if any, limitations exist as to who can serve as agent?
- Does the state permit co-agents?
- What standard of decision making should the agent use?
- Under what circumstances can the POA be modified or revoked, and what steps must be taken?
- What level of decision-making capacity is required to revoke a POA?
- Can the agent delegate his or her authority?
- How many witnesses are required?
- Must the documents creating the POA be notarized?
- Does the state have a registry for POAs?
- Are there any actions that cannot be delegated in a power of attorney for health care or property?
- Can a successor agent be appointed?
- Under what circumstances does the POA take effect?

For more information on POAs, consult your local agency on aging or state department on aging.

by the law of your father's state. If you are concerned about acting on your father's behalf, you should first determine whether the POA provides for a successor agent. If this is someone you trust to carry out your father's wishes, and if he or she is willing to take on the responsibility, then you may consider relinquishing your role as guardian. If this is not an option, you may want to consider petitioning a court to establish guardianship for your father. Guardianships are discussed in more detail in chapter 8.

Q. Can I be sued for something I do in my capacity as an agent under a POA?

A. Yes. As an agent, you can be held personally liable for any funds lost due to a breach of your fiduciary duty, whether the breach was purposeful or occurred by accident. This is yet another reason why it is important to feel comfortable with your role as an agent and to initiate the necessary discussions and planning with your parents prior to any incapacity.

Q. What is a living will?

A. A **living will** is a document that states whether a person wants extraordinary measures taken to keep him or her alive in the event of a terminal illness. **Extraordinary measures** can include placement on a ventilator or feeding tube. Living wills only take effect in the event of a terminal illness, and some states may also require that death be imminent. Living wills can be revoked at any time, regardless of the person's decision-making capacity. Some states have very strict guidelines regarding when a living will becomes effective, how long it will be effective, or even whether the living will is a recognized document under state law. If your parents are considering a living will, check with your area agency on aging or state department on aging for your state's requirements.

Q. Can an agent override a living will?

A. State law varies as to whether an agent can override a living will. Suppose your sister has been named as an agent for your

> ### ▶ GUARDIANSHIPS
>
> In some states, the term **guardianship** refers to the court-appointed power to make financial decisions, or personal decisions, or both. Some states divide this power into two kinds of guardianships: **guardianship of the estate** and **guardianship of the person**. Others combine the two forms of guardianship into a single type of power.

mother under a power of attorney. In any state, you could seek to have her removed as an agent for failing to follow your mother's wishes as specified in a living will. In that case, you would have to file a petition for guardianship and ask that you, or someone else, serve as your mother's guardian for the purpose of making these types of decisions.

Q. What are the main differences between a POA for health care and a living will?

A. With a **power of attorney for health care**, the principal names an agent to make medical decisions on his or her behalf. Under a POA, agents can make all kinds of medical decisions—not just those dealing with end-of-life decisions. Everyone should have a POA for health care.

By contrast, a **living will** is a statement that a person does or does not want extraordinary measures taken at the end of his or her life. A living will does not give anyone else the power to make decisions, and it only applies to end-of-life decisions when a person is terminally ill. Only people who do not want extraordinary measures at their end of life need to complete a living will. (In some states, POAs for health care also allow the principal to state his or her wishes as to end-of-life decisions.)

Q. Is a living will the same thing as a DNR?

A. No. "DNR" stands for "do not resuscitate." A **DNR** is a very limited type of document stating that a person does not want cardiopulmonary resuscitation performed on him or her. A living will is broader than a DNR, as it covers the use of feeding tubes and placement on a ventilator.

CARING FOR SOMEONE
WHO IS NOT YOUR PARENT

Caring for someone other than a parent who is aging—say, a neighbor or a family friend—can be a rewarding and necessary step to ensure that someone you care about receives appropriate care. However, some special legal issues should be considered in order to ensure that you have the ability to fully care for your neighbor or friend.

Q. *I have been helping my eighty-seven-year-old neighbor for about a year now. She has no children, and her other family members either cannot or will not help her out. Are there special legal considerations in this case?*

A. Yes. Planning is even more important in this case than in the case of a family member caregiver. Because you have no legal relationship to this person, you will need to ensure that the necessary documents (such as powers of attorney) are in place to allow you to step in and care for your neighbor. Planning tools are discussed earlier in this chapter and in chapter 1.

Q. *How much care should I provide for someone who is not a parent or relative?*

A. This will depend on your arrangement with the person for whom you are caring, the circumstances in your day-to-day life, and the degree to which that person needs help. For instance, perhaps you have a full-time job, and can provide care only on a part-time or as-needed basis. You may be the person on whom the individual can call when he or she needs help. Or you may have a more formal arrangement with a set schedule for providing help for a certain number of hours per week. You may also have a set list of responsibilities.

The care you provide may be sporadic and based on the type of work or support needed. For example, you may agree to take responsibility for help with transportation, shopping, managing bill payments, or household chores. Make sure it is clear which tasks you will take on, and which will need to be accomplished either by the person you are helping or by another helper. It is important to encourage and help the person do things for him or herself whenever possible. He or she may simply need help knowing how to do things, or learning what resources are available. If the person needs help with certain chores or tasks that you will not be assuming, you may want to consider arranging for supplemental care through a local home-care service.

Q. What happens if my neighbor is hospitalized? Will I be able to visit her?

A. It depends. In some cases, such as when a person is in intensive care and cannot communicate his or her wishes, only family members are permitted to visit. Again, careful planning can help provide for such situations. For example, an advance directive detailing your neighbor's wishes in the event of incapacitation may indicate that she would like you to have access to her room.

Q. Who will make medical decisions for my neighbor when she no longer has the capacity to make her own decisions?

A. If your neighbor has drafted a health-care power of attorney, her agent will be the one to make such decisions. Without any such directive, the health-care provider will first turn to the state health-care surrogacy law, assuming there is one, to determine who can be the decision maker (see chapter 4 for more information on such laws). The health-care provider will first turn to family members as directed by the statute. Some statutes also include friends as the very *last* people in the hierarchy of decision makers. It is important to note that the health-care provider is not permitted to make any determination as to whether the surrogate is an appropriate decision maker. This could mean, for example, that a niece who has not even seen your neighbor for twenty years may be chosen as a decision maker over a close friend or neighbor whom the individual would have preferred.

If your neighbor has no known relatives and "friend" is not an authorized type of decision maker under your state's health-care surrogacy statute, then a court may appoint a professional guardian. These cases are handled quite differently from state to state. In some states, a government agency called a state or public guardian's office accepts guardianship duties. Other states have private for-profit or nonprofit agencies to play this role when no family members are available. In other states, attorneys are appointed to serve as guardians. If a professional decision maker is appointed for your neighbor and your neighbor has the financial means, he or she will most likely be charged for the services of a professional guardian. In some states, there are volunteers who may serve as guardians without compensation, but they normally do not manage estates. (Guardianships are discussed further in the next chapter.)

Therefore, in order to ensure that your neighbor's wishes are followed, she must plan for incapacity before she is unable to make her own decisions.

Q. Who will make financial decisions for my neighbor when she no longer has the capacity to make them herself?

A. Just as a professional guardian may be appointed to make medical and personal decisions for your neighbor, a professional guardian also may be appointed to make financial decisions as guardian of her estate. As with medical guardians, a professional guardian of your neighbor's estate will charge a fee.

Government benefits such as Social Security, SSI, or veteran's benefits are a different story. In order for someone other than your neighbor to oversee these types of income, a representative payee must be appointed. (See chapter 4 for more information on the role of a representative payee.)

Q. If my neighbor no longer has the capacity to make decisions or name me as her agent under a power of attorney, can I become her guardian?

A. Yes. Anyone can petition for guardianship, but there is no guarantee that the court will appoint you. Some state statutes direct the court to give preference to relatives. If there are no relatives, a court may prefer to appoint a close friend over a professional guardian, depending on the circumstances. The court will consider your ability to care for your neighbor, your other responsibilities, and your knowledge of the older person's desires, among other factors. If you are appointed to manage your neighbor's estate, the court will want to ensure that you are sufficiently qualified to do so.

Q. If my state has an agency that will accept guardianship of my neighbor, should I defer to the agency since its employees are professionals?

A. It is not necessarily the case that a professional guardian will do a better job than you. Many of these agencies are severely overworked and underfunded. Even if the agency employees are very conscientious, they did not know your neighbor personally before she lost her decision-making capacity. Although they may do a fine job making decisions they believe are in her best interest, they might not be able to know what she would have wanted. It is also likely that you will be able to allot more time and attention to your neighbor's needs than would an agency. Additionally, if your neighbor is in a nursing home, your involvement as her guardian could mean that she may receive better care than she would otherwise have received (see chapter 9 for more information on nursing homes). Courts usually appoint agencies as guardians only when no suitable individual is able to act as a guardian.

If you think an agency may be appointed as your neighbor's guardian, research the agency to determine whether it will be able to handle issues that may arise in your friend's case.

Q. Are there any legal risks involved with helping out my neighbor?

A. As mentioned in the previous chapter and discussed in more detail in chapter 11, if you provide care for your neighbor and she becomes dependent on that care, and if you then stop providing that care and fail to arrange for alternative care, then you could be found guilty of neglecting your neighbor. If you are thinking of taking on this responsibility, make sure you will be able to fulfill all of the obligations to which you agree. In addition, if your neighbor has allowed you to help her with paying bills, purchasing groceries, or handling other financial matters, make sure you keep copies of all receipts and records that may help you to explain how her money was spent. While family members also need to be mindful of these things, non-family members must be particularly cautious. Sometimes the dependent person may become confused or paranoid, and could accuse you of taking his or her money or assets. Family members may also become suspicious.

If you are appointed as your neighbor's guardian, or as her agent under a power of attorney, all the responsibilities and potential liabilities discussed in previous chapters will apply to you. In addition, you may be more carefully scrutinized by family members who may question or resent your involvement.

There are personal risks as well as legal issues that are specifically associated with looking after any aging person who isn't your parent. These issues, and strategies for dealing with them, are outlined in chapter 13.

REMEMBER THIS

- If your family is beginning to plan for your parents' aging, consulting with an attorney is strongly recommended. Ideally this attorney will have a practice either dedicated to or concentrating in elder law, and he or she must be licensed to practice in the state where your mother lives.

- A power of attorney is a document that allows one person, the principal, to designate another person, the agent (or attorney in fact), to obtain private information and make decisions on the principal's behalf. Your parent's state may have two specific types of powers of attorney: for property and for health care.

- Many states offer "statutory form" powers of attorney. Although these may reduce the need for legal battles over the definition of terms featured in the documents, keep in mind that these forms may not meet your parent's specific needs.

- If your parent asks you to serve as an agent under a power of attorney, you should consider the following: your geographic proximity to your parent, any special skills or training that you or other family members may have, your other commitments, your willingness to carry out your parent's wishes, and your relationship with any other agents.

- If you are serving as an agent, you may be eligible to get paid for your work. Carefully read the document creating the power of attorney, and consult with an experienced elder law attorney.

- It can be incredibly beneficial for you and an aging neighbor or friend if you take on some responsibilities for providing care. However, it is extremely important to ensure that your friend or neighbor engages in proper planning that allows you to step in when necessary.

CHAPTER 4

Legal Interventions

When There Is No
Power of Attorney

Jason's dad recently suffered a massive stroke that has left him virtually incapacitated. His dad was never willing to discuss aging or plan for such a situation, so now Jason has no understanding of how to step in on his father's behalf. Medical bills need to be paid, treatment options need to be selected, and living arrangements must be determined. What can Jason do? Does he need to go to court?

If your parents never planned for their incapacity, or if their plans are thwarted—for example, if an agent dies and no successor has been appointed—then your family may face the frightening reality that no one can step in immediately and legally to help your parent. However, in this type of situation there are still some tools available to help your family. This chapter explores several types of legal interventions that may allow you to make decisions on behalf of your parents, even if they never drafted powers of attorney for health care or property. These include options under laws governing health-care surrogates, guardianship, and civil commitment. The laws that apply to your situation will depend on the state where your parents live and on the types of decisions you need to make.

HEALTH-CARE SURROGACY LAWS

Q. My mother needs someone to make health-care decisions for her. She has no power of attorney or living will. What can I do?

A. First, see if your mother lives in one of the forty-one states that have health-care surrogacy laws (as explained in the sidebar below). A **health-care surrogacy law** allows one person to make health-care decisions for another who has lost the ability to make his or her own decisions. These laws go into effect when one or more doctors state that the patient can no longer make his or her own decisions, and apply only when there is no valid power of attorney for health care in place.

Under health-care surrogacy laws, no court proceeding is needed. The statutes themselves list the possible types of decision makers and state the order in which they will become decision makers if they are ready and able to act as such. For instance, a health-care surrogacy law might state that a court-appointed guardian is the first in line to assume decision-making responsibilities. If there is no such guardian, then the spouse might be second in line; then parents; then adult children; then a close friend, and so on.

Q. What if the applicable health-care surrogacy law indicates that my mother's children are the decision makers, and my siblings and I are all willing to step into the role?

A. If all of you agree on the relevant decisions, there is no problem. However, if you don't all agree, then you must look at the law of the state where your mother is located. Some state laws indicate that the majority rules; others are silent on this issue and require the family to go to court if it cannot agree about a

▶ **HOW DOES YOUR STATE DO IT?**

To determine whether your state has a health-care surrogacy law, visit *www.abanet.org/aging/legislativeupdates/docs/Famcon_05–07.pdf*. You can then go to *www.findlaw.com* to obtain a copy of the law based on its citation.

▶ **STEPFAMILIES**

Vary rarely do health-care surrogacy laws address the issues of stepfamilies or remarriages later in life. These laws often don't make exceptions to fit specific family situations; instead, whatever the law says goes, regardless of what your parent would have wanted. This is yet another reason why prior planning is incredibly important in order to ensure that things play out as you would hope—and, more importantly, as your parent would have wanted.

parent's health care. Even in states where the majority rules, some physicians and hospitals may be unwilling to act when there is disagreement among the surrogate decision makers, and the family may still have to go to court.

Q. If so many states have health-care surrogacy laws, why are powers of attorney and guardianships necessary?

A. Although a state may have a health-care surrogacy law on its books, an individual health-care provider may not know about the law or understand how it works. Additionally, the laws may not reflect what you or your parents would have wanted. For example, under a health-care surrogacy law, your estranged uncle whom your mother hasn't seen in twenty years may end up having a say in your mom's health care. Also (as noted above), if there is any conflict among family members or if the patient herself objects to a procedure, it may be necessary to go to court to obtain a legal guardian for your parent.

Q. What happens in the event of a medical emergency?

A. If the patient cannot make decisions and there is no surrogate available, health-care providers will assume that the patient would want them to do everything possible to keep him or her alive.

REPRESENTATIVE PAYEES AND FINANCES

Q. What if my mother needs me to make financial decisions on her behalf and has no power of attorney for property?

A. It will first be necessary to determine whether your mother has income from a federal program such as Social Security, Social Security disability benefits (SSDI), or Supplemental Security Income (SSI). If your mother receives income from one of these government programs, then you will need to become her **representative payee.**

After determining the role a representative payee will play, you will next need to find out whether your mother is entitled to any pensions or other form of private benefits, and learn how to ensure that these benefits are protected. A guardianship of the estate may be a necessary tool to ensure that your mother is financially provided for. Each of these options is discussed below. (The health-care surrogacy laws discussed above do not apply to financial decisions.)

Q. What is a representative payee and how do I become one?

A. A **representative payee** is a person or an organization designated by the Social Security Administration to receive and manage funds on behalf of a recipient who is no longer able to do so. If you become your mother's representative payee, you will actually receive your mother's government benefits on her behalf, and will be responsible for managing those benefits and making sure they are spent as needed for your mother's welfare.

To become a representative payee, your mother or someone on her behalf must ask the Social Security Administration (or other program) to appoint a representative payee. Your mother must have some sort of disability or condition that prevents her from managing her own financial affairs. This disability may be physical or mental, and will need to be documented. For information on becoming a representative payee, contact the Social Security Administration at *www.ssa.gov* or call 1–800–772–1213.

Q. What are the responsibilities of representative payees?

A. Representative payees are required to set up special accounts for the funds coming from government programs. They are not allowed to commingle funds by depositing their own money in these accounts. The representative payee can only use the beneficiary's money to pay the beneficiary's expenses, and must keep receipts and submit annual reports to the Social Security Administration.

Q. If I am my father's representative payee, can I access the pension he receives from his former employer?

A. Some pension payors will permit a representative payee for government benefits to serve as a representative payee for their pension as well. Others will only release pension payments to the guardian of the person, while still others will release payments only to the guardian of an estate. Your parent should speak to a human resources representative at his or her former employer in order to determine who can receive payments and how to go about making proper arrangements. Pensions are discussed in more detail in chapter 5.

GUARDIANSHIP

Terminology relating to guardianships varies significantly from state to state. The information provided below is designed to give you a general idea of how things work in some states, but keep in mind that things may be very different in your state. Following this section is a list of what you will want to know about your state's law before you petition for guardianship.

Terminology and Procedure

Q. What options are available if my mom doesn't have a power of attorney, and if the applicable health-care surrogacy law would appoint someone my family opposes?

A. First, if your mom has capacity, she should immediately draft powers of attorney (for health care and property) and, depending on her assets, a trust (trusts are discussed further in chapter 5). This will ensure that your mother's wishes are carried out exactly as she would have wanted. If that is no longer possible, you may want to look into having a guardian or conservator appointed or, in some extreme cases, civil commitment. These options are all outlined below. Your choices will vary depending on where your parent lives and your exact circumstances.

Q. What is guardianship?

A. A **guardian** is appointed by a court to make personal or financial decisions on behalf of another person. Guardianship is a serious step. As such, it is generally not easy to obtain guardianship and, in order to do so, you will have to meet certain strict legal guidelines and requirements. To be a proper subject for guardianship, a person must be unable to make or understand

▶ **GUARDIAN VS. CONSERVATOR**

In some states, the guardian of an estate is referred to as the **conservator** and the court procedure relating to the estate is known as **conservatorship**. In other states, "conservatorship" refers to a court procedure that is similar but not identical to guardianship (see below).

the consequences of decisions. *Old age, mental illness, or disability alone does not qualify a person for guardianship.* Remember: a person has a right to make risky or even foolish decisions, as long as he or she understands the consequences of those decisions.

There are different kinds of guardianships. What follows is a list of some common ones. Your state may recognize all of these, some of them, or totally different types altogether.

Plenary or Full Guardianship

Plenary or **full guardianship** is established through a court procedure in which a court determines that a person is no longer able to make decisions, and appoints a guardian to make decisions on the person's behalf. In some states, a person under plenary guardianship is determined by the court to be incompetent, and may lose the right to vote, marry, drive, and enter into contracts.

Limited Guardianship

Limited guardianship is also established through a court order, but in this case the guardian has only those powers that are expressly granted by the court. Under limited guardianship, in some states the ward is not adjudicated incompetent and retains some rights—that is, the ward only loses those rights specifically removed or limited by the order. For example, a limited guardianship might allocate all financial decisions to the guardian, but allow the ward to write checks, withdraw cash, and make small purchases for household use. In this instance, the ward would still be able to drive and vote, but major financial decisions would be made by the guardian. A limited guardianship is appropriate when a person has cognitive deficits but can still make some decisions. In some states, a limited guardianship is reserved only for those individuals who are developmentally disabled prior to reaching the age of majority.

Conservatorship

In some states, the term **conservatorship** is similar in meaning to guardianship and involves similar court procedures. In others, a conservatorship is a voluntary procedure for turning over certain responsibilities to another party. With this type of conservatorship, the person whose estate is being conserved nominates a conservator to manage his or her estate. As with guardianship, an annual accounting is required. Although no finding of incompetence is needed to establish a conservatorship, if the individual whose estate is being conserved wants to fire the conservator, he or she must either prove competence to manage his or her own affairs or select an appropriate successor conservator to recommend to the court. These proceedings can vary greatly by state. If you are looking for such an option, it is wise to talk to an attorney in your state with experience in this area of law.

Guardianship of the Person

A **guardian of the person** is responsible for making all health-care and personal decisions for the ward. In most cases, the guardian of the person can make end-of-life decisions without court involvement. Some states require that the guardian seek and obtain court approval to move the ward and, in particular, to place the ward in a nursing home. If the ward objects to any moves, a court must decide the appropriate course of action.

Guardianship of the Estate

A **guardian of the estate** is responsible for making financial decisions and handling all legal matters for the ward. Most states require the guardian to file an annual accounting with the court detailing income, expenses, and assets on hand. Normally a guardian of the estate is required to obtain prior court approval for all expenditures of the ward's funds.

Temporary Guardianship

If there is an emergency situation and harm would result to the older person if action is not taken immediately, a court may order a **temporary guardianship** of the person or estate. Temporary guardianships are limited in scope and duration, and are only used in emergency situations.

Standby Guardianship

A **standby guardian** can be designated to act in the event that a primary guardian cannot act on the ward's behalf. If the guardian is no longer able to act, the standby guardian can step in and make decisions. As soon as possible, the standby guardian must petition the court to be appointed as successor guardian. The court will ultimately decide whether the standby guardian will be appointed as successor guardian based on the ward's desires and best interests.

Successor Guardianship

A **successor guardian** is appointed when a guardian is no longer able to act on the ward's behalf because of death, disability, or for any other reason. The court will determine whether a proposed successor guardian is appropriate.

Q. *How do I go about having a guardian appointed for my parent?*

A. While the details vary from state to state, a guardianship case is always initiated by filing a document with the court (sometimes called a **petition**). A hearing date will then be set, and the proposed ward personally served with the petition and notice of the date and time of the hearing. Some people find it odd that papers must be served on a person with advanced dementia. Nonetheless, our Constitution requires that every competent

> ▶ **WARDS**
>
> **Ward** is a general term that refers to someone who has a guardian. A ward may also be referred to as an **incapacitated person** or **conservatee**.

adult receive notice of any hearing at which his or her rights may be taken away. We are all presumed competent unless and until a judge has ruled otherwise.

In some jurisdictions, a **guardian ad litem** (GAL) or a court investigator (or both) will come to interview the proposed ward. A GAL may also interview the proposed guardian and other family members, and report back to the court on the ward's wishes and what the GAL thinks is in the ward's best interest. There will then be a hearing at which the court will hear evidence regarding the need for a guardian and whether the recommended guardian is appropriate. The length and nature of that hearing will vary depending on whether the case is contested or uncontested, as is discussed further later in this section (see "*What happens at the guardianship hearing?*").

Q. I am filing a petition to become my father's guardian. What rights does he have during these proceedings?

A. He has the right to an attorney, to be heard in court, to hear the evidence against him, and to present and cross-examine witnesses. In some cases, he may also have the right to have a jury determine the issue of capacity. It is important to note that he does not necessarily have the right to a *free* attorney. In the event that he opposes guardianship and cannot afford an attorney, the court may appoint a *pro bono* (free) attorney at his request. In some states, if the guardian will have the ability to administer psychotropic medications or to place your father in a facility that could restrict his movement, an attorney *must* be appointed.

Q. How will my father respond to my request for guardianship?

A. Older persons may respond in a number of ways to guardianship petitions. Your father's specific reaction will depend greatly upon his current cognitive ability. For example, let's say your father's dementia (or other cognitive dysfunction) has reached the point where he does not understand the nature of the proceedings. In this situation, your father may not be able to respond at all, or he may consent to or oppose guardianship without really understanding what it is you are seeking. If he opposes guardianship, he may exercise the rights described above, even though you and others feel that he clearly cannot make his own decisions. Remember: in the eyes of the law, he is presumed to be competent until a judge rules otherwise.

Q. How will my request for guardianship affect my father?

A. It is possible that your father may become depressed or hurt. It can be quite demoralizing to have your child file court documents saying you are no longer able to make decisions and asking that you be declared incompetent. The resulting depression may appear as further cognitive decline. For this reason, before filing the necessary documents, it is very important to make sure that guardianship is actually necessary.

Q. How will my request for guardianship affect the rest of my family?

A. In some cases, other family members may be very hurt and angry that you brought what they see as a private matter into court. As a result, they may oppose your guardianship petition and even seek to have one of them appointed as a guardian instead. This can be very divisive, time-consuming, and expensive for everyone, which is another reason why it is very important to have frank discussions with your family beforehand.

Q. How do I know that guardianship of my father is actually necessary?

A. There are a variety of factors to consider. The first question is whether there are trusts or powers of attorney for property and health care. If there are, guardianship may not be necessary if:

- the powers of attorney or trusts are valid, meaning that:
  - ○ your father is not objecting to the agent or trustee, or to the action he or she wishes to take;
  - ○ the powers of attorney or trusts cover the type of action the agent wishes to take; and
  - ○ the agent or trustee is acting properly; or
- your father's state has a health-care surrogacy act and you are comfortable with the family member designated by law to make decisions for your father.

If there are no powers of attorney or trusts, the next question is whether your father still has the capacity to execute them. Your father's ability to make decisions may vary significantly based on the type of decision he's being asked to make, the setting and manner in which he's asked to make it, and even the time of day (some elderly people may tend to think quite well in the morning, for example, but become easily confused in the evening). Furthermore, different levels of decision-making capacity are required for different types of decisions and legal actions.

If your father still has the ability to identify you and other family members, has knowledge of his income and property, and is able to articulate who he wants to make decisions for him, he may be able to execute powers of attorney and trusts despite other cognitive and memory deficits. In this instance, your father should contact an attorney directly for a consultation. If in doubt, the attorney may require a statement from your father's physician or a mental health professional before drafting the necessary documents.

If the only decisions that need to be made are health-care decisions, and if your father's state has a health-care surrogacy law, then guardianship may not be necessary. Exceptions would occur if:

- you want to make the health-care decisions, but there is another surrogate (above or equal to you under the law's hierarchy) who is willing and able to act and who is not in agreement with you; or

- your father suffers from cognitive dysfunction *and* he is being abused or neglected by another person and will not voluntarily do what is needed to end the abuse or neglect.

Finally, ask yourself precisely what authority guardianship will grant you that you absolutely need but do not currently have. If guardianship will not afford you some additional power that you need in order to help your father, it is probably not the correct solution.

Q. Who can serve as guardian?

A. Generally, to serve as a guardian a person must be an adult who is competent to act as a guardian. Some states impose other restrictions, such as barring people who have been convicted of felonies. In addition, some state statutes list relatives in order of preference, much as health-care surrogacy laws do.

Q. Do I need a lawyer to file for guardianship?

A. It is generally not a good idea to file a petition for guardianship without the assistance of an attorney. Some states require all guardians to be represented by attorneys; others only require this for guardianship of the estate.

Even if your state doesn't require an attorney, it is essential to obtain one if your petition is likely to be contested by either your parent or someone else, or if there have been allegations of abuse, neglect, or financial exploitation of your parent by you or someone else.

Q. What is a guardian ad litem?

A. A **guardian ad litem** (GAL) is an attorney or other professional who is appointed by the court to meet with the person for whom guardianship is being sought. The GAL will inform that person of his or her rights, and determine his or her preferences and desires. The GAL will then report back to the court with recommendations about what is in the best interest of the older person.

Q. Who pays for the lawyers and other expenses involved in a guardianship case?

A. This varies from state to state, and you should try to determine the answer before you file. The statute governing guardianship will indicate whom the court can order to pay, but this decision is usually made at the end of a case and is dependent on its outcome. In cases where a guardian is appointed, it is usually the ward (in this case, your parent) who will pay for the expenses. Older people who are either seeking or challenging a guardianship may be able to obtain free legal help through legal services programs or from lawyers who volunteer their services free of charge.

Q. What happens at the guardianship hearing?

A. At an uncontested hearing, the court reviews evidence of the need for a guardian and determines whether the proposed guardianship is necessary. This evidence can include oral or written testimony from a doctor, the GAL, the older person, the proposed guardian, and any other interested person.

At a contested hearing (or trial), each party introduces their own evidence and witnesses and the opposing party has an opportunity to cross-examine them. If the guardianship is contested, written medical opinions will be insufficient. In these cases, the courts will require actual testimony by a physician or physicians.

Q. How should the guardian make decisions on the ward's behalf?

A. There are two standards of decision making: substituted judgment and best interest. **Substituted judgment** is where the guardian does what the *ward* would have wanted. Under the **best-interest standard**, the guardian does what the *guardian* thinks is in the ward's best interest. States vary as to which standard applies. If you are unsure, check the court order creating the guardianship, talk to your attorney, or call the clerk of the court that appointed the guardian. Some state laws also specify what factors the guardian should take into consideration, such as the values of the ward, or the views of family members and others whom the ward would consult in making his or her own decisions. It is important to remember, however, that regardless of the standard that applies, if the ward is able to communicate, his or her preferences should always be sought and taken into account when making decisions.

Q. Can there be more than one guardian?

A. Yes. Depending on the law of your state, it may be possible to have co-guardians. But in order for this to work, the co-guardians must be able to agree on important care issues, such as where the older person is going to live and what kinds of treatment will be provided at the end of life. It is also possible to have one person serve as guardian of the person and the other as guardian of the estate.

Q. How long does guardianship last?

A. In most cases, the guardianship lasts indefinitely until the court rules otherwise, such as after a finding that the ward has regained competence.

Q. If I am appointed guardian of the person, am I required to care for my father personally?

A. If a court has appointed you as guardian of the person, you are not necessarily required to care for your father personally, but you are required to procure care for him. In other words, you must make sure that he is getting adequate care from *someone*.

Q. As guardian, do I have to use my own funds to pay for my father's care?

A. No.

Q. Can I be paid for my work as guardian?

A. Yes, you may be able to get paid for your work as a guardian with court approval. Consult an attorney as to the practice in your jurisdiction and the rate of pay.

Q. Can I ever be removed as the guardian?

A. Yes. You can be removed if you fail to follow the law, or if you act in a way that harms the ward's person or estate. For more about the remedies available when a guardian abuses, neglects, or financially exploits a ward, see chapter 11.

Q. What do I need to know about state law before I file for guardianship?

A. If you have determined that guardianship is the correct step for your family, make sure that you are fully aware of how guardianships work in the state where your parent lives. This includes finding out:

- what terminology the state uses for the options described above;
- whether the state requires you to have an attorney to be a guardian;
- whether the state distinguishes between guardianship of the person and guardianship of the estate;
- whether the state requires a court finding of incompetency before a plenary or full guardianship can be entered;
- what, if any, rights your parent will lose if you obtain plenary or full guardianship;
- whether the state has some form of limited guardianship or conservatorship;
- what standard of decision making the guardian must use;
- what record keeping and reporting requirements exist for guardians;
- whether the state allows co-guardians; and
- whether or not a guardian needs specific court permission to:
  - change the ward's residence;
  - place the ward in an institution;
  - review the ward's mental health records;
  - force the ward to take psychotropic medication, or obtain other kinds of mental health treatment against his or her will;

○ spend the ward's funds; or

○ buy or sell property.

For more general information about guardianship, visit the website for the National Guardianship Association at *www.guardianship.org*.

REMEMBER THIS

- Health-care surrogacy allows one person to make health-care decisions for another who has lost the ability to do so on his or her own. Health-care surrogacy statutes list possible decision makers and state the order in which they will become decision makers if they are ready and able to act.

- If your parent receives some form of government benefits (for example, Social Security), you may be appointed as his or her representative payee in order to receive and spend these benefits on his or her behalf. A representative payee is a person (or organization) designated by the Social Security Administration to receive and manage funds on behalf of a representative who is no longer able to do so.

- If your parent does not have a power of attorney or other legal document in place and can no longer care for him or herself, you may want to petition a court for guardianship. However, remember that a guardianship is a serious step and that old age, mental illness, or disability alone is not justification for a guardianship.

- There are many different types of guardianship, depending on your family's circumstances and the state where your parent lives. It is best to consult with an experienced elder law attorney to determine what is best for your parent.

- If you are filing a guardianship petition, know that your parent does have rights and will be able to contest the petition and be represented by an attorney.

CHAPTER 5

Money Matters

Identifying and Accessing
Income and Assets

Colleen's dad recently broke his hip and is now bedbound. He needs help taking care of his day-to-day tasks, and has appointed Colleen as his power of attorney for property so that she can help pay his bills. Colleen now realizes she has no idea about her dad's financial resources. Where does his money come from? How can she access it? Are there any other resources she doesn't know about?

A ssuming you have the legal authority to make decisions for your parent, you may decide that it is time to hire caregivers or other outside service providers to help you care for him or her. If that's the case, you will have to figure out a way to pay for these services. Understanding the sources of your parent's income and how to locate his or her assets can help you determine an appropriate care plan. As you try to locate this information, you may quickly realize that your parents have not organized their information. In that case, your first task will be to determine the resources available to your parents. This chapter provides tips on how to identify the sources of your parents' income, and then provides an overview of common sources of income and assets, as well as information on how to access the income and how to protect yourself.

GETTING STARTED

Q. Am I responsible for paying for any of the services my parent might need?

A. No. Assuming you have not signed any agreements saying you will take on such a responsibility, you are usually not required to pay for any services your parent may require.

Q. My parents are retired. What are their possible sources of income?

A. Income could come from a variety of sources, including government benefits such as Social Security and Supplemental Security Income, a pension or other employer benefits programs, investment income, trusts, life insurance, or rental income. Many of these possible income sources are discussed throughout this chapter.

Q. I would like to help my mother with her finances. Where should I start?

A. The first step is to talk to your mother. Even if she has experienced some cognitive decline, she may still know more about her finances than you do, and she may be able to tell you about certain income sources you may not otherwise have known about. Then you should collect as much information and documentation as possible.

The types of information and documents that will help you manage your parents' financial affairs include:
- wills;
- powers of attorney for health care and property;
- living wills;
- tax returns;
- trust documents;
- annuity plans;
- bank statements;
- the location of any safety-deposit boxes, including the location of the keys and a list of the contents;
- credit card statements;
- insurance policies, including home, life, long-term-care, and property policies;

- information on Medicare and Medicaid;
- information on veterans' benefits;
- titles to property (houses, cars, etc.);
- mortgage documents, including documents from any refinancing or home equity loans;
- documents relating to any other loans;
- information on any investments such as stocks, bonds, and mutual funds;
- information on any corporations owned in whole or part by your parent (including documents relating to limited liability corporations (LLCs), limited partnerships (LPs), or closely held corporations with which your parent may have been involved);
- the names, contact information, and any account numbers for your parents' lawyer, stockbroker, insurance agent, financial planner, etc.;
- documents relating to retirement plans, including Social Security, pensions, and 401(k) plans;
- information about burial plots and any prepaid funeral plans;
- birth certificates;
- Social Security cards;
- divorce decrees and related documents, such as separation agreements and qualified domestic relations orders (QDROs) (these are discussed in more detail later in the chapter); and
- immigration and naturalization documents.

▶ **GETTING ACCESS**

If your parent cannot help you locate the information necessary for you to provide care, then you may need to be named your parent's guardian or agent under a power of attorney for property. Chapters 3 and 4 discuss these legal tools in detail.

**Q. *Will I be limited in my ability to find out about my
parents' income and assets?***

A. Yes. In most cases, you will likely have to prove that you are
a guardian, a trustee, or your parent's agent under a valid power
of attorney.

**Q. *Should I consult an attorney for help with
managing my parents' income and assets
and planning for their long-term care?***

A. Through the process of identifying income and assets, you
may discover that your parents have engaged in planning for
their long-term care and have established a set plan for you to
follow. If not, you could simply spend their assets on their care
until those assets are depleted. Alternatively, you could meet
with an elder law attorney to determine whether any planning
options are still available to your parents. If your parents have
any assets, including equity in a home, consulting an elder law
attorney is strongly recommended. An attorney can advise you
on how to maximize these assets by minimizing tax liability and,
possibly, by qualifying your parents for public benefits. Consulting an elder law attorney is essential if your parents have assets
and if:

- one of your parents needs to go to a nursing home, but your
  other parent is able to remain at home;
- your parents have an adult disabled child who is dependent
  on them;
- an adult child has been living with your parents and caring
  for them for two or more years, which has prevented nursing
  home placement;
- your parents have $400,000 or more in cash assets; or
- your parents are interested in purchasing an annuity or drafting a trust.

In any of these situations, special and complex rules apply,
and an attorney can help you determine the correct course of
action.

As noted in previous chapters, a guardian or agent under a
power of attorney has a duty to do what his or her parents would

have wanted or, if that's not known, what is in their best interest. Depending on the complexity of your parents' estate, this can be a daunting task that requires the assistance of a knowledgeable professional. Information on how to locate an elder law attorney can be found in the appendix to this book.

UNDERSTANDING SOURCES OF INCOME

If you are assuming caregiving responsibilities for your parent, it will be necessary to determine the assets and income available for caregiving needs. (For example, if your parent needs a homemaker, you can't hire one until you know what your parent can afford.) This section outlines some of the more common types of income available for aging adults.

Social Security

Q. My mom relies a lot on her Social Security check. I am worried her benefits will run out, as she retired over thirty years ago. What exactly is Social Security? How does it work?

A. The Social Security Administration (SSA) administers **Social Security**, the country's most extensive insurance program for older and disabled people and their families. Your parent may receive benefits under Social Security if he or she is:

- aged sixty-two or older;
- the spouse of a retired worker;
- the divorced spouse of a retired or disabled worker;
- a worker who has become disabled;
- the spouse or dependent of a disabled worker; or
- the divorced spouse of deceased worker.

Social Security programs are complicated, and the law and regulations governing them can change. Contact your parents' local SSA office for information about their Social Security benefits or to ask specific questions about their cases.

▶ **CITIZENSHIP**

Don't worry if your parents aren't U.S. citizens—they may still be eligible for Social Security. Noncitizens who are lawful aliens are eligible for Social Security benefits provided that they meet coverage requirements. Your parents will, however, have to provide evidence that they are lawful residents of the United States. (Note, however, that there are different rules for Supplemental Security Income, which is discussed later in this section.)

Q. My dad only worked for a couple of years. Will he qualify for Social Security?

A. Under Social Security, as you work, you earn Social Security "credits." One credit is given for a specific amount of income, up to four credits per year. As a general rule, forty quarters of work (ten years of work) in a job that pays Social Security taxes will cover an individual, or the individual's beneficiaries, for life.

However, there are some exceptions to this rule, so do not assume that your parents are ineligible simply because they have performed fewer than ten years of covered work.

Q. How much money will my parents receive? Will it be enough for them to live on?

A. Social Security provides only a floor of protection. Generally, it replaces less than 40 percent of an average wage earner's earned income after retirement (not including any investment income). To be financially secure, your parents will probably need several sources of income in addition to their Social Security benefits.

The amount your parents will receive from Social Security depends on how much money they earned over their lifetime, their age at retirement, and other factors. If you are interested in finding out how much your parents will receive, try to locate their "Your Social Security Statements" form. Every year, approximately three months before their birthday, the SSA sends everyone such a form. This statement lists your parents' annual accredited earning and estimated retirement and disability benefits. It should help you estimate how much Social Security income your parents can rely on in the future.

If you can't find your parents' forms, you can obtain an estimate on the Social Security Administration's website using their Retirement Planner. Located at *www.ssa.gov/retire2*, the planner includes an online calculator that allows you to estimate retirement benefits using numbers you provide.

Social Security Disability Insurance (SSDI)

Q. My dad has Parkinson's disease and is unable to continue working. He has quite a large amount of savings in the bank, and is worried about losing it all by having to pay for his medical bills. Is there any program that can help him without requiring him to use his retirement savings?

▶ **CHANGES IN SOCIAL SECURITY**

Social Security laws, regulations, and benefits are complicated, and they sometimes change. The SSA's website (*www.ssa.gov*) provides the most up-to-date information. You can contact your local Social Security office for information, but you should also consider getting help from an elder law attorney or social work specialist with expertise in issues relating to Social Security. Don't be afraid to ask questions. The more you know, the better you can help your parents. Additionally, your parents' age will impact their benefits and responsibilities. For example, an upcoming birthday may seriously impact Social Security benefits. If your parent's birthday is approaching, make sure you and your parent are aware of any potential implications this may have on their benefits.

A. **Yes. Social Security Disability Insurance (SSDI)** pays cash benefits to people who are unable to work for more than a year due to a disability. SSDI is *not* a need-based program. Therefore, your parents may be eligible for SSDI even if they have money in the bank.

In order to be eligible for SSDI:

- An individual must have an eligible disability. **Disability** in this context means "inability to engage in any substantial gainful activity by reason of any medically determinable physical or mental impairment which can be expected to result in death or has lasted or can be expected to last for a continuous period of not less than 12 months";

- The individual must be unable to work due to the demonstrated physical or mental impairment (as described above); and

- The impairment (as described above) must have lasted for twelve months or be potentially expected to lead to death.

Q. *Once my parents qualify for disability benefits, will the benefits last for the rest of their lives?*

A. No. Their disability benefits will continue for as long as they remain medically disabled and unable to work. Your parents' health must be periodically reviewed in order to continue the benefits.

Q. *How long after a diagnosis of disability will my dad have to wait to apply?*

A. Your dad can apply for SSDI on the first day of disability. However, remember that the disability must be one that will last for at least one year.

▶ **SSDI INFORMATION**

For more information on SSDI, visit *www.ssa.gov/dibplan/ index.htm.*

Supplemental Security Income (SSI)

Q. *My dad doesn't have the necessary work background to qualify for Social Security benefits, and he really doesn't have a lot of money. Are there other government programs that can help him, or will I and my siblings be responsible for supporting him?*

A. Your dad is likely eligible for another government benefit program, Supplemental Security Income. **Supplemental Security Income (SSI)** is a social insurance program funded by general tax revenues to help the poor pay for basic needs like food, clothing, and shelter. Your dad may be eligible if he:

- is age sixty-five or older, blind, or disabled;
- has limited income and personal property; and
- meets certain citizenship or residency requirements.

Although Social Security runs the program, a recipient does not need to earn work credits to qualify. A person can receive SSDI and SSI at the same time. To qualify for SSI as a disabled person, the requirements are the same as those for SSDI.

In addition to the benefits offered through the SSA, some states offer state supplemental insurance. If you think your parent qualifies for SSI, check with the local Social Security office. The national phone number is 1–800–772–1213, or you can obtain more information online at *www.ssa.gov/pubs/11011.html*.

Q. *My parents have some assets, but no income at all. Will the fact that they have some assets disqualify them from receiving SSI benefits?*

A. Not necessarily. There is a limit on the amount of assets a person can have in order to qualify for SSI: generally no more than $2,000 for a single person and, for a married couple, no more than $3,000. However, the following assets are exempt and do not count toward this limit:

- a home and the land on which it is located;
- household goods and personal effects, plus wedding rings;

> ### ▶ WHY SO MUCH INFORMATION?
>
> It is important that you understand where your parent's income comes from, and where additional income could come from. If you are to coordinate services, support, and housing for your parent, it will first be necessary for you to determine how much you can spend. Although this may seem like a daunting task, it is a necessary one to ensure that you don't overcommit yourself or deplete your parent's resources.

- one car (if used for transportation);
- life insurance with a combined face value of $1,500 or less;
- trade or business property needed for self-support (e.g., office equipment, machinery, or tools);
- a burial space; and
- burial funds up to $1,500 (in an account earmarked for burial expenses).

Veterans' Benefits

Q. My dad is a World War II veteran and he thinks that he is entitled to additional benefits based on his service. Is this true?

A. Likely, yes. The United States Department of Veterans Affairs (DVA) administers a range of service- and non-service-connected benefits programs for veterans, their dependents, and their survivors. **Veterans' benefits** include cash benefits such as compensation and pensions, health benefits and services, burial and memorial benefits, vocational rehabilitation, education, and employment services, and special programs for certain groups such as homeless veterans and women.

Eligibility for DVA programs and services, and the level of those benefits, depends on several factors, including:

- the length and dates of the veteran's military service;
- the way in which the veteran was discharged from the military;
- the date and circumstances of the veteran's death, if applicable;
- the extent of any disability and whether the disability is service-connected;
- the relationship of the applicant to the veteran; and
- the applicant's income and resources.

If you think your father is eligible, or have questions about his benefits, contact your local office of the Department of Veterans Affairs or visit *www.va.gov.*

Pensions and Other Retirement Plans

Q. My parents worked their whole lives. Shouldn't they have pensions?

A. Your parents may have pension or other retirement income from former employers. However, employers are not legally required to provide retirement income for employees, so don't assume that your parents will have such income.

Q. What exactly is a pension?

A. There are generally two kinds of pensions: **defined-benefit plans**, which are the traditional type of pension, and **defined contribution plans**, a newer option that is becoming the norm.

Defined-Benefit Plans

In a **defined-benefit plan**, an employer—and also, perhaps, the employee—contributes funds to the plan with the understanding that the employee will receive a certain amount each month (a **defined benefit**) upon retirement. This amount is based on a formula that takes into account how long the employee worked, how much he or she earned, and any bargaining agreements between his or her union and the employer. These types of pensions are primarily funded by employers who pool individual funds to create one large pension fund, and then make decisions about where to invest the pooled funds. Most defined-benefit plans are insured by the Pension Benefit Guaranty Corporation (PBGC), so that if the pension funds are mismanaged, beneficiaries are still guaranteed payments upon retirement. Employees are not permitted to withdraw funds from a traditional defined-benefit plan while they are still employed.

Defined-Contribution Plans

The term **defined-contribution plan** usually includes individual retirement accounts (IRAs), 401(k)s, and profit-sharing and employee stock ownership plans. Defined-contribution plans do not guarantee a monthly payment upon retirement. The amount you receive at retirement is based on how much is in your individual account. Unlike defined-benefit plans, which are primarily funded and completely controlled by employers, defined-contribution plans are primarily funded by employees. The employee has some control over how the funds are invested, and can often begin withdrawing funds even if he or she is still employed, but a penalty will apply. On the other hand, if he or she makes poor investment decisions, his or her funds could be completely lost. Unlike defined-benefit plans, defined-contribution plans are not insured by the PBGC.

Another difference between defined-benefit and defined-contribution plans is that defined-contribution plans are not necessarily linked to a particular employer. This means that if your parents switched jobs, they could have moved their funds, or they may still have funds with an employer for whom they haven't worked in decades. Therefore, it can be much harder to determine whether your parents have a defined-contribution plan than to determine whether they are covered by defined-benefit plans.

Q. How do I figure out what kind of retirement plans my parents have?

A. If the answer is not clear from your parents' paperwork (for example, their written retirement and incapacity plans or their tax returns), the next step is to check their bank statements and ask the bank to tell you where their deposits are coming from. You can only obtain this information from your parents' bank if you are a joint holder on the account, an agent under a power of attorney for property, or a guardian of the estate.

Q. I think my father is entitled to a pension, but he is not receiving any pension income. How can I find out whether or not he is entitled to pension income?

A. If you know who your father worked for and if that company is still in business, contact the company's human resource department and ask them to identify the pension plan administrator. Then, write to the pension plan administrator and ask them to send you the **summary plan description** and his **individual benefit statement**. The pension plan administrator is required to respond to your request within thirty days. As with any other confidential information, in order to obtain it, you must first show that you are either your father's agent or his guardian. If you do not know the name of the company or if it is no longer in business, contact the Employee Benefits Security Administration of the U.S. Department of Labor by calling (866) 444–EBSA (3272) or visiting *www.dol.gov/ebsa*.

Q. I have located my father's employer, but they have told me that he is not entitled to benefits. Could this be true?

A. Possibly. First, make sure that you are looking in the right place. If your father was a member of a union, his pension plan may have been provided and administered through the union rather than his individual employer. See if you can find paperwork outlining his union membership and the responsibilities of the union. Then, make sure you're not dealing with a situation in which your father had a pension, but now, for whatever reason, there are no more funds in the plan. Your father may have been entitled to benefits at the start of his retirement and chosen to receive a lump sum rather than monthly benefits. Or, as discussed above, if your father had a defined-contribution plan or IRA, the funds may have been depleted or expended prior to his retirement. If there is no money left, you will have to try to help your father find other income.

As noted above, employers are not required to provide a pension or any other kind of retirement benefit. Moreover, even if your father's employer offered a pension plan, he may not have been eligible to participate. Employers can provide pensions to some of their employees and not others. There are very specific laws governing which employees may be excluded from pension plans. (For instance, part-time workers and workers in a particular division can be excluded, but lower-paid workers cannot be excluded simply because of their pay grade.) Another reason that your father might not be covered under the plan would be if he did not work for the employer long enough for his benefits to vest. It is only after benefits have **vested** that an employee has a right to those benefits. Federal law requires that vesting must occur no more than five years after the person has been employed.

The national Pension Rights Center (*www.pensionrights.org*) may be able to provide you with more information on how to ensure that your father is receiving any pension benefits to which he is entitled.

▶ **VESTING**

A pension is said to **vest** when you have the right to all the benefits you have earned. If your pension has vested, you have the right to the benefits even if you leave the job for another job or for any other reason.

Q. How can I make sure that my father is receiving the correct dollar amount each month?

A. The summary plan description and individual benefit statement from the plan administrator will help you figure out how much he should be receiving. After you review these documents, if you believe there is an error, you can follow the appeals process outlined in the summary plan description.

Q. My father worked for years, but is now sick. We are afraid that if he dies, my mom won't receive any of his pension. Is this true?

A. Perhaps. Defined-benefit plans provide a **joint and survivor annuity** for spouses. This means that when the beneficiary dies, his or her spouse receives a reduced monthly benefit for the rest of his or her life. However, it is possible to forego joint and survivor benefits. Some couples choose to do this in order to receive a lump sum or higher monthly benefits when the beneficiary is alive. However, your father would only have been able to do this with your mother's consent; a waiver of joint and survivor annuity can only be made if the employee's spouse consents in writing to the waiver.

Defined-contribution plans are somewhat different in this regard. With defined-contribution plans, payment may only be offered as a lump-sum benefit to spouses in the amount of 100 percent of the balance of the account at the time of death. Furthermore, under defined-contribution plans, the employee can withdraw funds without the consent of his or her spouse. This could mean that, prior to his death, your dad depleted the plan without your mom's knowledge.

Q. My parents divorced when they were in their sixties after forty years of marriage. My mother is now eighty-five and does not receive any of my father's pension. Is there anything I can do about this?

A. Your mother may still be entitled to a share of your father's pension. At the time they were divorced, the court should have entered a **qualified domestic relations order** (QDRO) that specified what, if any, share your mother was to receive of your father's pension. If your mother does not have a copy of this document, you can obtain it from the court or the attorney who represented her in the divorce. This document will tell you how much your mom should be receiving. If your mom is not receiving what she is owed, contact the plan administrator and, if necessary, file an appeal following the directions in the plan summary.

Unfortunately, many couples divorce without having the court enter a QDRO. If this occurs, the spouse waives his or her right to the beneficiary's pension. If no QDRO was entered when your parents divorced, and if your mom was represented by an attorney, this might even be the basis for a malpractice suit. You should consult with an attorney experienced in elder law or employee benefits in order to determine the appropriate next step.

Trusts

Q. What is a trust?

A. A **trust** is a legal arrangement, described in a document, that transfers ownership of property from a grantor to a trustee. A

▶ **OBTAINING MORE INFORMATION**

The following organizations and government agencies offer a wealth of free and easy-to-read information about pensions:

- The U.S. Department of Labor (*www.dol.gov/dol/topic/retirement/*)

- The Pension Benefit Guarantee Corporation (*www.pbgc.gov*)

- The Pension Rights Center (*www.pensionrights.org*)

trust generally involves at least three people: the **grantor** (the person who creates the trust, also known as the **settlor** or the **donor**), the **trustee** (who holds and manages the property for the benefit of the grantor and others), and one or more **beneficiaries** (who are entitled to the benefits). The property can be any kind of property—money, real estate, stocks, collections, business interests, or personal possessions.

Putting property in trust transfers it from your personal ownership to that of the trustee who holds the property for you. The trustee has legal title to the trust property. For most purposes, the law looks at these assets as if the trustee now owned them. For example, many (but not all) trusts have separate taxpayer identification numbers.

But trustees are not the full owners of the property. Trustees have a legal duty to use the property as provided in the trust agreement and as permitted by law. The beneficiaries retain what is known as **equitable title** or **beneficial title**—that is, the right to benefit from the property as specified in the trust.

Q. Why would my parents want a trust?

A. There are a number of reasons. First, a trust is a way for your parents to give a trusted person (which could include a family member, an attorney, or a trust company) control over property when they no longer have the desire or capacity for such control. A trust therefore may provide some important peace of mind to your parents as they age. Through a properly created trust, your parents can give another person (the trustee) the day-to-day responsibilities of maintaining their property and investments and, at the same time, your parents can still receive income from the property. They can set up the trust so that they receive monthly payments, and anything left over in the trust at their death passes to their beneficiaries. A trust may be a good idea for anyone who is worried about losing the ability to manage his or her money and assets prudently. It is also an effective way to avoid the expense and undesirable aspects of a court-appointed guardian. To manage the property contained in a trust, it is not necessary to appoint an agent under a power of attorney or have a guardian appointed. This can be particularly advantageous if your parent is planning on splitting time between two locations.

In addition, a trust can be set up so that it generates a stream of income—not only for the grantor, but also for other family members, loved ones, or a charity after the grantor no longer needs the income.

Additionally, an irrevocable trust may offer tax advantages, allow the grantor to qualify for public benefits such as Medicaid, and protect assets from creditors. For some government benefits, your parents may be required to "spend down" some of their assets before they become eligible to receive the benefits, and a properly created trust may protect some of your parent's assets from this spend-down requirement. For more information on spend-down requirements, see chapter 9.

Finally, by reducing the number of steps that will legally need to be taken, a living trust may shorten the time between your parent's death and the time that his or her heirs receive property. A trust can give your parent a sense of participation in the distribution of his or her estate, and allow your parent the chance to refine his or her wishes regarding the disposition of his or her property at death.

Q. If my parents are thinking about buying a trust, what should they consider?

A. First and foremost, setting up a trust can be expensive. Depending on the size of the estate, the cost of creating a trust may be much higher than the cost of going through probate or drafting a power of attorney. A trust, like a will, should be a document that is carefully tailored to the needs of the person creating it. While there are "trust mills" and form trusts available for creating trusts using boilerplate (i.e., standardized) language, these should be avoided.

As a general rule, trusts make the most sense for people with cash assets of $400,000 or more. Depending on the size of your parent's estate and the law and practice in his or her state, creating a trust may be more costly or burdensome than drafting a power of attorney for property or going through the probate process. Your parent's individual circumstances will dictate which planning tools make the most sense and are the most cost-effective. It is absolutely necessary to consult with an experienced elder law attorney when considering these trust options. A trust should only be created as part of a comprehensive plan developed by an attorney who is knowledgeable about the tax implications and the effect a trust may have on public benefits such as Medicaid.

In addition, managing a trust may be complicated, and may require the services of a professional trustee, such as a bank, who will charge a fee. This can sometimes be quite expensive. While a trust allows the family to step in to help when an older person loses capacity, it may not cover everything that the older person owns, and therefore a power of attorney for property will still be necessary. (If the person has died, a will may also be necessary in order to place the remaining property into the trust.) It may be much less expensive to draft a power of attorney that gives an agent control over all of your parent's property than it is to create a trust. If your parents have substantial assets (and the necessary capacity), you and they should consult with an experienced attorney to determine which planning tools are the best and most cost-effective.

Last but not least, a great deal of fraud often takes place in the marketing and sale of trusts. This problem is discussed further in chapter 11.

Q. What is the difference between a revocable and an irrevocable trust?

A. The grantor can change the terms of a **revocable trust**, or even dissolve it completely at any point during his or her lifetime. In contrast, the grantor cannot modify or dissolve an **irrevocable trust**. Generally, a revocable trust gives the creator great flexibility but no tax advantages, whereas an irrevocable trust (where the beneficiary is someone other than the grantor) offers less flexibility but considerable tax benefits. In addition, an irrevocable trust may protect trust property from the creditors of the trust creator. However, an irrevocable trust often doesn't avoid death taxes entirely. Because of these advantages and disadvantages, your parent should consult with an elder law attorney before setting up a trust.

Q. My dad set up an irrevocable trust. Can we now revoke it?

A. Possibly, but termination is very difficult and costly. If an irrevocable trust does not state how it can be terminated, then it may be terminated if all beneficiaries consent and if the purpose of the trust is not defeated. An irrevocable trust may also be terminated if there was fraud, duress, undue influence, or some other problem when the trust was set up. There may also be other ways in which an irrevocable trust can be terminated, depending on the law in your state. The best advice is to talk to an attorney to determine your options.

Q. My mom is talking about setting up a special-needs trust for my dad, who is under guardianship. What is a special-needs trust? Is this different from a regular trust?

A. A **special-needs trust** is a trust set up for the benefit of a person with a disability. These trusts vary by state and can be rather complicated. The benefit of this type of trust is that it allows the person with the disability to qualify for needs-based public benefits programs such as Medicaid and Supplemental Security Income. If created correctly, the assets of the disabled person are held in the trust, and thereby removed from consideration (for eligibility purposes) for various government benefits such as SSI and Medicaid. The disabled person can then receive public benefits and access funds from the trust. These funds can only be used for very limited purposes, such as paying for services and equipment that are not covered by Medicaid.

There are very strict requirements for creating a special-needs trust, and the requirements can vary greatly by state.

▶ SPECIAL CAUTION FOR IRREVOCABLE TRUSTS

Irrevocable trusts require careful consideration before drafting, precisely because they are irrevocable even if circumstances change.

For example, let's say Bob, age seventy-eight, transfers his house to a trust, naming his son John as his beneficiary for the sole purpose of qualifying for Medicaid should he ever need to go into a nursing home. John promises Bob that he will care for him, in his home, until it's absolutely necessary for him to go into a nursing home. At the age of seventy-six, Bob, who is mentally alert and otherwise healthy, falls and breaks his hip. Bob is placed in a nursing home following his hospital stay for rehabilitation. Bob reaches a point where he is ready to go home, but will still need assistance with bathing, dressing, food preparation, and other household chores. John has since married Jane, who refuses to let Bob move in with them. And John, because of his work and personal obligations, is neither willing nor able to visit Bob every day to help take care of him. Bob cannot afford to pay for the services he would need to stay at home, Medicaid will not cover them, and John will not chip in. As a result, Bob is forced to move into a nursing home.

If Bob had not put his house into a trust, he may have been able to obtain a reverse mortgage, which would have provided him with the funds to pay caregivers. (Reverse mortgages are discussed in chapter 13.) Or Bob could have sold his house and used the proceeds to move into an assisted-living facility, or found some other way to use his home to generate income.

Therefore, if you or a family member are considering such a trust, you should work with an attorney who is knowledgeable about your state's Medicaid law and policies.

Q. How can I find out if my mother created a trust?

A. Carefully review her tax returns, and speak with any attorneys she may have contacted over the years. If any checks or other account information list her as "trustee" or mention "the living trust of [your mother's name]," it is more likely than not that she has set up a trust.

Annuities

Q. What is an annuity?

A. An **annuity** is a financial product that allows a person to deposit funds and receive periodic payments. An annuity allows a person to convert a lump sum of money into a future income stream. There are various types of annuities, and each comes with certain benefits and restrictions; consequently, if your parent is considering such an option, the guidance of an elder law attorney is valuable.

Q. Why would someone purchase an annuity?

A. Annuities earn interest, and therefore can allow a person to increase current income if they are willing to receive payments over a period of time and have nothing left at death. Additionally, an annuity may offer tax advantages. In the past, annuities were also used as a way to qualify for Medicaid. However, recent changes to federal laws have limited the usefulness of using annuities to qualify for Medicaid.

Q. If my dad is thinking about purchasing an annuity, what should I talk to him about?

A. Tell your dad to be careful. As with trusts, there is a high degree of fraud in the marketing and sale of annuities. The purchase of an annuity should be part of a comprehensive plan developed with the help of an elder law attorney who is knowledgeable about the tax implications and the impact of the annuity on his eligibility to collect SSI or Medicaid.

Q. How can I find out if my mother purchased an annuity?

A. The first step, of course, is to ask your mother if she purchased such a policy. If she doesn't remember or no longer has the capacity to answer accurately, you should next look at her tax returns and other insurance policies. An annuity is a type of insurance, and often is sold by a company that also sells life insurance. Therefore, the best place to start your search is with the company who holds your mom's life insurance policy, if she has one. If she doesn't have such a policy, or if she hasn't purchased an annuity from that company, look for documents in her files from other insurance companies.

Life Insurance

Q. Why is a discussion about life insurance included in a chapter about income and assets?

A. Your parent may be able to cash in his or her insurance policy for cash. If the reasons your parent purchased life insurance are no longer applicable, then your parent may be able to cash in the policy and receive a cash payout. Additionally, a person may be able to sell a life insurance policy during his or her lifetime. This is known as a **viatical settlement**. The amount the insured receives will be only a fraction of what their beneficiaries would have received if premiums were paid until the insured person's death.

Q. Why would someone want to sell a life insurance policy if he or she was only going to receive a small percentage of the value?

A. A viatical settlement can raise much-needed funds quickly. It probably shouldn't be the first option for obtaining money, but it can be an important option for someone facing tough financial choices.

Q. Are there risks or disadvantages to a viatical settlement?

A. Yes. First, your parent's beneficiaries will likely no longer receive any benefits from the life insurance policy after the parent's death. There is also a risk of fraud. For this reason, it is best to have an attorney review the terms of a viatical settlement. And

▶ **BUYING A VIATICAL SETTLEMENT**

Be aware that some older people may be interested in buying (rather than selling) viatical settlements. Buying a viatical settlement involves purchasing the health insurance proceeds of an elderly or terminally ill individual, with the idea that the seller (i.e., an ill or elderly person) will receive an immediate sum of money for current expenses and the buyer will get the full value of the policy when that person dies. This type of arrangement is often pitched as having a high return on investment, with the added benefit of helping a sick person. Such arrangements are rare, but are still an option that you should be aware of.

Keep in mind that these arrangements are breeding grounds for fraud, and involve an incredibly risky gamble: betting on the death of another person. In some cases, investors have discovered that they have actually purchased the policies of a healthy person who lied about being ill, or that a sales agent has scammed them into buying from a fake company. If this happens to your parent, he or she may end up having to pay the premiums on the insurance policy until the seller actually does die—or, in the worst-case scenario, he or she may end up losing all of the invested money. Moreover, any proceeds that are actually received under such a settlement will be taxed as ordinary income.

if your parent is considering a viatical settlement, research the company and the broker to ensure that they are upstanding and properly licensed in your state. The North American Securities Administrators Association (*www.nasaa.org*) can help you identify the regulators in your state and provide their contact information.

ACCESSING YOUR PARENT'S INCOME

Q. When can I have access to my parent's income and assets?

A. You will need to have a legal relationship or document in order to access your parent's income (and perhaps even to determine what income your parents have, as is discussed earlier in this chapter). You will need to be your parent's agent, guardian, trustee, or joint tenant, or have some other court order granting you this right. As this can take some time, it is important to determine as early as possible which option will serve your parent's needs best. A consultation with an elder law attorney may help you identify the correct path and the necessary steps.

Q. My mother receives Social Security (or SSI or SSDI) and can no longer figure out how to pay her bills. How can I receive these benefits on her behalf?

A. You can contact the Social Security Administration and apply to become your mother's representative payee. As representative payee, you will receive your mother's government benefits on her behalf, and can then spend that money for her care and support as needed. Chapter 4 provides more information on the duties of a representative payee.

Q. Do I need to be my mother's agent under a power of attorney or her court-appointed guardian in order to become her representative payee?

A. No. In fact, even if you are your mother's agent or guardian, you will still need to apply to the Social Security Administration to become your mother's representative payee. This is because the SSA is a federal agency that makes its own determination as to whether a recipient needs help with his or her finances.

Q. My father is receiving pension benefits. How do I access them on his behalf?

A. Some defined-benefit plans may allow your father to appoint you as representative payee for his pension benefits if you are his representative payee for Social Security or his agent under a power of attorney for property. Other plans may require that guardianship be established. Talk to the plan administrator to determine the necessary steps and paperwork.

PROTECTING YOURSELF WHEN CONTROLLING YOUR PARENT'S MONEY

Q. How do I know how I should spend my parent's money?

A. First, make sure that you are acting in accordance with the state's decision-making standard: substituted judgment (which hinges on what your parent would have wanted) or best-interest (which hinges on what you think is best for your parent). The standard will vary depending on the type of role you have and the state where your parent lives. If you have any questions, review the paperwork creating your role and, if still in doubt, contact a local elder law attorney.

You should also consult with your parent as to his or her wishes, and keep your parent informed of your expenditures on his or her behalf whenever possible. Even if he or she has started to lose some mental capacity, your parent may still be able to communicate certain wishes or desires.

Q. If I am legally permitted to control my parent's finances, can I get in trouble (i.e., be sued) for any mistakes I make? I am not very good with math and finances.

A. Yes, you can be held liable for any errors that you make. If you feel that you need help with your responsibilities, ask the court for permission to use your parent's funds to hire professionals to help you, such as an elder law attorney, accountant, or financial planner.

Q. How do I protect myself from charges of financial mismanagement or exploitation?

A. If you are caring for your parent, you may want to take some steps to protect yourself from claims that you are financially exploiting him or her. Although you may think that the chances of someone raising such claims against you are slim, if such claims do arise, you will be happy for any steps you have taken. Such steps may include:

- Learning the applicable recordkeeping and reporting requirements:
  - If you are a **guardian**, be familiar with your guardianship order and with the law and practice of the state. In particular, know the circumstances under which you must petition the court for approval before expending funds.
  - If you are an **agent**, be familiar with the document that creates the power of attorney, and with the law and practice of the state.
  - If you are a **representative payee**, know the Social Security Administration's requirements for representative payees.
  - If you are a **trustee**, look to the trust document and the law and practice of your state.
- If you have any doubts about your recordkeeping and reporting responsibilities, talk to an attorney in your parent's state who is experienced in elder law issues.
- Always obtain and keep receipts for any goods or services you purchase or obtain on behalf of your parent.
- If you are being paid for your services, keep a log specifically noting the day and time you perform work for your parent.
- Know your limitations: ask the court for permission to use funds to obtain assistance from other professionals when necessary.

REMEMBER THIS

- **If you are starting to care for your parent and determine where income and resources are located, the first step is to talk to your parent. Even if he or she has experienced some cognitive** decline, your parent may still know more about his or her finances than you do, and may be able to tell you about certain sources that you may not otherwise have known about. Next, you should collect as much information and documentation as possible.

• There are a variety of sources from which your parents may receive income as they age, including: Social Security, veterans' benefits, private pension benefits, trusts, and life insurance. Once you identify where your parents' income will come from, you can identify the steps you will need to take in order to access that income if your parent can no longer do so.

• In order to access or control any of your parent's income or assets, you will need to assume some sort of legal role. This is another reason why advance planning can be so important. In an emergency situation, for example, you don't want to be waiting for a court to grant you a guardianship order just so you can pay your parent's doctors' bills.

• If you are spending or controlling your parent's money, you will want to protect yourself from claims of mismanagement or exploitation. The steps you should take include: if you have any questions about what is expected of you, talking to an attorney in your parent's state who is experienced in elder law issues; always obtaining and keeping receipts for any goods or services you purchase or obtain on behalf of your parent; if you are being paid for your services, keeping a log specifically noting the day and time you perform work for your parent; and knowing your limitations (i.e., asking the court for permission to expend funds to obtain assistance from other professionals when necessary).

CHAPTER 6

Health-Care Help

Becoming Involved in
Health-Care Decisions

*Ben's mom was recently admitted to the hospital after suffering
a stroke, and Ben rushed to the hospital to help her. He was
shocked when he got to the hospital and the doctors wouldn't
share any information with him about his mother's condition.
Can they do this? After all, he is her son.*

Privacy and self-determination are central to our rights as
Americans. As a result, with few exceptions, you are the
only person who can find out about your personal medical issues, and the only person whom your doctor can consult about
your medical treatment—unless you have given someone else
the authority to access your health-care information. On the one
hand, this rule makes complete sense and provides individuals
with privacy and peace of mind. On the other hand, if you are
caring for an aging parent, it can be incredibly frustrating to
learn that doctors cannot discuss your parent's medical condition with you without his or her consent. Nonetheless, the rule
exists because medical professionals owe certain privacy and
confidentiality rights to their patients, regardless of a patient's
age or mental status.

Some states have health-care surrogate laws that allow doctors to turn to family members if a patient lacks decision-making
capacity. (These laws are discussed in more detail in chapter 4.)
However, health-care surrogacy laws are often applied inconsis-
tently and may not be of much help to you. For these reasons, it
is essential that you and your parent take the necessary steps to
ensure that you (or someone else your parent chooses) are able
to work with his or her doctors. This chapter outlines some of

your parent's privacy rights, and explains how you can become involved in health-care decisions.

Q. My dad gets upset talking about his declining health. Can I work directly with his doctor and remove my dad from the process?

A. Not without your father's permission. Contrary to some depictions on television and in the movies, physicians cannot shield competent patients from their own medical information or turn to family members for direction on how to proceed. Medical decisions are governed by the doctrine of **informed consent.** This means that physicians must explain treatment options to patients and provide them with enough information to make an informed decision about how to proceed.

Unless there is a court-appointed surrogate (i.e., a guardian) or an agent under a power of attorney, or unless a health-care surrogacy law applies, your parent's physician must make an effort to explain medical conditions and treatment options directly to your parent, and to elicit his or her directions about how to proceed. This can be particularly troubling when there has been a diagnosis of Alzheimer's or some other type of dementia. In those cases, family members may prefer that the physician withhold information from a parent, but unless your parent has been judged by a court to be incompetent or you have power through a valid power of attorney, the physician is required to work directly with your parent.

Q. Why can't I just be given this information about my parent? I only want to help.

A. The principles described above are based on the individual rights provided by the U.S. Constitution, and further developed in federal and state laws and the ethical codes guiding professionals. Since 2003, the federal Health Insurance Portability and Accountability Act (HIPAA) has further restricted many health-care professionals from providing any information about a patient to a third party, including whether a particular person is even a patient in the first place. States have additional confidentiality laws that protect medical and financial information. Mental health records are often given the highest degree of protection.

In addition to these federal and state laws, the ethical codes governing doctors, lawyers, social workers, and psychologists also require protection of client or patient confidentiality. Without a court order, such confidentiality can only be breached under very specific circumstances, such as when there is evidence of an imminent risk of serious bodily harm or death, or when a health-care surrogacy law applies. If these circumstances do not exist, sharing information with you without the express permission of your parent would be an ethical violation that could result in professional sanctions or even the loss of a professional license.

Q. Can my dad tell the doctors to keep me updated?

A. Of course. While your parent is capable of making decisions, he or she can inform professionals and institutions that they may share information with you and authorize you to make decisions on his or her behalf. Ideally, this should be done through a power of attorney for health care. Your parent may also be able to provide written permission for specific health-care providers or service organizations to share information with you. Some institutions, such as banks and hospitals, may have their own form for your parent to fill out indicating that information can be shared with you.

It is important to note, however, that in order for your parent to authorize you to obtain information and provide assistance, he or she must have a sufficient level of decision-making capacity. The level required will depend on the complexity of the decision and the law in your parent's state. Once an individual no longer has the required level of decision-making capacity, such authorization can no longer be validly given.

Q. What is covered under a health-care power of attorney?

A. In general, a health-care power of attorney can be used to delegate the power to:
- review medical records;
- make medical decisions, including end-of-life treatment decisions (although many states only allow such decisions to be made by the agent if the document creating the POA contains specific language authorizing it);
- authorize organ donation;
- authorize an autopsy; and
- dispose of remains.

Q. How can I obtain information about my parents' health?

A. Without authorization from your parent, doctors and their office staff cannot reveal any confidential information to you, or even reveal whether your parent has kept an appointment. Likewise, financial institutions cannot give you information that you may need to determine whether bills have been paid. Chapter 3 contains information about how to plan ahead for such circum-

▶ **KNOW WHAT IS IMPORTANT TO YOUR PARENTS**

A critical aspect of advance planning is clearly understanding your parents' values. To assist in helping your parents articulate what is important to them, consider asking them to list their goals and values or to complete a **values history form**. (These can be obtained from various agencies that serve the elderly). This may help your parents to complete their health-care directives, and it will help you understand what is important to them in case you have to make decisions for them later on. For instance, if a new technology arises for the treatment of a medical condition, or if a new type of housing alternative emerges, you may be able to make a decision for your parents even if you never discussed that specific scenario before.

stances, and how to make sure that those individuals who need information about your parents can get it.

Q. What if my parent has already lost cognitive ability completely, but never drafted a power of attorney for health care?

A. If a health-care surrogate law exists in your parent's state, then the law may allow you to obtain medical information and make medical decisions for your parent. (These laws are discussed further in chapter 4.) If your parent's state does not have a health-care surrogate law, or if it has one but the law does not apply to your situation, then you will need to file for guardianship. (Guardianship is discussed further in chapter 3.)

Q. My mom has some cognitive ability, but sometimes she makes strange (and sometimes dangerous) decisions. I am worried about her making a medical decision that isn't in her best interest. What can I do?

A. This is complicated. Until someone is adjudicated incompetent or a health-care surrogate act applies, he or she has the right to make his or her own decisions. In order to make decisions for your parent, you must have some legal authority—for example, through guardianship or a power of attorney.

Regardless of your legal authority, start by talking with your parent about your concerns. Try to determine whether he or she really understands the decisions that need to be made, and the options for treatment and their consequences. If your parent cannot understand the decisions he or she needs to make, or is making decisions that are not consistent with what he or she would have wanted before the decline in cognitive ability, then it is time to have your parent's capacity evaluated by a mental health professional. If your parent will not cooperate with such an evaluation, you will need to begin the guardianship process and ask the court for an order compelling your parent to comply with the capacity assessment.

Q. My dad gets confused very easily and sometimes can't express complex ideas very well. Can I attend doctor's appointments with my dad? We both think it is important that I understand what is going on.

A. Ask your dad to allow you to accompany him to the doctor. Chances are that he won't object, and that he'll welcome your help with understanding complex medical issues and making tough decisions. However, if your dad requests privacy, you will have to abide by his wishes.

Q. How will I know if my parent has had an emergency? Will the hospital call me? What can I do to make sure I am notified?

A. There are several ways to ensure that you are notified in case of an emergency. The easiest option is for your parent to have a **medical alert call plan.** For instance, if your parent lives in a facility, such a plan would list you as the next of kin, and a request for notification will already be in place in the event of an emergency. A hospital will always ask for family names and a contact person to call in case of an emergency.

Q. If my parent has to go into the hospital, who will be able to visit?

A. This will be determined by the nature of your parent's illness, and by the policy of the hospital. Certain visiting restrictions may apply depending on the unit where your parent is placed. The restrictions are usually in place in order to enforce a certain level of rest and permit a particular level of care. Sometimes if a hospital's restrictions and your own schedule entirely preclude visits (for example, because of your work schedule or the need to arrive from out of town), a call to your parent's doctor or a hospital administrator may help to alter the restriction. However, such restrictions are usually imposed by the hospital, and not at the patient's request.

Your parent can also tell the hospital that he or she does not want a particular person to visit. If your parent has not been adjudicated incompetent by a court, then the hospital will have to abide by his or her wishes.

REMEMBER THIS

- Medical decisions are governed by the doctrine of informed consent. This means that physicians must explain treatment options to patients and provide them with enough information to allow them to make an informed decision as to how to proceed.

- The ethical codes governing doctors, lawyers, social workers, and psychologists usually require that these professionals honor client and patient confidentiality. In general, such confidentiality can only be breached under very specific circumstances, as when there is evidence of an imminent risk of serious bodily harm or death, or if a health-care surrogate law applies.

- Until someone is adjudicated incompetent or a health-care surrogacy law applies, he or she has the right to make his or her own decisions. In order to make decisions for your parent, you must have some legal authority—for example, through guardianship or a power of attorney.

CHAPTER 7

Paying For Health Care

Understanding Insurance, Government
Benefits, and More

Both of Nick's parents have started to experience medical is-
sues, from high blood pressure to diabetes and a broken wrist.
Nick knew to expect increased medical bills as his parents aged,
but he had no idea how high the costs would be—especially for
the nursing home that his parents say they would like to move
into. Should his dad's health insurance cover these costs? Are
there any government programs that can help Nick and his
parents? What can Nick tell his parents about Medicare and
Medicaid?

I f your parent has recently experienced a change in health-care
needs, it is likely that health insurance is an important topic
in your family. Understanding the coverage to which your parent
is entitled, and the various options available to him or her, will
save everyone a lot of worry and uncertainty later. This chapter
describes the benefits and limits of health-care programs available to your parent, including government-supported and private
programs.

GOVERNMENT-SPONSORED
HEALTH-CARE OPTIONS

**Q. What are the parameters of a government-
sponsored health-care program?**

A. There are a number of government-sponsored health-care
options that provide important benefits and coverage for older
Americans. It is important to note up front that most of these

programs are not free. Some require monthly premiums, deductibles, and co-payments. None provide full coverage for all treatments, and you should not assume they will cover the long-term care your parents may need. (Long-term-care options are discussed later in this chapter.) Despite their limitations, however, such programs do provide support for many of the health-care needs your parent may face, and can be supplemented by private health-care insurance or long-term-care insurance.

Q. My mom keeps asking me questions about Medicare and her prescription drugs. I don't understand these programs any more than she does. Help!

A. The federal government administers a number of health-care programs. The two largest, and likely the most relevant to your older parents, are Medicare and Medicaid. This chapter will examine each of these programs individually.

Q. Why do I need to know all the details about Medicare and Medicaid? Shouldn't my parents' doctors take care of this?

A. As your parents' advocate, it is important that you understand the details of their health-care coverage for a variety of reasons. First, you will want to ensure that your parents are getting all of the benefits for which they are eligible. It is also important that you understand the limits of such coverage, so that you can help your parents engage in proper planning and research other options.

Medicare

Q. What is Medicare? Are all the parts different?

A. Medicare is a program of basic health-care insurance for older and disabled persons. Practically everyone sixty-five and older is eligible. The exact coverage rules and limitations are complex. The actual coverage determinations and payments to care providers are handled by insurance companies under contract with Medicare.

Medicare is divided into four main parts. The hospital insurance part, or **Part A**, covers *medically necessary care* whether you receive it in a hospital, skilled nursing facility, inpatient psychiatric hospital, or through hospice care. **Part B** relates to medical insurance benefits, and covers *medically necessary physician's services*, as well as outpatient hospital care, many diagnostic tests, rehabilitation services, and a variety of other medical services and supplies not covered by Part A. (These two parts together are often referred to as **Original Medicare**.)

Medicare beneficiaries also have the option of joining a **Medicare Advantage Plan** (or **MA plan**). Collectively, these programs are known as **Part C**. MA plans are health plans run by private companies. If you choose one, Medicare pays a set amount each month to the plan, and in return, the plan must provide all of your Part A (hospital insurance) and Part B (medical insurance) benefits, and must cover at least the medically necessary services that Medicare A and B covers. These plans may offer extra benefits such as hearing, vision, dental, or wellness programs, and must also provide Part D prescription drug coverage at no extra cost. Your parent will be required to pay a monthly Part B premium to Medicare, and may be required to pay an extra monthly premium for the extra services provided by the Medicare Advantage Plan.

The newest benefit under Medicare is **Part D**, the Prescription Drug Coverage Program. Provided through private insurance companies or Medicare Advantage Plans, it is an optional benefits program in which an eligible person may choose to enroll. It covers part of the cost of outpatient generic and many brand-name medications. Within certain guidelines established by the government, each plan has significant flexibility to decide what drugs to cover (i.e., its **formulary**) and to set its own premiums, deductibles, coinsurances, and co-payments. Each plan may limit coverage to a specific list of drugs, and the list can change during the year upon sixty days' notice to your parent and his or her treating doctor.

Q. What does Medicare Part A (hospital insurance) cover?

A. Part A coverage, while generally referred to as "hospital insurance," actually covers a complex category of services. To understand the coverage, it is best to look individually at each type of Part A coverage: hospital care, skilled nursing care, home health care, and hospice care.

Q. What does hospitalization under Part A include?

A. Part A hospitalization coverage includes:
- a semiprivate room and board;
- general nursing;
- the cost of special-care units, such as intensive-care or coronary-care units;
- drugs furnished by the hospital during the patient's stay;
- blood transfusions;
- lab tests, X-rays, and other radiology services;
- medical supplies and equipment;
- operating and recovery room costs; and
- rehabilitation services.

Q. What will my parents have to pay to get Part A coverage in a hospital?

A. Although there are deductibles and co-payment costs for Part A, there is no monthly premium for individuals who have paid adequate Medicare taxes. In 2008, the Part A deductible was $1,024 per benefit period. For exact information on the current deductible, you should talk to your parents' primary health-care provider or the local Medicare office.

Q. If my mom is admitted to the hospital, will Part A kick in as soon as she is admitted?

A. For hospital care, Part A will pay hospital costs from the first day of admission through the sixtieth, after your mom has met her yearly deductible. After the sixtieth day, there is a co–payment; however, once this has been paid, all other costs are covered up to the ninetieth day. From the ninetieth day to the 150th day, there will be another co-payment, and again, once this is paid, Part A then covers all costs. After the 150th day, Medicare will no longer pay for hospital care, and your mom will have to assume all costs or find other funding.

If your mom remains out of a hospital or skilled care for sixty days in a row, then the benefit period ends. A new benefit period will begin again upon admission to a hospital. Once again, a deductible will have to be paid and the payment method (as described above) will resume. There is no limit to the number of benefit periods.

While psychiatric hospitalization is also covered, it has different benefit periods than general hospitals for Medicare purposes. Medicare offers a lifetime benefit of 190 days in a specialized psychiatric hospital.

Q. What types of skilled nursing care does Part A cover? If my parent needs to move into a nursing home directly from the hospital, will we have to worry about paying for it?

A. Probably not. To obtain coverage under Part A, your parent's condition must require skilled nursing or skilled rehabilitation services on a daily basis that, as a practical matter, can be provided only in a skilled nursing facility. Part A will cover skilled care in a nursing home or rehabilitation hospital, but only after a minimum three-day hospital stay for a related illness or injury. In order for coverage to apply, your parent's doctor will have to prescribe treatment that requires daily skilled care, such as intravenous injections or physical rehabilitation. Medical equipment and medical social services may also be covered.

Your parent must have stayed in a hospital for at least three days and be admitted within a short time (usually thirty days) after leaving a hospital, and the skilled care received must be based on a doctor's order. Most nursing home residents do not re-

quire the level of nursing services considered "skilled" by Medicare. Consequently, Medicare pays for relatively little nursing
home care. In addition, not every nursing home participates in
Medicare or is a skilled nursing facility. Ask the hospital discharge staff or nursing home staff if you are unsure of the facility's status.

It is important (and often a source of much frustration) to
note that custodial care and long-term care do not qualify as
"skilled care" for purposes of Medicare coverage. The term **custodial care** generally refers to assistance with the activities of
daily living. **Skilled care** refers to specialized services that require the expertise of professional skilled and rehabilitation
staff, including registered nurses, physical or occupational therapists, speech therapists, or audiologists.

▶ **MEDICARE COVERAGE OF SKILLED
CARE IN NURSING HOMES**

Generally, Medicare does not pay for long-term care. However, if a person needs skilled care in a nursing home after three days or more in the
hospital, some benefits will be provided by the Original Medicare Plan.
As with hospitalization coverage, there are some co-payments required
depending on how long your parent has been using the services. (The following numbers reflect applicable amounts in 2008.)

For Days	Medicare Pays	You Pay
1–20	Everything	Nothing
21–100	Everything after co-payment	Daily co-payment of $128
Beyond 100	Nothing	Everything

Remember: if custodial care is the only type of care needed, it will not be
covered. Many families are unaware of this important coverage distinction until it is too late.

▶ **COVERAGE DENIAL BASED ON CUSTODIAL CARE**

If your parent is denied coverage on the basis of the distinction between skilled nursing care and custodial care, find out if your parent needs the skills of a professional nurse or therapist to administer injections, to change sterile dressing, or for rehabilitative services. If this is the case, you may be able to appeal the denial.

Q. What types of services are covered by Part A home health-care coverage?

A. Medicare Part A covers part-time or intermittent skilled nursing care; physical, occupational, and speech therapy services; medical social services; part-time care provided by a home health aide; and medical equipment for use in the home. However, the benefit does not cover general household services. From a practical standpoint, coverage for these services is actually very limited due to the restrictions outlined below.

Q. Is my parent eligible for such services?

A. To be eligible for home health-care services, your parent must meet four conditions:

1. He or she must be under the care of a physician who determines the need for home health care and sets up a plan.

2. Your parent must be homebound, although he or she need not be bedridden. An individual is considered **homebound** if leaving home requires a considerable and taxing effort, and if any absences from the home are either for medical care or to attend adult day care or religious services, or are infrequent or for periods of relatively short duration.

3. The care your parent needs must include intermittent skilled nursing, physical therapy, occupational therapy, or speech therapy.

4. The care must be provided by a Medicare-participating home health-care agency.

A general need for homemaker services will not satisfy these requirements.

In 2008, if your mom meets the eligibility requirements, she will not pay for home health services, but she will be required to pay 20 percent of the Medicare-approved costs of durable medical equipment. **Durable medical equipment** is equipment that is customarily and primarily used solely for medical purposes, and includes oxygen equipment, wheelchairs, leg braces, and surgical dressings. In some cases, Medicare will only pay the cost of renting the equipment.

Q. What counts as hospice care under Part A?

A. A **hospice** is an agency or organization that provides primarily pain relief, palliative care, symptom management, and supportive services to terminally ill people. Medicare Part A will pay for physician services and twenty-four-hour availability, illness-related supplies, and all pain management drugs for a patient who is receiving such services through hospice care. Hospice services may also include physician or visiting-nurse services, individual and family psychological support, inpatient care when needed, medications, social services, counseling, and respite care for family caregivers. Short-term homemaker and home health aides may also be available. Some co-payments will likely be required for prescription medicine.

Q. How will we know if my parent is eligible for hospice coverage under Medicare?

A. To be eligible for hospice care, your parent must have a doctor certify that he or she is **terminally ill** (which is defined as having a life expectancy of six months or less); your parent must choose to receive hospice care instead of standard Medicare benefits; and the hospice must be a Medicare-participating program. Generally, this means that other medical interventions for terminal illness and benefits to pay for them are stopped—that is, Medicare will no longer pay for treatments to "cure" the terminal condition.

Benefits will still be provided for standard care in cases of illness or injury not related to the terminal illness. If your parent requires hospice care in the home, this is generally also covered through special benefit periods. There is usually no time limit on such coverage.

Q. My mom is on a feeding tube and we want to get her hospice care. Will Medicare still cover the costs of her feeding tube?

A. Possibly, but only if insertion of the feeding tube (or other medical equipment such as a ventilator) does not prolong life expectancy beyond six months.

Q. I need a break from helping to care for my mom— she's a hospice patient, and it's just getting to be too much. Will Medicare's hospice coverage cover respite care?

A. Yes. A unique Medicare benefit included as a part of hospice care is an allowance for respite care. This means that Medicare will cover your parent's placement in an inpatient facility for up to five days so that you and the rest of your family can have a break. In order to be covered, this respite care must be short-term, and you may be required to pay 5 percent of the Medicare-approved costs of the inpatient respite care. If your parent requires hospice care in a facility for longer than the coverage period, then you and your parents may be responsible for some room and board.

Q. How can my family obtain access to this type of respite care?

A. You can apply for respite care through the hospice providing care for your parent. A physician may need to request the service, and the facility offering the respite services must be Medicare/Medicaid certified in order to qualify. If you have questions about how these services work, or about how to set them up, talk to the staff providing care for your parent.

Q. What if my parent breaks a leg while in hospice care? Will these costs be covered by Medicare?

A. If there are injuries or required treatments that are not related to the terminal condition, then standard Medicare benefits will provide coverage.

Q. My mom has some pretty hefty doctors' bills and limited assets and income. Can Medicare help cover her visits to her doctors?

A. Part B pays for doctors' services and other services not covered under Part A. For this reason, it is sometimes called **Supplemental Medical Insurance.** Medicare Part B offers limited coverage for these services regardless of where they are provided—at home, in a hospital or nursing home, or in a private office. Covered services include:

- doctors' services, including some services provided by chiropractors, dentists, podiatrists, and optometrists;
- outpatient hospital services, such as emergency room services or outpatient clinic care, radiology services, and ambulatory surgical services;
- diagnostic tests, including X-rays and other laboratory services, as well as some mammography and Pap smear screenings;
- durable medical equipment, such as oxygen equipment, wheelchairs, and other medically necessary equipment that a doctor prescribes for use in the home;
- kidney dialysis;
- ambulance services to or from a hospital or skilled nursing facility;
- mental health services, although Medicare generally pays only 50 percent for such services;
- certain services of other practitioners who are not physicians, such as clinical psychologists or social workers;

- certain vaccinations such as those for flu, pneumonia, and hepatitis B;
- prostate cancer screenings;
- pelvic examinations;
- diabetes screening and monitoring;
- colorectal cancer screening;
- bone mass measurements; and
- many other health services, supplies, and prosthetic devices that are not covered by Medicare Part A (Part B also covers some home health services).

Medicare B does not cover:

- routine physical examinations;
- most routine foot care and dental care;
- examinations for prescribing or fitting eyeglasses or hearing aids;
- prescription drugs that do not require administration by a physician;
- most cosmetic surgery;
- immunizations, except for certain persons at risk;
- personal comfort items and services; and
- any service not considered "reasonable and necessary."

Q. What will my parents have to pay for Part B coverage?

A. There is a monthly premium required for enrollment in Part B. Your parents will also have to meet an annual deductible before Part B benefits will kick in. Then Medicare generally pays 80 percent of Medicare-approved amounts for covered services for the rest of the year. Your parent will have to pay the other 20 percent of the approved amount. There is no cap on the patient's share of the cost. (Note that this approved amount changes annually.)

If a physician or other provider charges your parent more than the Medicare-approved amount, then your parent's liability depends on whether the provider accepts assignment. **Accepting assignment** means that the provider agrees to accept the

Medicare-approved amount as payment in full. If the provider does not accept assignment, then generally your parent must pay for any excess charge over the Medicare-approved amount, but only up to certain limits. If your parent receives Medicaid, however, then the physician must accept assignment.

The government presently sets the limit on physician's charges at 115 percent of the Medicare-approved fee schedule. Doctors who charge more than these limits may be fined, and your parent should receive a refund from the doctor.

Let's look at an example that illustrates the effect of accepting assignment. Say that Mrs. Jones sees Dr. Brown on June 1 for medical care. She has already paid her $100 annual deductible for covered Part B medical care. Dr. Brown charges $230 for the visit. The Medicare-approved amount for such services is $200, so Medicare will only pay 80 percent of $200, or $160.

If Dr. Brown accepts assignment, then Mrs. Jones must pay a $40 co-payment (that is, 20 percent of the $200 approved amount). If Dr. Brown does *not* accept assignment, then Mrs. Jones *still* must pay that same $40, but she *also* must pay the extra $30 that Dr. Brown is charging her (i.e., the amount in excess of the Medicare-approved amount). Her total payment will be $70. Note that Dr. Brown's actual charge ($230) is within 115 percent of the Medicare-approved amount ($200), and is therefore permissible.

▶ **CURRENT INFORMATION**

Because annual deductibles, co-payments, and other Medicare requirements can change quickly and seriously impact your parents' coverage and eligibility, it is important to stay up-to-date with this information. For current information, contact an experienced elder law attorney, or contact the U.S. Department of Health and Human Services directly at *http://www.medicare.gov/* or 1–800-MEDICARE.

Certain services have higher co-payments. For example, mental health services require a 50 percent co-payment from patients. Often because of these co-payment and deductible requirements, some patients opt out of Part B, preferring to rely on their own private insurance.

Q. My parent is asking me for advice about enrolling in Part C. What should I say?

A. Medicare Part C plans vary significantly by state. Most of these plans provide more benefits and lower co-payments than Parts A and B alone. However, your parents will be restricted to seeing only those doctors that belong to the plan, and must go to certain hospitals to receive services. Any decision to opt into Medicare Part C should be made with the careful guidance of a professional who is knowledgeable in Medicare benefits. Your local agency on aging can help with this. Selecting the proper Part C program is important. To join, your parents must have Medicare Part A and Part B. They will still have to pay their monthly Medicare Part B premium to Medicare. In addition, they might have to pay a monthly premium to the Medicare Advantage Plan for the extra benefits.

If your parents decide to join a Medicare Advantage Plan, they will use the health card that they get from their Medicare Advantage Plan provider for their health care.

Q. My parents have a number of prescriptions. Will we have to find a way to pay for all of these ourselves?

A. Your parents' prescriptions may be covered by Medicare. The prescription drug benefit of Medicare is referred to as **Part D**. The Part D program only covers some of the costs of some drugs; it will not necessarily cover all of your parents' medications. There are many Medicare drug plans, and in most states your parents will be presented with a confusing array of stand-alone prescription drug plans (PDPs) and Medicare Advantage Plans (such as HMOs or PPOs) from which to choose. State Health

Insurance Assistance Programs (SHIPs) can help you and your parents identify the most important factors to consider in making their selection, including the annual cost of a plan (i.e., the cost of premiums, deductibles, and co-payments), whether the drugs they need are included, and whether their local pharmacy is in the plan network. Your parents can change plans annually, and because plan coverage and prices change yearly, they should review their coverage annually to make sure they have a plan that best fits their circumstances.

Q. What will Part D cost my parents?

A. Usually, a deductible must be paid first. After that, Medicare will pay up to a set percentage of the prescription costs, and up to a set amount. After that set amount, your parents will again have to assume full responsibility up to another predetermined amount. If the cost of your parents' medicines still exceeds that final amount, Medicare coverage will kick in again at the set percentage. For example, let's say that individuals who sign up for Part D have to pay the first $275 of their prescription medicine costs as a deductible. Then Medicare pays 75 percent of the next $2,235 of the costs of drugs. After the $2,235, there is a gap in coverage. This is often referred to as the **Donut Hole**. This means that after Medicare has paid 75 percent of the next $2,235 worth of drugs, your parent will have to pay another $3,216.25 in out-of-pocket costs. After that, Medicare will begin to pay 95 percent of the cost of covered drugs until the end of the calendar year. These numbers can change annually, so it is important to talk to your local Medicare office or State Health Insurance Assistance Program to determine the actual deductibles for your parent under a given Part D plan.

Q. My mom needs to enroll in Medicare. How does she do this?

A. The Medicare enrollment process depends upon the type of Medicare in which your parent wishes to enroll.

Part A and Part B

Parts A and B are open to all individuals sixty-five and older who are eligible for Social Security, even if they are still working. Enrolling is not a problem for most people; everyone applying for Social Security or railroad retirement benefits is automatically enrolled.

If your parents aren't eligible for Social Security, they can enroll after age sixty-five, but they will have to pay a sizable monthly premium. Additionally, some younger persons who have received Social Security disability for more than twenty-four months are eligible, as well as certain persons with kidney disease.

Part C

When your parents are first eligible for Medicare, they will decide whether to join a Part C plan. (If they make no selection, then they will become part of the Original Medicare Plan, which includes Parts A and B.) Each year they can review their health and prescription needs and, if desired, switch to a different plan in the fall.

Part D

Regardless of health, income, or prescription drug needs, everyone who has Medicare can enroll in a prescription drug plan. Part D is optional, and no one is automatically signed up for this benefit. However, if your parents delay enrollment after their initial eligibility, this will result in an increased premium. Enrolling in Part D is a separate process from enrolling in Medicare, but it usually occurs at the same time.

Q. Can I enroll my parent in Medicare?

A. You cannot enroll your parent in Medicare unless you have been appointed as guardian or are your parent's agent under a power of attorney, or his or her designated representative (a form available from *www.medicare.gov*).

▶ **OTHER DRUG COVERAGE**

Your parents do not have to enroll in a Medicare Part D prescription plan if they have other prescription drug coverage that is equal to or greater than Medicare Part D coverage.

Q. What if my parents can't afford all of these deductibles and co-payments? Will I have to find a way to pay?

A. There are two options for your parents: purchasing a supplemental Medigap policy, or seeing if they qualify for certain government programs to help with the costs. Medigap insurance policies are sold by private insurance programs and may cover deductibles and co-payments. Such policies are discussed later in this chapter.

If your parents cannot afford Medigap insurance policies and they meet certain income and resource tests, then their state's Medicaid program may assist them in paying Medicare costs. These programs may help your parents pay for their Medicare premiums, deductibles, and co-payments. The income and resource tests for Medicare Savings Programs are more generous than the tests for regular Medicaid eligibility, so even if your parents are not eligible for Medicaid, they may still be eligible for help with Medicare costs. (Medicaid is discussed further later in this chapter.) If you think your parent may qualify for this type of financial help, call the State Medical Assistance Office at 1–800-MEDICARE.

Q. How are Medicare claims filed and paid? Will I need to make sure my parents can pay up front?

A. Again, the answer differs depending on the type of Medicare. For Part A benefits, the provider submits the claim directly to the fiscal intermediary (i.e., the insurance company). The provider will charge your parents for any owed deductible or coinsurance payment. For Part B claims, doctors, suppliers, and other providers are required to submit your parents' Medicare claims to the carrier (the insurance company) in most cases, even if they do not take assignment. The provider will charge your parents (or their private supplemental insurance) directly for any deductible, coinsurance, or excess charge owed. If your parents belong to a Medicare Advantage Plan, there are usually no claim forms to be filed, although there may be a co-payment for any covered services. For prescription drugs covered under Medicare Part D, the plan pays the covered portion directly to the pharmacist, while your parents pay deductibles and co-payments at the time of purchase.

Q. What if we disagree with a Medicare decision? How can my parents appeal?

A. Your parents have the right to appeal all decisions regarding service coverage or the amount Medicare will pay on a claim. If a claim has been denied in whole or in part, it is usually a good idea to appeal, especially if the basis for denial is unclear. A surprisingly high percentage of denials are reversed on appeal. In any case, the appeal will make clear the reason for the denial.

Medicare Parts A, B, and D require different procedures for appealing an adverse ruling. There are several steps in the appeals process. Procedures differ somewhat depending on whether your parents are enrolled in the Original Medicare Plan or in a Medicare Advantage Plan. After the initial levels of review, if the dispute hasn't been resolved, all parts of Medicare include the option of a hearing before an administrative law judge—and even a review by a federal court if sufficient amounts of money are at stake.

Help your parents to be conscious of the time limits for filing appeals, because they may lose their rights if they wait too long. It may be a good idea to get assistance with an appeal from a legal-services office or a private lawyer, particularly if large medical bills are involved. Nonlawyer volunteers and nonlawyer staff members of legal-service programs also help a number of people with their appeals without charging fees.

Medicaid

Q. Is Medicaid the same as Medicare?

A. No. Medicaid is a health benefit program for people with low incomes. (However, some older people may qualify for both Medicaid and Medicare programs.)

Medicaid coverage (and rules regarding benefits and eligibility) can vary from state to state, whereas Medicare coverage is the same in every state.

Q. Who qualifies for Medicaid?

A. To qualify for Medicaid, a person must have limited assets and income and either be over sixty-five or disabled. (Additionally, Medicaid applies to certain children and families whose income and assets fall below certain levels.) If your parent is over sixty-five or disabled and living on a fixed income, he or she may be eligible for Medicaid.

Q. What are the asset and income qualifications limits for Medicaid?

A. The limits can change frequently, so it is important to contact your local Medicaid office to determine your parents' eligibility. For example, in New York in 2008, if your mom or dad had only $4,350 in assets, or $6,400 as a couple, then they would likely qualify. However, in other states, the limits are $2,000 for individuals and $3,000 as a couple. In some states, if your parents qualify for SSI, they will also qualify for Medicaid. (SSI benefits are discussed in detail in chapter 11.) Because there is so much variation, the best way to determine the asset and income limits for Medicaid in your parents' state is to contact their local Medicaid office. You can find the number for the state Medicaid office by visiting *www.cms.hhs.gov/home/medicaid.asp*.

Q. *My mom's neighbor apparently had to sell her house in order to qualify for Medicaid. My mom is terrified that the same thing will happen to her. Is this really possible?*

A. No. Tell your mom there is a good chance she won't have to sell her house in order to qualify.

In all states, your home is exempt from being considered a countable asset so long as you, your spouse, or certain other qualified individuals live in it. If your parent must leave his or her home in order to receive nursing home care or other long-term care, the home is still exempt, as long as there is a likelihood that your parent will return to the home. States differ as to how and when they determine the likelihood of return. Therefore, it is important to know the specific rules in your state.

All states allow you to keep a very limited amount of cash and personal property. There are variations from state to state, but these exemptions generally include:

- household goods and personal effects up to a certain amount (e.g., a wedding ring);
- the cash value of life insurance, if the face value of all policies the individual owns is $1,500 or less (if the face value is higher, then the cash value is counted as a resource);
- trade or business property needed for self-support;
- the value of burial plots for the individuals and their immediate family;
- up to $1,500 per person in a burial expense fund (the money must be in an account earmarked for burial expenses); and
- money or property the individuals have set aside under a plan to become self-supporting, if they are disabled or blind.

Q. *What about for nursing home coverage? Will we have to sell my parents' house so they can qualify?*

A. Special income and asset rules apply to people who need help paying nursing home bills. Additionally, each state has eligibility rules for individuals going into nursing homes whose spouses are remaining in the community or who are supporting an adult disabled child. These policies are outlined later in this chapter and in chapter 9. More specific information can be obtained from your state Medicaid office.

Q. I have read about older people having to "spend down" their assets to be eligible for Medicaid. Does this mean that my mom will have to get rid of all of her assets?

A. Some states are "spend-down" states and others are "income cap" states. The term **spend down** refers to the spending of any income or assets that exceed the eligibility limits set by the state. If your parents do not have enough money to pay their medical bills, but they have more money than the Medicaid eligibility limit set by their state, then they can take advantage of the Medicaid spend-down provision.

For example, say your dad's income is $5,000 per month and the asset cap in his state is $2,000 per month. Once your dad's medical expenses equal $3,000 in a given month (the difference between his income and the cap), then Medicaid will begin to pay his medical bills for the remainder of the month. When your dad is approved for Medicaid coverage, he will receive a notice indicating the spend-down amount and providing a further explanation of this provision.

It is important to note that some states have other income caps and do not allow individuals to take advantage of a spend-down provision. This means that if your parents' income exceeds the cap by even one dollar in such a state, they will be ineligible for Medicaid benefits for any covered services.

Q. Will Medicaid cover everything? Or should my parents expect to pay something?

A. Medicaid covers a broad spectrum of services. Certain benefits are mandated by federal law. They include:
- inpatient and outpatient hospital services;
- doctors' and nurse practitioners' services;

- inpatient nursing home care;
- home health-care services; and
- laboratory and X-ray charges.

Other services may include those provided by podiatrists, optometrists, and chiropractors; mental health services; personal in-home care; dental care; physical therapy and other rehabilitation; dentures; eyeglasses; transportation services; and more. In all cases, you may receive these services only from a Medicaid-participating provider. Providers may choose whether to participate in Medicaid, and they must meet certain standards in order to do so. Some states have contracted with managed-care organizations to provide comprehensive care to Medicaid-eligible individuals. In these states, your parent may be limited to using the designated care provider for regular care. For outpatient prescription drugs, your parent must enroll in a Medicare prescription drug plan, although he or she will be eligible for a no-cost or low-cost plan.

Q. Will Medicaid pay for nursing homes?

A. Medicaid will cover nursing home expenses if your parents meet the income and resource eligibility requirements. In order for your parents to be eligible, they must require nursing home care and the home must be certified by the Medicaid agency.

Q. What if my dad goes into a nursing home, but my mom stays at home? Will Medicaid pay for his services? Will my mom have to spend down all of her assets first?

A. If your dad has to move into a nursing home and your mom plans to stay at home, their income and resources will be evaluated by the state to determine their eligibility for Medicaid benefits. These rules vary from state to state. It is likely that your mom will be able to continue to live in the community and keep all of the money and assets that are *solely* in her name. However, joint income and assets are different—though she may be able to retain some or all of the joint income under certain circum-

▶ **COMMUNITY AND NURSING HOME SPOUSES**

If one of your parents goes into a nursing home and the other one doesn't, Medicaid lingo provides specific names for their new roles. The parent who goes into the nursing home is referred to as the **nursing home spouse**, and the parent who stays at home is referred to as the **community spouse**.

stances. Otherwise, the state will require part, or perhaps all, of the joint income and assets to go toward paying for the nursing home expenses before Medicaid will make payments.

Q. My dad was receiving Medicaid benefits for his nursing home bill. He has since passed away. Now the state is asking me, as his executor, to pay money out of the estate to cover some of the bill. Can they do this?

A. Likely, yes. After a Medicaid beneficiary (here, your father) dies, federal law requires the state to seek recovery from the beneficiary's estate of some of the payments made by Medicaid. This is called an **estate recovery program**. No recovery can take place until after the death of the Medicaid beneficiary and the death of his or her spouse. While every state is required to have such a program, there are significant variations. If you have concerns about what is happening, talk to an attorney experienced with Medicaid planning.

Q. My parents are adamant about staying at home. They feel more secure at home and want to choose who takes care of them. Will Medicaid pay for home care?

A. Your parents are not alone; many older adults would prefer to stay out of nursing homes. Whether Medicaid will pay for home care varies from state to state. In some circumstances, Medicaid may cover a variety of home- and community-based services including home health, home health aide, and personal-care services. Some states are implementing more consumer-based programs in which the older person gets to choose caregivers and participate in decisions regarding services. Some states have instituted Medicaid waiver programs that allow their residents to use Medicaid dollars for home- and community-based services. (These services are discussed in greater detail in chapter 13.) Personal care, adult day care, housekeeping, care management, chore and companion services, and respite care programs that give caregivers a break can also be covered under these waiver programs. (Again, these programs will be discussed further in chapter 13.)

If you think one of these Medicaid-funded programs is appropriate for your parent, be aware that such programs tend to have limited funding, and therefore limited enrollment. Some programs have waiting lists. More information can be found at the website for Home and Community Based Services, part of the Clearinghouse for the Community Living Exchange Collaborative, at *www.hcbs.org*.

▶ **ASSET TRANSFER LIMITATIONS**

If it is possible that your parent will need Medicaid in the next five years, you should become familiar with asset transfer limitations in your state. If your parent gives you gifts or transfers property to you for less than market value, this will trigger a period of Medicaid ineligibility. See chapter 9 for more information on such "look-back" periods. If your parent is planning on applying for Medicaid soon, then it might be helpful to consult with an attorney who has experience in Medicaid planning in order to ensure that nothing he does now will render him ineligible for Medicaid later.

Q. How are Medicaid claims filed and paid?

A. Medicaid providers bill Medicaid directly, and Medicaid pays the providers directly. Medicaid will not reimburse your parent for a service he or she pays for out-of-pocket. However, if your parent has paid a provider and that provider gets paid by Medicaid, then the provider should reimburse your parent.

Q. If my parents disagree with a decision made by their Medicaid program, what can we do?

A. Your parents have the right to appeal all decisions that affect their Medicaid eligibility or services. When a decision about their Medicaid coverage is made, they should receive prompt written notice of the decision. This will include an explanation of how they can appeal the decision. The appeals process includes the right to a fair hearing before a hearing officer. You may want a lawyer or a public-benefits specialist experienced in Medicaid law to work with you and your parents.

PRIVATE SUPPLEMENTAL HEALTH INSURANCE

Q. In order to apply for Medicare, my mom is thinking about giving up the health insurance provided by her old employer. Can't she be covered by both?

A. Yes. If your mom receives benefits from her previous employer's health insurance program, or if she is covered by her spouse's plan, then she can still apply for Medicare. However, if she is covered by a private plan, then Medicare is usually the secondary payer after the other insurance pays. If she hasn't enrolled in Medicare and she loses the other insurance, then she may sign up for Medicare during a seven-month enrollment period beginning in the month in which the other program no longer covers her.

To make sure she receives maximum coverage without penalty, she should talk to her employer's benefits office, a Center for Medicare & Medicaid Services, or her local Social Security Administration office.

Q. What are the private health insurance options for my parents?

A. There are various possibilities, depending on your parents' needs and their available money and assets. Medigap policies, retiree group-health benefits, and long-term-care insurance are all possible options. Each of these options is discussed further later in this section.

Q. When talking to my parents about private health insurance options, what considerations should we keep in mind?

A. There are a variety of factors that will impact the best choice for your parents when considering private health insurance options, including:

- the assets and money your parents have available for health-care costs;
- their current health insurance coverage, including the extent of the coverage, its costs, and how long it lasts;
- your parents' past and current health status; and
- the doctors and other health professionals your parents would like to continue to see (i.e., you will want to make sure that whatever plan you choose includes these professionals).

Although it may be difficult to talk to your parents about such issues, especially concerning future health worries, it is important for everyone to be on the same page, and for you and your parents to have the information necessary to make the best decisions.

Q. How can we tell if extra coverage is appropriate for my dad? He already receives Medicare— shouldn't that be enough?

A. If you have already determined that your father does not qualify for Medicaid or any of his state's Medicare Savings Programs, and if he does not have Medicare Part C, then your father could benefit from purchasing supplemental health and long-term-care insurance for the following reasons:

- Medicare does not always pay the entire amount of the hospital bill, and will not pay for an unlimited number of days in a hospital. (This concept was discussed earlier in this chapter.)
- Medicare does not cover as much as a supplemental insurance plan. For example, Medicare does not cover routine physical or eye exams, hearing aids, dental care, or a private room in a hospital (unless medically necessary).
- Medicare offers a limited choice of doctors. As discussed above, doctors are not required to accept Medicare or Medicaid patients. In some cases, these programs pay less than private insurance for care, and some doctors are choosing to opt out.
- Medicare offers limited coverage for long-term care. Medicare only covers nursing home care that becomes necessary following a hospital stay of at least three days, and may not cover as much as private insurance options.
- Medicare offers very limited home care. Medicare will only pay for home care in a limited number of situations, as outlined above.

MEDIGAP POLICIES

Q. What are Medigap policies?

A. **Medigap policies** are private health insurance plans that are highly regulated by the federal government. There are twelve types of these plans, but every policy is not available in every state, and some states have their own specific programs. Medigap insurance policies are sold by private insurance programs and, at a minimum, cover at least some of Medicare's deductibles and co-payments. Some Medigap plans provide coverage for prescription drug costs, home care, and preventive examinations. Medigap policies do not have income or resource tests, but some

> **FINDING MEDIGAP POLICIES**
> The Internet can prove helpful when comparing Medigap poli-
> cies. Visit *www.medicare.gov* and click on "Compare Health Plans and
> Medigap Policies in Your Area." This will allow you to compare Medigap
> policies that will fill the "gaps" in Original Medicare Plan coverage.

options may be more appropriate than others for your parent's
particular financial circumstances.

There is considerable variation in the premiums charged by
different companies, so it is advisable to shop around for plans,
many of which offer identical coverage at different costs.

Q. When should my father apply for a Medigap policy?

A. Your father should apply within six months of enrolling in
Medicare Part B.

**Q. My father has battled diabetes for years. Can a
Medigap insurer refuse to give my father insurance
or decline coverage for a preexisting condition?**

A. No, but only if your father applies within six months of enrolling in Medicare Part B. After that, Medigap insurers can determine eligibility based on health, and could deny for preexisting
conditions.

Q. Do Medigap policies cover prescription drugs?

A. Since the creation of Medicare Part D in 2003, Medigap
policies no longer include prescription drug coverage. Medigap
policies in existence prior to 2003 may include prescription
drug coverage, and may continue to provide that coverage to existing recipients. If your parent has one of these policies, he or
she must decide which is better—Medicare Part D or the drug
coverage provided by the Medigap policy. Both policies cannot
cover your parent's prescription drugs, and he or she will need
to pick one.

Q. *My mom has a Medigap policy, and her doctor's bill is also covered by Medicaid. Which program will cover it?*

A. In a case where there is dual coverage, Medicaid pays first.

Q. *Do Medigap policies cover nursing home care?*

A. Yes, but only to a very limited degree. Medigap policies only cover the co-payments and deductibles for the long-term care provided by Medicare. Medigap policies do not cover additional days in a nursing home above what is covered by Medicare.

Q. *Are there any risks to purchasing Medigap policies?*

A. Yes. There has been a tremendous amount of fraud in the marketing and sale of these policies. The biggest risk is that your parent will pay for coverage of services that are already covered by Medicare.

Q. *How should we protect my parents from unscrupulous sellers? Is there any way to know that we are working with a company we can trust?*

A. If your parents are considering a Medigap policy, they should check with their state department of insurance for additional information on the policies available in their area and for information on state licensing requirements. Additionally, the federal and many state governments provide buyer's guides.

Q. *How can we know if a Medigap policy is the right choice for my parent?*

A. For certain people, a Medigap policy isn't necessarily the best option. While most people need Medigap coverage, your parents may already have enough coverage without it in the following cases:

- If they are already covered by Medicaid, then they do not need a Medigap policy. Medicaid covers the gaps in Medicare and more.

▶ **MORE INFORMATION ON MEDIGAP**

The Kaiser Family Foundation (*www.kff.org*) offers a listing of all State Health Insurance Assistance Programs (SHIPs), which can help you identify and compare the Medigap plans in your area. Additionally, you can find more information through your parent's state department of insurance, or through the federal government's Medicare office (*www.medicare.gov/medigap/*).

- If they are eligible for help under the Medicare Savings Program. (These programs are discussed in further detail earlier in this chapter.)
- If they have retiree health coverage through a former employer or union, it is *possible* that they do not need Medigap insurance. This coverage may be comprehensive, but alternatively, it may be expressly designed to coordinate its coverage with Medicare. You will need to examine the coverage, costs, and stability of your parents' coverage to determine whether it is a better option than Medigap.
- If they belong to a Medicare Part C plan, then your parents probably do not need a Medigap policy, since coverage is normally comprehensive. But they shouldn't give up their Medigap coverage too quickly if they are joining a Medicare Advantage Plan. If they can afford it, they should keep Medigap long enough to be sure they are satisfied with the managed-care organization.

RETIREE GROUP-HEALTH BENEFIT PLANS

Q. My father has recently been hospitalized. He used to be covered by his former employer's insurance. Should they be covering him now?

A. He might have a supplemental plan from his employer, although such plans are increasingly rare. Check with the human resources office of your father's former employer to find out if they offer a supplemental plan and, if so, if your father is covered.

Q. My father's employer provided health insurance when he was working. Shouldn't they have to provide it after he retires?

A. No. The decision to offer health benefits after retirement is completely up to individual companies.

Q. My father's employer promised him health insurance upon his retirement, but is now telling him that such insurance is no longer offered. Is this legal?

A. Probably. Unlike pension benefits, retiree health-care benefits do not necessarily vest—that is, there is no absolute right to such benefits after a certain period of employment. If your father had a written employment contract, check to see whether it unconditionally promised health benefits upon retirement.

Q. My father's employer provided him with health insurance for five years after his retirement, but then stopped offering it. Is this legal?

A. As with the previous question, probably yes. Again, if your parent has a written employment contract, check the contract to see if it addresses the issues of health insurance after retirement.

Q. My dad is thinking about applying for retiree health-care benefits. Are there any risks?

A. The only risk is that your father may later determine that Medicare Part B and a Medigap policy would have provided more coverage in the long run, and at the same or less cost. Medicare Part B premiums increase by 10 percent per year, whereas private insurance companies can raise rates as much as they want. If your father delays applying for Medigap, insurers will not be required to insure him for preexisting conditions, and they may even deny him coverage completely.

Q. *My dad is about to retire and won't look into Medicare—he just assumes his job will continue to offer him health insurance. What can I do? Will he still be covered by his employer's plan?*

A. You should use your father's retirement as an opportunity to have discussions about such important planning topics. Even if your father is initially reluctant to think about the need to take advantage of government benefits, you should at least talk to him about the *options* that are available.

If your father's employer provides him with health insurance that ceases upon retirement, he should ask about COBRA. Under **COBRA** (which stands for the Consolidated Omnibus Budget Reconciliation Act), your father can continue his employer-sponsored health insurance for eighteen months after the benefits end (or twenty-nine months if he is disabled as determined by the Social Security Administration). You father will have to pay the full cost of the premiums (without the employer's contribution), but this is still likely to be a better deal than any insurance he could purchase on the open market. However, because COBRA does eventually end, you and your father will ultimately need to explore other options.

Q. *My parents just divorced. My mom always relied on my dad's employee health insurance. Will she still be entitled to this insurance now that she is divorced? Should I be helping her research her Medicaid/Medicare options?*

A. You should be helping your mother research her options, including government benefits and private health insurance that she can afford on her own. Your father's former employer will cover your mother's health insurance only if, as part of the divorce, a specific order was entered requiring that her health insurance benefits be maintained. Even if this is the case, such benefits will last only for a limited period of time. Regulations regarding this type of coverage are provided by COBRA (discussed above).

In order to determine whether such an order was entered, try to locate the documents relating to your parents' divorce, or contact the clerk of the court that granted the divorce or the attorneys who represented your parents.

Regardless of whether your mother is still covered, use this as an opportunity to talk to her about planning and outlining her options for the future.

LONG-TERM-CARE INSURANCE

Q. I am worried about having to pay for my parent's nursing home care. Are there insurance options to cover such care?

A. You may want to talk to your parents about purchasing a long-term-care insurance plan, which is a type of private insurance plan that may cover such costs. In addition, certain government benefits may cover some nursing home care (these options and their limitations are outlined earlier in this chapter).

Q. What is long-term-care insurance?

A. Long-term-care insurance is private insurance that covers some portion of the costs of long-term care, which may include nursing home care, assisted living, and even home care, depending on the terms of the policy.

Q. How much does long-term-care insurance cost?

A. Premiums vary significantly, based on the age of the applicant, the amount of time coverage will be provided, and whether the policy offers inflation protection. Premiums range from $1,500 a year to over $4,000 a year.

Q. Aren't my parents too old to purchase such policies?

A. If a policy is available, then your parents aren't too old. The average age of people purchasing policies is sixty. The mid-fifties is generally believed to be the best period during which to purchase long-term-care insurance. It is important to note that premiums increase with age.

Q. My mom has diabetes. Will this preclude her from obtaining a long-term-care plan? Do these plans have preexisting-condition clauses?

A. Most long-term-care insurers will issue policies to people with minor preexisting conditions. However, the policy benefits may be denied for a specific period of time. This is an area where policies can vary greatly. Consequently, it is important that you and your parents understand the specific limits of the particular policies you are considering.

Q. Are there deductibles and co-payments?

A. Most policies have an **elimination period** (also known as a **reservation period** or **waiting period**) that must expire before benefits will kick in. During the elimination period, the beneficiary must be receiving the type of care covered by the policy and paying for it out-of-pocket. This works, in essence, like a deductible. Additionally, most plans do not cover the entire cost of care, so the beneficiary will need to make co-payments.

Q. Can premiums increase over the years?

A. Yes. It is likely that the insurer will raise premiums periodically for a class of policyholders. In most cases, premiums will not go up because of a policyholder's illness.

Q. Are there tax benefits to long-term-care insurance?

A. Yes. Long-term-care expenses are deducted as medical expenses. Long-term-care insurance premiums are deductible as

> ### ▶ WHAT ARE LONG-TERM-CARE INSURANCE PARTNERSHIP PROGRAMS?
>
> Some states have established **long-term-care insurance partnership programs**. These partnerships involve collaboration among the state government, the insurance companies selling the long-term-care programs in the state, and those individuals who buy policies. In states with these programs, long-term-care insurance purchasers are assured that they can receive Medicaid without completely depleting their assets should their insurance no longer cover long-term-care expenses. These policies are highly regulated, and provide strong consumer protections. At the time of publication, only nine states had established long-term-care partnerships. But recent changes in federal law now encourage states to form these partnerships, which means that the number of states offering this option will likely increase. The National Clearinghouse for Long-Term Care Information (*www.longtermcare.gov/LTC/Main_Site/index.aspx*) provides up-to-date information on which states offer this program. Your state department of insurance can also provide more specific information about the program available in your state.

well, but only if the long-term-care insurance plan is a **qualified plan.** This means that the following must be true:
- the plan only provides services to someone who is determined to be chronically ill;
- the determination of chronic illness is made by a physician, nurse, or social worker;
- the beneficiary is unable, or needs substantial assistance, to perform at least two of the six basic activities of daily living (as described in chapter 1);
- the policy does not pay for expenses covered by Medicare;
- the policy cannot be cancelled because the policyholder (i.e., the insurance company) is likely to incur expenses; and
- the policy does not have a cash surrender value.

Long-term-care insurance premium deductions are capped based on the age of the taxpayer. However, in order to be deductible, medical expenses as a whole must equal more than 7.5 percent of the taxpayer's adjusted gross income. This means that if the taxpayer's adjusted gross income is $25,000, in order for his or her health-care expenses to be deductible, they must total more than $1,875.

An additional advantage to purchasing a qualified plan is that benefits are not subject to federal taxes when they are received. Depending on where your parents live, there may also be state-tax incentives for purchasing qualified plans.

Q. How do my parents purchase long-term-care insurance?

A. Long-term-care insurance is sometimes available from employers. Your parents' state department of insurance provides a list of qualified plans at *www.consumeraction.gov/insurance.shtml*. Long-term-care insurance can also be purchased directly from insurance companies. The Federal Long Term Care Insurance Program's website (*www.ltcfeds.com*) offers helpful information about general programs and features.

Q. If we have a problem with the long-term-care insurer, whom do we contact?

A. Long-term-care insurance is regulated by the states; federal law only governs the *federal tax* benefits of qualified plans. Therefore, concerns or complaints should be directed to your state department of insurance.

Q. My mom has asked if she should buy a long-term-care policy. Are there any risks I should tell her about?

A. Yes. Long-term-care policies are very complicated, and your parent may end up purchasing a plan that lacks features that are important to him or her. Before purchasing a policy, consider the following questions:

- What levels of care are covered? The most desirable plans cover custodial care in nursing homes, assisted-living facilities, and other residential care facilities, in addition to medically necessary care.
- Where can care be provided? The best plans cover home care (including custodial care and assistance with the activities of daily living) and hospice care.
- What extra benefits are covered? Possibilities include respite care, caregiver training, adult day care, the services of a care coordinator, home accommodations, and alternate plans of care (i.e., any other services or items that your parent needs for care).
- Will the amount of benefits be adequate in the future? The plan should have an inflation adjuster that increases benefits each year by a set percentage, compounded annually.
- How many years of coverage does your parent want? Most people spend less than five years in a nursing home.
- What is the exclusion period for preexisting conditions? Six months is generally reasonable.
- Under what circumstances will the policy begin to pay for benefits? In order to be a tax-qualified policy, the policy must pay benefits when the purchaser is unable to perform at least two activities of daily living for at least ninety days, or when he or she requires substantial supervision to protect him or her from threats to health or safety because of severe cognitive impairment.
- Is a prior period of hospitalization required before benefits are paid out? It is better to purchase a policy without this requirement.
- What is the waiting period during which your parent must pay for services before the benefits will pay out? Most policies have a waiting period of twenty to ninety days.
- Does the policy cover Alzheimer's disease and other forms of dementia? Dementia is a common reason why nursing home care is necessary.
- Will the premium remain the same over the life of the policy?

- Is the policy guaranteed renewable?
- Is the insurance company licensed in your parent's state? Ideally, the insurance agency will have offices and employees present in your parent's state (this can be important in the unfortunate event that you have to sue or otherwise pursue the company for legal purposes).
- Is the policy tax qualified?
- Does your parent's state have a long-term-care insurance partnership program? And, if so, is the policy qualified?

Q. Should my parents have an attorney review a long-term-care insurance policy before they purchase it?

A. Not necessarily, but to do so could be advantageous. If your parent is consulting an elder law attorney for planning purposes,

▶ **MORE INFORMATION ON LONG-TERM-CARE INSURANCE**

The following organizations and agencies may be able to provide you and your parents with more information on long-term-care insurance programs:

- National Clearinghouse for Long-Term Care Information (*www .longtermcare.gov/LTC/Main_Site/index.aspx*)
- Americas Health Insurance Plans (review its Guide to Long-Term Care Insurance at *www.ahip.org*)
- AARP (*www.aarp.org*)
- Federal Long Term Care Insurance Program (*www.opm.gov/insure/ ltc/index.asp*)
- Long Term Care Partners (see its Benefits and Features worksheet at *www.ltcfeds.com/documents/index.html#forms*)

the purchase of long-term-care insurance should be a part of his or her discussions with the attorney. If you have questions about any portion of the contract, don't be afraid to ask the insurance company for clarification or to have the contract tailored to your parents' needs.

FRAUDULENT CONVEYANCE LAWS

Q. My mom is getting ready to apply for Medicaid. Can she simply put all of her assets in my name in order to become eligible?

A. No! Your parents cannot attempt to get around Medicaid eligibility requirements by simply putting everything in your name. This is illegal and could result in your parents being declared ineligible for benefits for a set period of time. In order to ensure that no gift or transfer of property has taken place that would be considered a fraudulent conveyance, Medicaid will look at all conveyances that your parents have made for up to five years prior to them applying for Medicaid.

Q. What is a fraudulent conveyance?

A. If the state Medicaid agency learns that a beneficiary transferred property for less than fair market value, or made substantial gifts to a third party during the five-year "look-back" period, then the Medicaid agency may seek to have a court deem that transfer or gift a **fraudulent conveyance** and require the third party to reimburse the agency. If a Medicaid applicant is found to have made a fraudulent conveyance, it may render him or her ineligible for Medicaid benefits for a specified period of time. This **look-back period** allows the state Medicaid agency to review all gifts and property transfers made by an applicant during the five years prior to application. These laws vary greatly from state to state, and there are important exceptions.

Q. So does this mean that my father can never give me a gift?

A. No, but it does mean that he must be very careful about any substantial gifts or transfers of property if there is any chance he may need to apply for Medicaid within the next five years.

Q. What can we do if my dad honestly wants to give me a gift?

A. Proper planning can help ensure that any gifts are made in keeping with appropriate Medicaid laws and requirements. Talking with an experienced elder law attorney or Medicaid professional can help ensure that your dad doesn't violate Medicaid law.

Q. What could happen if my dad gives me a gift of $10,000 and then shortly thereafter applies for Medicaid?

A. If the gift is revealed to Medicaid, which it will be if your dad's application is filled out honestly, then your dad will be ineligible for Medicaid for a specified period of time. The length of this period will be determined by dividing the amount of money given by the average monthly cost of nursing home care in your father's region. So, for example, if nursing home care costs $5,000 a month, your dad will be ineligible to receive Medicaid for two months from the date of application (10,000 divided by 5,000 is 2, hence the two months).

If for some reason the gift is not revealed at the time of application and Medicaid learns of it later, then Medicaid may ask a court to deem the gift a fraudulent transfer, and Medicaid may recover that amount back from you to reimburse the state for the cost of providing care for your father.

REMEMBER THIS

- Medicare is the government program of basic health-care insurance for older and disabled persons. It has four parts: Part

A (which covers medically necessary care in a hospital, skilled nursing facility, or inpatient psychiatric hospital, or hospice care), Part B (which covers medically necessary physician's services as well as outpatient care and other services not covered by Part A), Part C (which is a health plan run by a private company), and Part D (the prescription drug programs). These are complex programs with complex coverage and eligibility requirements.

- If you or your parents disagree with a Medicare claim decision, you have a right to appeal. There are different appeals procedures depending on the type of claim being made, but many denials are reversed on appeal.

- Medicaid is a health benefit program for people with low incomes. To qualify, a person must have limited assets and income and either be over sixty-five or disabled.

- If your parent has private insurance coverage (for example, from an employer) and is eligible for Medicare, then Medicare will be the secondary payor after the other insurance pays.

- Long-term-care policies can be very important if your parent ends up needing long-term care that would require him or her to deplete funds in order to become eligible for government benefits. However, these programs can be complicated, and your parent may end up purchasing a plan that lacks features that are important to him or her. For this reason, it may be helpful to have an attorney review any long-term-care insurance policies before your parents purchase one.

CHAPTER 8

In-Home Assistance

Service Options

Leo's parents are starting to have difficulty with everyday tasks such as laundry, cooking, and cleaning. Leo doesn't think his parents need to move into a nursing home (and they are adamant that they don't want to do so), but what other options do they have? What is the difference between homemakers and personal attendants? How can Leo help his parents acquire such services?

If you have started to notice that your parent is having difficulty accomplishing some daily activities, this doesn't necessarily mean that he or she has to move into a nursing home. However, it does mean that it is time to ask whether having services provided in your parent's home is appropriate and feasible. This chapter examines various community-based services, discusses how to pay for such services, and outlines how to find the appropriate services for your parent.

AGING IN PLACE

Q. Can my parents stay in their home as they age?

A. This is often the first choice of many older Americans. **Aging in place** is a term used to describe older people who have lived in a place for a number of years, and who plan to stay there even as their needs change. These individuals typically engage home- or community-based services to help them with daily chores.

Some continuing-care communities and assisted-living facilities also provide care services in the community, but these require that your parent first move into the community. (See chapter 9 for more information on supportive housing options.) If your parent chooses to age in place, you may have to work with your parent to find the services that are already in place in the community where he or she chooses to live.

Q. Why would my parents want to stay in our family home? It would be so much easier for everyone if they just moved into an assisted-living community.

A. Your parents, like many others, may want to hold on to the memories, security, and sense of control that can come with staying in their own home. Aging in place allows your parent to remain in a home and community that is familiar and comfortable. Your parent may fear losing his or her independence by moving into a facility.

In some cases, the neighborhood where your parents live may be home to a number of other aging adults, and the neighborhood may thus become a naturally occurring retirement community. **Naturally occurring retirement communities (NORCs)** are those neighborhoods and communities where residents remain for many years. The neighborhood (or even apartment building) may have started as a group of young families who continue to live there, even as parents age and children grow up and move out. Community agencies and even government grants may provide services to enhance the independence and quality of life for residents of these communities.

If your parents' neighborhood resembles a NORC, and if your parents wish to remain in their home, then you may be able to help them work with other community members to their advantage. In many cases, the aging residents in such a community can work together to hire services in bulk. They may even draft informal or formal arrangements outlining how these services will be secured.

There are some other advantages to naturally occurring retirement communities. Such communities can:

- help your parent maintain a sense of independence;
- provide your parent with a sense of safety and security;

- provide a sense of familiarity and eliminate the stress of moving to a strange environment;
- make it easier to obtain services to accommodate the physical, mental, and psychological changes that may accompany aging;
- make it easier to secure contractors to make physical changes to homes, which can facilitate independence and the capacity to accomplish activities of daily living; and
- create a strong sense of loyalty and caring amongst community members, which may prevent feelings of isolation and depression.

Q. I am nervous about my mom staying at home. What if she falls? Or if there is a fire? Her hearing isn't very good, and a fire alarm might not wake her up.

A. A variety of physical changes can be made to your parents' home to help them safely age in place. These include installing grab bars in the showers and bathrooms, elevating toilets, widening doorways and hallways to allow for wheelchairs, installing phones with large buttons and a higher volume, and installing smoke detectors with strobe lights. Your parents may also want to bring in services to assist with some daily tasks. Such services could even include therapy or exercise classes, or assistance with gardening and landscape. As your parents' needs change, they will likely need to reevaluate the services and changes they have in place to see if additional modifications are needed. Constant alertness may make it possible for your parent to safely age in place.

Q. My parents are going to age at home. Where can I get help finding them services and identifying the important issues associated with this decision?

A. The National Aging in Place Council (*www.naipc.org*) offers a variety of resources for helping individuals to continue living in their housing of choice, including information on health-care, financial, legal, design, and building concerns. The website lists many resources for those who decide to age in place. AARP's website (*www.aarp.org*) also offers many resources for those who decide to age in place.

MONEY MATTERS:
PAYING TO AGE IN PLACE

Q. How will my parents afford to stay in their home?

A. With proper planning, your parents may be able to afford to live in their home as they age (if that is what they want to do). In addition to the income options outlined in chapter 5 (including government benefits and pensions), there are some other options for income that can originate from your parents' home and allow them to remain in it. These include home equity conversion plans, reverse mortgages, and renters' or other home exchange programs. These options are each discussed later in this section.

Q. How would a home equity conversion plan help my parents pay to stay in their home?

A. Home equity conversion plans can add to your parents' monthly income without forcing them to leave their home, thereby creating money that can be used to pay for services.

▶ **USING THE HOME AS INCOME**

As the options in this section highlight, if used carefully and correctly, your parents' home can provide them with a source of income as they age, and possibly provide them with needed funds for obtaining services such as home health aides or a geriatric care manager. If your family is considering one of these financing options, make sure you have fully researched the options and companies you are working with, and that you understand the specifics of any agreements.

These plans fall into two broad categories: sales and loans. **Sales** permit the individual to lease back the residence or retain a life estate. They are less common than loans, and need to be worked out carefully and with the benefit of legal advice.

Loan plans, which include reverse mortgages and special-purpose loans, permit your parents to borrow against the equity in their home. These plans involve repayment that is deferred until your parents sell their house, move out, or die. These options should not be confused with home equity loans and home equity lines of credit, which require an individual to make monthly payments immediately or risk losing his or her house.

Q. How does a reverse mortgage work?

A. **A reverse mortgage** allows your parents to borrow against the equity in their home in exchange for a lump sum, monthly payments, or a line of credit. The amount they receive will be based on their age, the value of their home, the value of their equity in the home, the interest rate, the term of the loan, and other factors. Except for some special-purpose state- or local-government-sponsored plans (such as those designed to pay for home repairs), there are no restrictions on how they can use the money. This means that your parents could use the money to pay for various services needed to help them remain at home—

> ### ▶ WHY YOU NEED TO KNOW
>
> You may be wondering why this section provides so much information about how your *parents* can access the equity in their home. Regardless of what you may initially think, this is important information for *you* to know. First, the more information you have, the more you can help your parents evaluate their options. Second, you can't help your parents access services for aging in place if they don't have any money to pay for those services. And lastly, if you one day must step in to control your parents' assets or finances, it is important that you understand the decisions your parents have made.

for example, a physical therapist to come in once a week and a contractor to make changes to a bathroom to accommodate a wheelchair.

A reverse mortgage usually does not have to be repaid until your parents die, or until they sell or move from their home. When the loan does come due, the amount to be repaid cannot exceed the appraised value of the property.

Q. Is my parent eligible for a reverse mortgage?

A. Your parent is eligible for a reverse mortgage if he or she is at least sixty-two years of age and owns and occupies the home as a principal place of residence. Your parent's home should be free of liens or mortgages, except for those that can be paid off at closing by the proceeds from the reverse mortgage. Unlike traditional loans or home equity lines of credit, your parent's income is not considered. Mobile homes and cooperatives are usually not eligible for reverse mortgages.

Q. How will a reverse mortgage affect my parents' other benefits?

A. The income from a reverse mortgage will not affect eligibility for Social Security, Medicare, or other retirement benefits or pensions that are not based on need. However, without careful planning, the income from a reverse mortgage could affect eligibility for Supplemental Security Income, Medicaid, food stamps, and some state benefit programs.

In general, a reverse mortgage payment is considered a loan and will not affect need-based benefits if the money is spent during the month in which it is received. If your parents receive money and do not spend it during that month, it will be counted as a resource and may lead to loss of benefit eligibility. Leaving the money available as a line of credit may avoid this problem.

Be aware that payments received under an annuity mortgage plan will be considered income, even if they are spent in the month in which they are received. Because of the potential impact on public benefits, it is very important that your parents consult an elder law attorney before entering into a reverse mortgage.

Q. What happens to the reverse mortgage when my parents die?

A. When the owner of a home under a reverse mortgage dies, the amount due to the mortgage company immediately comes due. Anyone inheriting a home with a reverse mortgage will have to satisfy the lien—for instance, by paying the remaining amount of the loan, or by obtaining their own mortgage to cover it. If the heirs don't pay off the mortgage, they may lose the home to the mortgage company.

Q. My parents already have a regular home equity loan. Is this the same as a reverse mortgage?

A. No. A traditional home equity loan is very different from a reverse mortgage, and can be risky for an older person on a fixed income. With a reverse mortgage, your parents will borrow against the equity they have already built up in their home. But with a home equity loan, they will have to make regular monthly

▶ **SALE-LEASEBACKS**

In a **sale-leaseback**, your parents sell the equity in their home but retain the right to live there, often paying a monthly rent. The buyer usually makes a substantial down payment to them. Your parents act as a lender by granting the buyer a mortgage. Your parents receive the buyer's mortgage payments, and the buyer receives their rent payments, which are set lower than the mortgage payments, so your parents gain a positive net monthly income. Your parents remain in the home, and can use the down payment and the mortgage payments as income. The buyer can deduct the mortgage interest payment from his or her income. The buyer also will benefit if the value of the property increases.

However, be aware that the IRS requires both the sale price and the rental payments to be fair. Today, there are few tax advantages to sale-leasebacks, so finding an investor may be difficult.

payments of principal and interest or else risk losing their home altogether.

Q. My parents don't want to take out another home loan. Are there other ways they can use their home to generate income?

A. In addition to loan plans, your parents may be able to generate income from the equity they have acquired in their home through sale plans. Sale plans include sale-leasebacks, life estates, and charitable annuities.

Q. My sister has extra money and is willing to buy my parents' house and let them live in it for the rest of their lives. Is this possible?

A. Yes. In a **life estate**, also known as a **sale of a remainder interest**, your parents will sell their home to a buyer, but retain the right to live in the home during their lifetimes. The buyer pays your parents a lump sum, or monthly payments, or both. Your parents are usually responsible for taxes and repairs, but pay no rent. Upon the death of the last living parent, full ownership passes automatically to the buyer. This arrangement is most common within families, as part of an estate plan. Your family should work with an experienced attorney in order to ensure that there are no problems with this plan.

Q. Is home equity conversion the only way to increase my parents' monthly income?

A. Not necessarily. If your parents find that their monthly income does not meet their expenses, they may be eligible for government benefits, such as Supplemental Security Income, food stamps, or Medicaid. Some states also have property tax credit or deferral programs for which they may be eligible. To find out more about these programs, call your area agency on aging. Your parents should consider all of the available options before they make any decision.

> ▶ **DO YOUR RESEARCH**
>
> Your parents should not enter into any of the transactions discussed in this section without first consulting an elder law attorney. All of these transactions may have an impact on receipt of public benefits and on tax liability. You and your parents should make sure that they are working with lending institutions and other organizations that are fully licensed and have good reputations–these transactions can easily be misused as a way to financially exploit older homeowners.

Q. My parents are not sure that they can continue to live in their own home, but they would like to stay in their community. What other choices do they have?

A. They may have several choices, depending on their current and future health needs, their financial circumstances, and their personal preferences. Not all choices may be available in their community. There are home-sharing programs, in which homeowners are matched with individuals seeking housing in exchange for rent or services; accessory units that provide private living in (or next to) single-family homes; or assisted living (described in chapter 9), which combines a homelike setting with services designed to meet individual needs. For more information on programs available in your area, contact your area agency on aging.

COMMUNITY-BASED SERVICES

Q. What kinds of services are available in the community to help my parents age in place?

A. Depending on where your parents live, there are likely a variety of community-based services available to help them. Many are privately run and funded. Some may be provided by state-supported agencies on aging. These services include a broad range of home-health and medical services; homemaker, personal-attendant, and homemaker services; respite services; and adult day care. Some community agencies may charge a fee. Others are subsidized by government funds or private nonprofit agencies and may offer services at little to no cost.

Q. How do these government-funded community-based services work?

A. Every state has an agency devoted to aging residents. Specific programs and funding vary from state to state. Most government-funded or government-supported community-based services for older Americans are administered through the local area agency on aging (AAA). The AAA in your parent's community likely plans programs and services for older adults, as well as advocating on behalf of the senior citizens in the community (such as for tax breaks and housing rights). Many AAAs contract with local agencies to provide a wide range of community-based services.

Q. Will I be responsible for coordinating all of my parent's services?

A. This will depend on the type of agency you and your parent work with (and, of course, on the condition of your parent and his or her desire to coordinate services on his or her own).

▶ **COMMUNITY-BASED SERVICES**

Community-based service is a term used to signify a wide range of services that are available to the community at large. These are services that do not require your parents to be housed in a certain nursing home or hospital in order to access them. Many of these services are available in your parents' home.

▶ **FINDING SERVICES IN YOUR PARENT'S AREA**

To find community-based services in your parent's community, call the state Medicaid office or visit *www.eldercare.gov/eldercare/Public/Home.asp*.

Community-based services may be offered to your parent as services directed either by the agency or by the consumer (i.e., your parent). Agency-directed services will not allow you and your parent much choice regarding who provides the services. An assessment team from the agency will evaluate your parent and send out personnel to provide particular services. For consumer-directed services, you and your parent will have the option to participate in service decisions and to hire the provider of your parent's choice (which may include hiring a family member or friend). Your parent will have a say regarding the level and type of services and the hiring or firing of the specific caregiver.

Q. Who hires the service providers?

A. Your parent will be the client, and if he or she has the capacity, then he or she should be involved in the hiring process. If someone has been appointed as your parent's guardian, then the guardian has the ability to hire such services for your parent.

HIRING AGENCY AND NON-AGENCY SERVICES

Q. Hiring an agency to provide home care to my mother is going to cost much more than simply hiring a woman who lives down the street. Is the care the agency provides that much better?

A. The answer to that question is likely to depend in part on the extent to which your state licenses and regulates home care agencies. It also depends on the extent to which an agency conducts criminal background checks on workers, provides training and supervision, and has liability insurance. Some states require agencies to take these types of steps in order to obtain a license. In states where these steps are not required, some agencies take them voluntarily. While criminal background checks, training and supervision, and liability insurance do not guarantee better care, they can help ensure that the person providing the care has the appropriate background and knowledge and, at a minimum, has not committed crimes in the past. Also, should something happen to your mother or the caregiver, the agency will have liability insurance to cover resulting expenses.

Q. Are there tax concerns if I hire our neighbor?

A. Yes. If you hire someone directly to care for your mother, it is likely that he or she will be considered your mother's employee for tax purposes. This would make your mother responsible for paying income and payroll taxes (i.e., Social Security and Medicare) and possibly unemployment insurance. You or your mother will also be responsible for ensuring that the employee can work legally in the U.S. Even if you and the worker agree that he or she is an independent contractor and will handle these issues herself, the IRS may disagree, and may still be able to seek repayment from your mother in the future.

Q. Does hiring an agency always solve this problem?

A. Not necessarily. In some cases, the agency will tell you that the caregiver is an independent contractor and ask you to pay the caregiver directly. If you do pay the worker directly, the IRS may later determine that he or she is actually your mother's employee, and may therefore seek repayment from your mother even if the initial arrangements were coordinated by the agency.

Q. Are there any other benefits to using an agency?

A. An additional consideration is your schedule and how much flexibility you have. An agency may be able to provide a substitute should their caregiver become ill or otherwise unable to work. (If you have hired a neighbor who falls ill, you may have to provide the care yourself or else find alternative arrangements on your own.) The agency will also provide oversight and offer you other options should you or your mother determine that a different caregiver is needed.

Q. *If agencies have so many benefits, why do people hire caregivers directly?*

A. One factor is cost. The hourly rate for a friend down the street or someone hired through the classifieds will likely be less than what you would have to pay an agency. In some cases, non-agency-based caregivers are not eligible to work legally in the U.S., and will therefore accept an even lower hourly rate. However, hiring such a worker is illegal, and could end up being very costly for both you and your parent.

Quality control and consistency are other factors. If you hire someone directly, this will be a person of your choosing and there will be no variation in caregivers over time, as there might be with an agency.

Q. *I am my mother's court-appointed guardian. Must I hire an agency caregiver, or can I still hire our neighbor?*

A. You may be required to hire an agency that is licensed and insured. The court that ordered the guardianship has jurisdiction over your mother and her care, and the court may require this. Read the court order to determine whether there are any provisions for your mother's care. If you are unsure, talk to the attorney who helped you obtain the guardianship.

Q. *Is there a registry of care workers who have abused or neglected the elderly?*

A. Some states do maintain such registries. Your area agency on aging should be able to tell you if there is one in your state.

Q. *Could I be found legally responsible if a worker I hire harms or neglects my mother?*

A. Possibly. A court may find you liable if you were negligent in the hiring or supervision of the care worker. Therefore, it is important to check the references of any care workers you might consider hiring. Try to hire only service providers who are fully insured and bonded.

Q. Are there any guidelines for hiring home care workers or agencies?

A. AARP's website provides checklists of questions to ask individuals or agencies at *http://assets.aarp.org/external_sites/care giving/planAhead/index.html*. Also, check with your AAA for state-specific guides to home care services.

REGULATIONS AND COMPLAINTS

Q. Does anyone regulate or certify community-based agencies?

A. Yes, but this a complicated area and varies greatly depending on state laws and the source of an agency's funding. Some states license agencies depending on the purpose of the agency. Talk to your local AAA to find out about the various regulatory agencies in your area.

Q. Where do I go if I am concerned about the home care my mother is receiving through an agency?

A. First, speak with your mother and find out how she would like to proceed. Your mother may interpret the questionable behavior differently than you do. For instance, she may not be troubled by what you perceive as sloppiness on the part of the care worker, especially if she is fond of him or her. Reporting the care worker may lead to termination or transfer. If this is done without informing your mother or against her wishes, your mother may feel demoralized and resent your interference.

On the other hand, if you suspect that there is abuse or neglect that needs an immediate response, you should report this directly to the agency that investigates abuse and neglect in that particular community. You can locate the appropriate agency by contacting your area agency on aging.

If the care worker is routinely late or not as careful as you would like, and if there is no risk of immediate harm, you should start by speaking with the caregiver directly. If you do not receive an adequate response, the next step is to report the problem to his or her supervisor at the agency.

Q. What if my mother no longer has capacity, but is telling me I shouldn't report her caregiver?

A. This question is not easy to answer. If you suspect abuse or neglect or see the potential for abuse or neglect, and if your mother is not capable of understanding what is happening to her, then you may have to override your mother's wishes, report the worker to the abuse and neglect agency, and take other protective measures as described in chapter 11. However, these steps should not be taken lightly.

If the problem is something less than abuse or neglect (or potential abuse or neglect), then you must carefully consider the impact that reporting the worker will have on your mother. Even if your mother is not fully cognizant of what is going on, she may still have bonded with the worker and feel a real sense of loss if he or she is replaced.

Q. I am not concerned about immediate harm to my mother, but both my mother and I are displeased with the worker's performance. I have contacted the caregiver's supervisor and nothing has changed. Where do I turn next?

A. If you do not get a sufficient response from the worker's supervisor, or if your problem is with the agency as a whole, contact the area agency on aging (AAA) in your community. As outlined above, AAAs are responsible for using public funds to contract with independent agencies to provide services, such as home care and elder abuse and neglect investigations. If the care provided to your mother is publicly funded, then the funding is likely to come through the AAA, and its staff can tell you which government agency is responsible for handling complaints.

If you are paying the agency privately, you can still turn to the AAA to find out which (if any) agency is responsible for handling complaints. The regulation of private home care agencies varies significantly from state to state. If there is no specific agency that handles complaints about private home care agencies in your state, you can always report them to the Better Business Bureau.

TYPES OF SERVICES

Q. What types of services are available to assist my aging parent?

A. The available services will vary depending on your parent's needs and community. Common examples of home- and community-based services include:

- transportation;
- senior centers;
- outreach;
- legal assistance;
- information and referral;
- housing services;
- case management;
- respite care;
- home health care;
- personal-care services;
- protective services;
- homemaker services;
- employment services;
- chore services;
- counseling;
- home-delivered meals;

- volunteer programs;
- congregate-meal programs;
- residential repair;
- friendly visitors;
- crime prevention and victim assistance;
- adult day care;
- money management; and
- other supportive services.

Some of the more common services will be explored in further detail throughout this section.

Home Health-Care Services

Q. My mom needs medical care: nursing services to change her dressings, some physical therapy, and someone to help coordinate her medicine. Is a nursing home the only option available for her?

A. No. Depending on the level of care your mom needs, and the services available in her community, you may be able to engage a home health-care service to provide these services for your mom in her home.

Q. What are home health-care services?

A. Home health-care services enable older people to receive medical services at home rather than in institutions such as nursing homes. For some individuals, home health-care services may make it possible for them to return to their homes after hospitalization or short-term nursing care. Home care programs will vary depending on the person's individual needs. Some of the services available through home health care include:

- physical therapy;
- occupational therapy;
- speech therapy;
- social work services;

- wound or dressing changes;
- monitoring of vital signs;
- medication management;
- end-of-life care;
- meal services; and
- personal-care services.

Q. How will we know if this sort of care will help my parent?

A. Sometimes a physician will order home health care following an acute hospitalization (meaning for a single "episode" of illness), or else you and your parent may simply determine that your parent's needs now dictate such assistance. The exact type of assistance needed will depend on the older person's ability to independently perform the activities of daily living. Questions to ask include:

- What are your parent's physical limitations?
- Can your parent manage his or her medications?
- Can he or she keep medical appointments?
- Can he or she manage money matters?
- Can your parent do housework?
- Can he or she manage personal hygiene?
- Is he or she eating properly?
- Is your parent's home set up to accommodate any problems created by impairment in vision or hearing?
- Is your parent able to exit the residence or contact someone in an emergency?
- Is your parent confused or depressed?

Q. Who pays for home health-care services?

A. Some private insurance companies provide short periods of coverage for home health-care services after a hospital stay, if ordered by a physician. Medicare Part A may pay for limited home care from a certified agency, if skilled nursing care or physical, occupational, or speech therapy is also required and prescribed by a physician.

Homemaker Services and Personal Attendants

Q. *My mom needs help with daily chores. I work full-time and have two kids at home. Are there any services available that can help my mom with things like grocery shopping, cleaning, and showering?*

A. Yes. Homemaker services or a personal attendant may be the appropriate choice for your mom. If your parent needs more intensive medical assistance, you will likely need to consider engaging a home health-care service as well.

Q. *What are homemaker services?*

A. A **homemaker** provides basic household assistance, including:

- assistance with personal hygiene;
- essential shopping;
- laundry;
- light housekeeping; and
- light meal preparation.

Q. *What are personal attendants?*

A. Similar to homemakers, **personal attendants** allow older adults to stay in their homes by providing personal support. While homemaker services provide more home management assistance, personal attendants provide more help with daily personal routines. Basic services include assistance with:

- transfers in and out of bed, a wheelchair, and/or a motor vehicle;
- health maintenance activities, such as scheduling regular checkups, providing nutritious meals, and ensuring that your parent gets appropriate levels of exercise;
- bathing and personal hygiene;
- dressing and grooming; and
- eating (including meal preparation and cleanup).

Q. When would a personal-attendant service make sense for my parent?

A. A personal attendant may be the correct choice if your parent needs hands-on help with everyday activities. Personal-attendant services are not typically associated with post-acute care (i.e., care after hospitalization or other institutionalization). Personal attendants are available at any time, either based on a set schedule or sporadically as needed. Generally, personal attendants provide hands-on care, often under the supervision of nursing, social work, or medical staff.

Q. How does someone pay for homemaker services or a personal attendant?

A. For most families, homemaker services are paid for out of private funds. Government benefits rarely pay for homemaker services. If your parent needs such services and funds are limited, then you may need to find additional private funding.

Medication Management Services '

Q. My mom is on a lot of medication. If she is living at home, can someone help her regulate them?

A. Yes. In addition to home health-care services, medication management services may be appropriate to help your mom regulate and monitor her medicines.

Q. What exactly are medication management services?

A. Some community-based agencies offer **medication management services.** These services may include home visits by nurses to assess an individual's safety regarding his or her medication. For instance, the medication manager may recommend and help facilitate large-text instructions or color-coded prescription bottles, pillboxes with designated sections for each day of the week, or even phone calls to remind your parent of the dosage and timing of medications. This is yet another service that allows older people to age in their homes safely.

An increasingly popular program of this type is the Medication Management Improvement System (MMIS). MMIS allows community-based agencies to address the safety and quality-of-life concerns associated with in-home medicine management. MMIS creates a system that allows care managers to use computer programs and consultations with pharmacists to screen medications for older adults. This screening is intended to prevent the problems that can sometimes be associated with multiple medications. Any problems noticed during the screening are brought to the attention of the older person's physician. These systems are relatively new and must be implemented by trained individuals. In many communities, these programs are administered by licensed nurses working through home health-care agencies.

Q. Why would my parents need a medication management service?

A. Seniors remaining at home in their communities may be vulnerable to medicine mix-ups. Residents of skilled nursing facilities that receive federal funds are required to undergo monthly drug reviews by consultant pharmacists, but seniors outside of such facilities do not have such oversight. A medication management service can thus help ensure that your parent is using medication safely.

Q. Are there restrictions on who can give my mother her medications? Can't I just ask a neighbor to help?

A. In some states, the person administering a medication must be, at a minimum, a licensed practical nurse. The rationale for requiring that a licensed nurse dispense medications is that some medications can affect older people in unforeseen ways. The thought is that the person administering the medicine should therefore be qualified to observe reactions and notice any adverse reactions or complications. Some families get around this requirement by setting up the medications ahead of time and then having a non-nurse caregiver simply remind the older person to take the medicine. However, in order for this to work, the older person must be able to understand the reminder and be physically able to take the medication on his or her own.

Respite Care and Adult Day Care

Q. I am taking on a lot of responsibilities to help my parent, on top of my job and taking care of my kids. What if I need a short break? I don't need to put my parent in a home just to go to the grocery store, do I?

A. If they are available in the community and your family can afford it, a respite care program or adult day care center may be the appropriate choice.

Q. What are respite care services?

A. For families with older adults who are remaining in their homes, but who also require daily care and assistance, respite care services may provide valuable relief. By providing an alternate short-term caregiver, **respite care** allows a primary caregiver to take a break from caregiving. Although respite care is actually for the benefit of the caregiver, it can also improve the situation of the older person and extend the period for which he or she can remain at home. Respite care may be provided by a family member, friend, neighbor, community volunteer, or local institution.

Q. What will my parent do while at respite care?

A. Respite care services can be anything from simple companionship for your parent (i.e., simply spending time with your parent) to actual personal-care services. The specifics of your family's respite care, including the frequency and schedule, will be determined by your parent, you, and the respite care provider.

Q. How much will respite care cost my family?

A. In most cases, the cost of respite care services will vary depending on the agency and the services needed. Medicaid funds may pay for some limited respite care services. There are also some federal, state, and local programs that may help your family pay for respite care. Such programs can help you determine your parent's eligibility and locate available services. For more information, contact your local agency on aging.

Q. What exactly are adult day care centers?

A. Adult day care is a type of respite care. **Adult day care** centers provide protection and activity for older adults who are unable to stay at home alone while caregivers are at work or away from home for other reasons. This is an attractive alternative for many families who want to help an older family member stay at home, but have other daily responsibilities. Adult day care can also be beneficial for the older individuals themselves. Many centers provide social activities and interactions that older adults might not otherwise enjoy. Often transportation is provided door-to-door, and meals and snacks are provided during the day.

▶ **GRANNY CAMS**

Some respite care facilities and adult day care centers have started to offer an adult version of a "nanny cam." These "granny cams" allow family members to access a website that provides video feed directly from the respite or day care center. For many families, these cameras may relieve some caregiver guilt and provide peace of mind. However, they are not without legal issues. In some states, "granny cams" at adult day care centers and nursing homes have been the source of litigation over privacy rights, and have spurred fears that the number of people interested in working at such facilities will decrease. Talk to the agencies you are thinking of working with to determine whether and where such programs are available.

Aides are present to provide personal assistance to the older adult, including assistance using the bathroom, eating, bathing, or meeting other personal needs.

Q. Are there different types of adult day care centers?

A. Yes. The specifics of the day care centers in your area may vary. In general, there are three types of adult day care:

1. social programs (which provide meals, recreation, and some health-related services);

2. medical and health programs (which provide social activities as well as more intensive health and therapeutic services); and

3. specialized programs (which provide services only to specific care recipients, such as those with diagnosed dementias or developmental disabilities).

REMEMBER THIS

- Aging in place (i.e., remaining in one community as he or she ages) may help your parent maintain a sense of independence and provide him or her with a sense of safety and security.

- There are many financial options available to help your parent age in place, such as home equity conversion plans. However, it is important that your parent explore all options and work with an elder law attorney to ensure that he or she will not fall victim to consumer fraud.

- The regulation and licensing of community-based agencies is very complicated, and varies depending on your area and the services the agencies will be providing. Work with your local AAA to ensure that the agency you are thinking of hiring is reputable.

- Community-based services can provide important services for those individuals who want to age in place.

CHAPTER 9

Supportive Housing Options

Assisted-Living Facilities, Nursing Homes, and More

Francesca's parents have always taken their independence very seriously—they never ask her for help unless it is the last option. But over the last year, the upkeep on their home has really started to take its toll. And last month, Francesca's mom suffered a heart attack, and now she requires around-the-clock monitoring. Between the house and her mom, Francesca's dad just can't handle it anymore. Francesca and her dad have decided it is time for her parents to move, but where will they move to? Does her dad have to move into a nursing home if her mom goes into one? Are there any "in-between" options? How can Francesca tell if the facilities are any good?

A t some point, whether due to physical limitations or a loss of cognitive ability, your parents may reach a point at which they can no longer live safely in their home. However, depending on their abilities and the available services, a nursing home or similar facility may not be the only option, or even the best one. Sometimes an interim solution, often referred to as **supportive housing**, may be the appropriate choice. This type of housing includes various types of assisted-living communities and continuing-care retirement communities.

This chapter outlines various types of supportive housing options, and explains how to find the one that will best fit your parent's needs. It will also provide advice about how to avoid some of the legal hassles that often accompany structured-living arrangements.

SUPPORTIVE HOUSING OPTIONS (THAT AREN'T NURSING HOMES)

Q. My parents are both relatively healthy, but they need a little help. Sometimes they skip meals because it is too much trouble to prepare them. My mom has a laundry basket that is always full. They both have some mobility issues and simply cannot get up the stairs anymore. As a family, we don't think it is safe for them to continue to live in their home anymore. What are their options?

A. There are several types of supportive housing that may be suitable for your parents' needs, including assisted-living communities and continuing-care retirement communities. To determine which option is best, you will need to assess your parents' capacity, long-term funding options, and lifestyle choices.

Between the extremes of independent living and nursing home care, a variety of alternatives offer endless combinations of shelter plus services or amenities. Physically, facilities range from single-family-type housing, to high-rise or garden apartment buildings, to campus-like developments.

Facility definitions differ among states, and sometimes even within states, but generally there are three types of housing that are classified based on the services provided. At one end of the continuum are **independent-living communities**. These offer little or no health and supportive services, though they usually provide recreational and social programs. Next are facilities that offer a wide variety of housing and health or supportive services, but no nursing home care. Today, these are commonly referred to as **assisted-living communities**, but they include facilities variously known as **housing with supportive services, congregate-care homes, board-and-care homes,** and **personal-care homes.** At the opposite end of the continuum are **continuing-care retirement communities (CCRCs)**. These provide a fairly extensive range of housing options, care, and services, including nursing home services. This chapter discusses assisted-living facilities, and then turns its attention to CCRCs.

Q. How do we get my parent into one of these communities? Do we purchase or rent?

A. Conventional independent-living communities without health-care services typically offer home ownership or rental arrangements that are similar to standard real estate purchases or rentals. These transactions are governed by local real estate and landlord-tenant law. Residents pay the costs of their mortgage or lease, as well as condominium or association fees. In facilities that provide additional services, accommodations, or health care, there are three basic types of contracts, typically categorized according to payment arrangement (though keep in mind that state regulations may categorize facilities differently):

1. **Entrance-fee-plus-monthly-fee contracts.** Entrance fees, ranging from $20,000 to over $400,000, are charged by most continuing-care retirement facilities. An entrance fee may represent a partial prepayment for future services, but it normally does not purchase an interest in the real estate. Increasingly, CCRCs are providing greater refundability of entrance fees, even up to 100 percent, although this usually results in higher monthly fees. Residency rights and obligations are governed by a long-term lease or occupancy agreement. Monthly fees are subject to periodic inflation adjustments, and possibly to further adjustments when the resident's level-of-care needs change.

2. **Pay-as-you-go contracts.** With no entrance fee, these contracts are essentially straight rental arrangements with a defined set of services included in the fee (or available when needed for an additional charge). Most assisted-living facilities and an increasing number of continuing-care facilities offer this type of arrangement. This type of contract involves no initial investment, but is subject to

greater changes in monthly fees, since the resident assumes most or all of the financial risk for services.

3. **Condominiums or cooperatives with continuing-care contracts.** Some retirement communities offer residents an ownership interest under a condominium or cooperative arrangement with a service package included. These ownership/contractual arrangements are unavoidably complex, and present special advantages and risks that need to be weighed carefully.

Assisted-Living Communities

Q. What exactly is an assisted-living community?

A. Assisted-living communities are designed for those older adults who need an extra level of assistance, but who are generally able to live somewhat independently. These facilities vary greatly, as do the services they offer. Typically assisted-living communities offer independent apartments for their residents, and many offer a communal dining room. Some offer services such as housekeeping, laundry, fitness programs, shuttle services for day trips to the grocery store or movie theaters, and some home health care. These additional services are available at an additional cost, and will be contingent on the unique needs of each individual client. Depending on the community, your parents may be able to select the exact level of services that they need.

Q. Do assisted-living communities offer health and medical services?

A. Some may offer on-site medical centers. However, the care offered at such facilities is not as intensive as that available to residents of nursing homes. If your parent needs skilled care for an extended period, he or she will likely have to relocate to another facility.

**Q. What are the options for paying for
assisted living?**

A. For the most part, assisted-living facilities are **private pay**—
that is, your parent must come up with the rent and fees from
his or her own income and assets, or through a long-term-care
insurance policy (these policies are discussed further in chapter 7). Average monthly rents can reach $3,000 to $4,000, with
additional fees tacked on for services.

Some states allow assisted-living residents to receive
Medicaid-funded home- and community-based services. In addition, some states have received waivers from the federal government allowing them to use Medicaid dollars to completely
fund assisted-living facilities. In states that fund such facilities,
the facilities may actually be called by a different name, such as
supportive-living facility. Because the residents of such facilities are receiving Medicaid, they must turn all of their income
over to the facility, and are only allowed to keep a small amount
(around $100) per month. To determine whether your state op-
erates a waiver program, contact your area agency on aging or
state Medicaid office.

**Q. My mother is thinking of moving into an assisted-
living community, and has asked me to review the
contract. What should I be looking for?**

A. Assisted-living community contracts vary depending on the
facility and the state in which the facility is located. However, it
is helpful to ask a few general questions:

- What services does the facility provide? Which of these services are included in the monthly payment, and which ones
  cost extra?
- Can your parent have care providers come in who are not
  employed by the facility? For instance, can your parent have
  Medicaid or privately funded care providers come into his or
  her unit to provide care?
- Can the monthly payments be raised, and under what circumstances?
- What are the residents' rights?

- Does the contract try to limit the facility's liability? (For more information, see the sidebar later in this section on negotiated risk.)
- Under what circumstances can the admissions contract be terminated? (This clause should be reviewed very carefully.)
- What is the facility's "bed hold" policy? If the resident leaves temporarily for hospitalization, how long will his or her apartment be held, and how much will this cost?
- Does the facility have a special unit for residents with dementia? If so, what are the criteria for moving a resident to this unit? How will this decision be made and by whom?

The contract should be reviewed carefully, and you or your parent should obtain clarification on any clauses you don't understand. If you have serious questions about the fairness of the

▶ NEGOTIATED RISK

Unlike a nursing home that is completely responsible for a resident's care, assisted-living facilities provide residents with a high degree of independence. This is the very reason that your parent may choose an assisted-living facility over a nursing home. But what happens, for example, if your parent trips on her way out of the building and breaks her hip?

The tension between allowing the resident to live independently and holding the facility responsible if something goes wrong has led to the concept of **negotiated risk**. At least fifteen states have incorporated the notion of negotiated risk into their assisted-living laws. This usually means that, at the time of admission, an individualized plan is developed stating the types of risks the resident would like to take and, in exchange, the types of risks for which he or she will absolve the facility of liability. In practice, many facilities offer a preprinted agreement that residents are expected to sign and that will become a part of their contract. This agreement should be reviewed very carefully to ensure that it is appropriate for your parents. When in doubt, ask questions or talk to an experienced elder law attorney.

contract, do not hesitate to talk to the facility director or contact an elder law attorney, or both.

Q. Are assisted-living fees tax-deductible?

A. To some extent. Depending on how much assistance the resident needs, he or she may be able to deduct part of the cost of assisted living. If there are questions, your parent should work with the facility or talk to an experienced elder law attorney to determine which part of the fees will be tax-deductible.

Q. How can we tell that an assisted-living facility is "good?" Are there signs of poor quality that we should look out for?

A. There are a variety of signs that may indicate the quality of an assisted-living facility. You should feel comfortable asking questions about staffing and services. When considering a facility, appropriate questions to ask include:

- Does the staff seem to know the residents?
- Are there residents in the common spaces? Are they interacting with each other?
- Is there an activity list available with a weekly schedule?
- How often does the staff "turn over"?
- How is the food service? The maintenance? The quality of planned activities? (If possible, try to talk to the residents about these issues.)
- Are the elevators in working order, and are there enough to accommodate all of the residents? (Sometimes in assisted-living facilities, elevators are "held up" due to a move or emergency medical needs. There should be enough elevators to accommodate such potential obstructions and still allow residents to get up and down easily.)
- What medical services are available on-site? Is there a medical professional on call? Is there a wellness center in the facility? Is nursing help easily available if necessary? What other support services are available? Is there a social worker on the staff?

- Are there short-term caregiver services available for hire if necessary?
- Can meals be delivered to the resident's apartment if he or she is ill or unable to come down to the common area?

Q. How are assisted-living facilities regulated? Where do I file a complaint if something goes wrong?

A. There is no federal regulation of assisted-living facilities. State regulations vary significantly. To find your state licensing agency, go to *www.ccal.org/agencies.htm.*

In some states, the Long Term Care Ombudsman Program investigates complaints about assisted-living facilities in addition to nursing homes. To locate your state's Long Term Care Ombudsman Program, visit *www.ltcombudsman.org/static_pages/ombudsmen.cfm.* Your area agency on aging should also be able to tell you where to file a complaint.

Q. My father's assisted-living community is attempting to evict him. Can they do this?

A. The first place to look for the answer to this question is in the admissions contract. Chances are that the contract will outline the circumstances under which your father can be evicted. In addition, some states specifically apply general landlord-tenant laws to assisted-living facilities. Others have created administrative procedures or do not have laws specifically addressing this issue. To find the laws governing assisted-living facilities in your state, visit the website for your state department on aging or area agency on aging.

A particularly difficult circumstance arises when a facility argues that it can no longer care for a resident. For example, if a resident becomes bedbound and is no longer able to help him or herself in the event of an emergency, an assisted-living community might decide it is no longer safe for that resident to remain in the community. Although most states do not allow assisted-living facilities to accept bedbound residents in the first place,

> ### ▶ WHO SPONSORS AND WHO REGULATES RETIREMENT COMMUNITIES?
>
> Most retirement communities are developed privately. Some are sponsored by nonprofit groups and agencies, including churches and charitable organizations. All states regulate one or more types of assisted-living communities. Most states regulate continuing-care communities, but the extent of regulation varies considerably between the states.

some allow facilities to continue providing care to residents who become bedbound after admission. When such a facility is no longer willing to provide care, a legal issue may arise. If this happens to your parent, try to work with the facility to find another housing option that will better serve your parent's needs. If the facility will not give you sufficient time to make other arrangements, an elder law attorney or your local ombudsman may be able to help you determine your immediate options and recourse.

Continuing-Care Retirement Communities (CCRCs)

Q. What are CCRCs?

A. Continuing-care retirement communities (CCRCs) are communities that provide a continuum of care, from independent living to skilled nursing-care facilities. They allow seniors to "age in place." This means that a resident will be able to access different levels of support and care without having to relocate to a different facility every time his or her needs change. If a resident needs skilled care, it will likely be available within the community. Then, if the resident becomes well enough to no longer require the care, the care will cease and the resident can resume an independent lifestyle within the same community.

Q. What is the difference between a CCRC and an assisted-living community?

A. The main difference is that assisted-living communities usually do not offer the extensive levels of care provided by CCRCs. Many CCRCs have sections that provide skilled nursing care, which allows residents to remain in the facility if their care needs increase. Most assisted-living facilities do not offer this level of care. So if your parent's needs change while he or she is living in an assisted-living community, he or she will probably have to move to another facility.

Q. What should I be concerned about when evaluating CCRCs?

A. Some CCRCs have faced financial crises and even gone bankrupt. In these instances, the resident, who may have made a huge initial payment, could lose his or her entire investment. Therefore, it is very important to evaluate the solvency of the CCRC. The following checklist outlines some issues to be on the lookout for.

Q. Is there anything my parent and I should look out for when reviewing a CCRC contract?

A. Yes. Many CCRCs require a large admission fee, some or all of which may not be reimbursed if the resident dies before using nursing home care or chooses to leave the facility after the probationary period ends. If your parent chooses to leave the CCRC for a valid reason, he or she may still have problems getting back the admission fee. CCRC contracts are governed by state contract laws, which generally require that the resident show a breach of the contract and damages in order to get out of the contract. Therefore, it may be very hard, if not impossible, to get out of many CCRC contracts. Residents usually do not succeed with breach of contract claims.

▶ CHECKLIST: WHAT TO CONSIDER
WHEN SELECTING A CONTINUING-
CARE COMMUNITY FOR YOUR
PARENTS

SOLVENCY AND EXPERTISE OF THE PROVIDER

- What is the provider's background and experience? The provider is the person or entity who is legally and financially responsible. Some facilities may claim to be "sponsored" by nonprofit groups or churches that in reality have no legal control or financial responsibility. Be wary if such illusory sponsorship is trumpeted in the facility's sales literature.

- Is the provider financially sound? Ask a professional to review the facility's financial, actuarial, and operating statements. Determine whether the facility has sufficient financial reserves.

- Are all levels of care licensed or certified under applicable state statutes that regulate continuing care, assisted living, and nursing home care?

- How does the facility ensure the quality of care and services provided? Is the facility accredited by any recognized private accrediting organization?

FEES

- What is the entrance fee, and when can your parents get back all or part of this fee? The facility should provide a formula for a pro rata refund of the entrance fee based on the resident's length of stay, regardless of whether the facility or the resident initiates the termination.

- What is the monthly fee? When and how much can it be increased? What happens if fee increases exceed your ability to pay? Some facilities have a program that grants financial assistance to residents whose income becomes inadequate to pay increasing monthly fees and personal expenses.

- Will fees change when the resident's living arrangements or level-of-care needs change (for example, in the event of transfers from independent living to assisted living or nursing care)?
- For owner arrangements, are there limits on the people to whom your parents can sell their property? What happens to the residence and financial obligations if your parents move from the residence?

SERVICES AND HEALTH CARE

- Exactly what services are included in the regular fees? Especially inquire about coverage, limitations, and costs of the following:

Housing/Social/Recreational

- meal services
- special diets/tray service
- utilities
- cable television
- furnishings
- unit maintenance
- linens/personal laundry
- housekeeping
- recreational/cultural activities
- transportation

Health and Personal Care

- physician services
- nursing services outside a nursing unit (for example, assistance with medications)
- private-duty nursing
- dental and eye care
- personal-care services (that is, assistance with eating, dressing, bathing, and using bathroom facilities)
- homemaker/companion services
- drugs
- medication

- medical equipment/supplies
- facility services
- If the facility provides a nursing unit, what happens if a bed is not available when your parent needs it?

- To what extent does the facility have the right to cut back, change, or eliminate services, or change the fees?

- Does the facility limit its responsibility for certain health conditions or preexisting conditions? When are you considered too sick or impaired to be cared for by the facility?

- Can your parents receive Medicare and Medicaid coverage while in the facility?

- Does the facility require residents to buy private insurance or participate in a special group insurance program?

- What are the criteria and procedures for determining when a resident needs to be transferred from independent living to assisted living, or to a nursing care unit, or to an entirely different facility? Who is involved in these decisions?

RESIDENTS' RIGHTS

- What does the living unit consist of, and to what extent can your parent/parents change or redecorate it?

- What happens if your parent marries, divorces, becomes widowed, or wishes to have a friend or family member move in?

- What rights do residents have to participate in facility management and decision making? How are complaints handled?

- On what grounds can residents' contracts or leases be terminated against their wishes?

- What other rules and policies cover the day-to-day operation of the facility?

- Does the contract release the facility from any liability for injury to a resident or guest resulting from negligence by the facility or third parties? (Such waivers should be avoided.)

Q. Do I need to have an attorney review a CCRC contract?

A. If you are paying a large admission fee that may not be refundable, it is a good idea to have an elder law attorney review your parent's CCRC contract before he or she enters into it.

Q. How are CCRCs regulated? Where do I go to file a complaint?

A. State insurance agencies regulate CCRC contracts in most states. If the CCRC receives any Medicare or Medicaid funds, then the CCRC is also subject to federal regulation for those services that fall under Medicare or Medicaid. For information on where to go to report a problem with a CCRC, visit the websites of the American Association of Homes and Services for the Aging (*www.aahsa.org*), the Continuing Care Accreditation Commission (*www.carf.org*), or your local area agency on aging.

Subsidized Housing

Q. My parents have limited funds, but we all think they would benefit from supportive housing. Are there less expensive options?

A. Possibly. Some federally funded programs administered by the U.S. Department of Housing and Urban Development (HUD) may provide low-cost housing for your parents. Eligibility for these facilities is usually based on age and income. Residents generally must be at least sixty-two years old and have incomes below 50 percent of their area's median income.

These housing options provide independent living accommodations for older persons who need some assistance with the tasks of daily living. Typically, such accommodations are studio or one-bedroom apartments with kitchens and baths. Often they feature special amenities like walk-in tubs, grab bars, and ramps to accommodate older adults with walkers or wheelchairs.

It is important to note that there is a shortage of subsidized supportive housing, so it may not be easy to find such housing

► ## AGE-RESTRICTED COMMUNITIES

If your parents are worried about joining a new community and are interested in living around other aging seniors, they may want to consider an **age-restricted community**. These are communities, often gated, that impose age requirements for residency and ownership. This means that your parents would likely be surrounded only by other individuals over a certain age. Some age-restricted communities also offer various levels of supportive services that your parents may need as their needs and abilities change. Many such communities create a "resort" lifestyle that is consistent with wellness and activity. They may offer swimming pools, college-level classes, fitness centers, biking trails, and golf courses.

Although on its face the establishment of such communities may seem to constitute illegal age discrimination, the Fair Housing Act of 1968 and the Housing for Older Persons Act of 1995 allow communities to enforce these types of age restrictions, so long as the community is one of the two approved types:

- A community in which at least 80 percent of the units are occupied (not owned) by at least one person fifty-five years of age or older; or

- A community in which 100 percent of the units are occupied by persons sixty-two years of age or older.

If your parents are considering such a community, review the building's lease agreement or contract very carefully. Age-restricted communities are permitted to restrict residents in ways that are not permitted in the general community. For instance, an age-restricted community can bar residents from having children spend the night. Or the community might bar relatives, including spouses, from living in the community if they are under a certain age.

for your parents even if they are eligible. The number of available subsidized homes has been decreasing as the number of older adults seeking subsidized housing increases. This is yet another reason why planning for your parents' retirement early is incredibly important.

Q. How much does subsidized housing cost, and how does my mother apply for it?

A. Income and asset limits vary depending on where your parent lives. The local Public Housing Agency (PHA) is the agency that sets income and asset limits and processes applications. You can locate your local PHA by visiting *www.hud.gov/offices/pih/pha* or by calling 1–800–685–8470.

Q. My mother's application to a subsidized apartment was denied. Can we appeal?

A. Because subsidized housing is publicly funded, it is possible to appeal denial of an application. Federal law permits the PHA to restrict the following groups from residing in public housing: those who have been convicted of a crime, those who have been evicted from a federal housing facility for drug-related criminal activity within the last three years, and those who owe a debt to a PHA. In addition, local PHAs are authorized to adopt their own residency requirements.

The Multifamily Housing Clearinghouse is a source of information on the initiatives, programs, and policies of HUD's Office of Multifamily Housing Programs. It can be reached by visiting *www.hud.gov/offices/hsg/mfh/hc/mfhc.cfm* or by calling 1–800–685–8470.

Q. My mother is in subsidized senior housing and her apartment is not being properly maintained. Where can she file a complaint?

A. Because she is a renter, she might have recourse through her state and local landlord-tenant laws. She should try to contact her landlord and pursue legal remedies available under the ap-

propriate landlord-tenant laws in her jurisdiction. She can also
contact HUD's Housing Complaint Line at 1–800–685–8470.

NURSING HOMES

Nursing homes are often thought of as the last option for aging
individuals. Many older people make the statement, "I don't
want to be put into a home." However, if your parent soon may
no longer be able to manage on his or her own, even with supportive services or housing, then your family may need to consider a nursing home as an option. Understanding what to
expect when looking for a nursing home and what to do if something goes wrong will help you, your parents, and your family
feel comfortable with any decisions. In this section, we will discuss nursing homes, the types of care they provide, quality as-
surance issues, costs, and the difficult choices your family faces
when only one parent needs nursing home care.

Q. What are nursing homes?

A. **Nursing homes** are institutions run by for-profit or not-for-
profit organizations that provide skilled nursing and medical
care, rehabilitation services, custodial care, and other health-
related services. Nursing homes must be licensed under state
law and are regulated at both the state and federal levels. However, a license is not a guarantee of quality.

Q. Why do people move into nursing homes?

A. There are a variety of reasons. Not everyone moving into a
nursing home plans to remain in the facility long-term. Many people who enter nursing homes are discharged directly from a hospital or within a month after hospital care. For these residents,
their time in the nursing home is for receiving specialized medical
care or rehabilitation. After a one- or two-month stay, these people may be able to return home and continue receiving some services such as physical therapy from a home health-care agency.

Other nursing home residents require long-term care. They

may suffer from chronic illness and need nursing care in addition to help with daily activities. Other residents of nursing homes may not need continuous nursing or medical care, but may require twenty-four-hour supervision.

Some individuals may not need the full-time care of a nursing home, but may still choose to move into one. For these people, an assisted-living facility or CCRC may be more appropriate, but financially unavailable. Because Medicaid will pay for some nursing home care, for some families, nursing homes may be their only options for care and supervision.

Q. When is nursing home placement necessary?

A. A move into a nursing home may be necessary when your parent can no longer manage the activities of daily living or has a sudden health crisis that cannot be treated at home or in an assisted-living facility. A nursing home may be appropriate if your parent:

- can no longer care independently for himself or herself (this usually means that your parent cannot provide for his or her own personal needs, such as eating, bathing, using the bathroom, moving around, or taking medications);
- is going to be discharged from the hospital and requires temporary skilled nursing care or rehabilitation before returning home or to an assisted-care facility;
- has suffered a sudden serious health crisis;
- has recently been diagnosed with significant physical or cognitive decline;
- requires temporary or long-term care with available twenty-four-hour medical assistance;
- requires more care than can be provided by a caregiver, or cannot live alone;
- might wander away when unsupervised; or
- has extensive medical needs requiring daily attention or monitoring by a registered nurse supervised by a doctor.

Of course, individual decisions will be based on your family's situation. Even if your parent doesn't meet the above criteria, that doesn't necessarily mean that a nursing home isn't the right choice for your family. Alternatively, even if your parent meets *all* of the above criteria, a nursing home won't necessarily be the guaranteed solution.

Most often, admission to a nursing home is preceded by a recommendation from a physician, though some homes will accept your parent directly without such a recommendation.

Q. What's the best way to choose a nursing home?

A. There are many criteria to consider when choosing a nursing home. No home is perfect; however, there are signs of both good quality and bad quality. As a starting point for acquiring information, you can obtain a facility's inspection report. States usually inspect homes once a year. Inspection reports detail major and minor deficiencies in the operation of facilities. Virtually every facility, even the very best, will have some problems. After all, the job of caring for highly impaired individuals is difficult. But beware of facilities that have demonstrated serious deficiencies in administering medication, managing incontinence or bedsores, or using restraints, or that repeatedly experience the same problems. Compare the facility's last three or four inspection reports. If the same problems never get resolved, then even minor deficiencies may constitute major shortcomings.

Nursing homes are required to have their inspection reports available for you to read. If a home doesn't have its report available, or if the facility makes it difficult for you to examine the report, consider its reluctance a serious "red flag" that could indicate quality problems. State nursing home licensing agencies—usually part of the state health department—can also make inspection reports available to you; often state or local ombudsman programs will have them as well. Nursing Home Compare, a federal government website, posts inspection and other information about nursing homes around the country that are certified by Medicare or Medicaid. For more information, visit *www.medicare.gov/NHCompare/Home.asp*.

Visit the facility you are considering on more than one occasion and at different times throughout the day. Observe mealtimes, resident activities, and the interaction between staff and residents. Be wary of administrators who make access difficult or evade your questions. Look for both positive and negative signs, including the following:

	Signs of Good Quality	Signs of Poor Quality
Staff	Numerous staff interact personally with residents in a friendly and respectful manner.	Few staff are on duty. Staff does not interact with residents, or does so in an impersonal or brusque manner.
Food/ Mealtimes	The food is appetizing to you and served in a dining room that encourages people to socialize. Staff is available to help residents who need assistance. Residents needing help are integrated with other residents. Residents have water and other fluid easily accessible.	Food is unappetizing or cold and served in a setting that does not encourage socializing. Staff is not available to provide assistance. Residents needing assistance are fed elsewhere or at a different time than other residents. No water or pitchers are easily accessible to residents.
Building Appearance	The most important rooms are residents' rooms. Rooms are personalized and homey.	Residents' rooms are drab and institutionalized looking, indicating that residents are not encouraged to personalize their rooms.
Resident Appearance	Residents are reasonably well groomed, clean, and appropriately dressed.	Residents are inappropriately dressed, dirty, or unkempt (indicates inadequate staffing).

Restraints	Few (and preferably no) residents are restrained, physically or by medication. (Ask the administrator how many residents are restrained, and why.)	Many residents are in restraints, or the facility cannot give you a clear answer as to the number of residents who are restrained (indicates inadequate care planning or inadequate staffing).
Bedsores	Preferably no residents suffer from bedsores, though you probably cannot gather this information during a brief visit. (Check recent state inspection reports and ask the administrator for numbers.)	Bedsores are more than a rare occurrence, or the facility cannot give you a straight answer regarding the incidence of bedsores (indicates inadequate care planning or inadequate staffing).
Smells	Facility is generally free of offensive odors.	Lingering, offensive odors throughout building (indicates inadequate staffing).
Activities	Substantial numbers of residents enjoy frequently scheduled activities.	The activity calendar is fairly empty or uncreative in its offerings. Most around in day rooms doing nothing.

What To Expect

Q. *My mom's doctor says she has to go to a nursing home, but my dad does not agree. My mom doesn't know what's going on. What is my role in such a situation?*

A. Depending on your previous role in your parents' lives, a supportive position is probably the best. Listen to each of their views and concerns and help them recognize the options. Will your mom's nursing home stay be short-term? Is there any possibility that her nursing needs could be served by a good home health-care plan? You may want to consult a geriatric or clinical social worker to determine all of the options available to your parents, and then work with the social worker to assure yourself that your parents understand the various options available.

From a legal perspective, the answer depends on your parents' decision-making capacity and whether they have been adjudicated incompetent. If your parents still have the ability to make their own decisions and they choose not to involve you in the process, then there is nothing you can do. However, if your mother can no longer make her own decisions and she doesn't have a power of attorney for health care or property, you can petition to become her guardian. It is important to realize, however, that your father may have negative reactions to this type of situation, and may feel angry and alienated. Therefore, this option should only be pursued if absolutely necessary.

Q. What kind of issues should I be alert to? How will this move impact my parents (and me!)?

A. This is a very difficult situation, as couples who have been together for fifty or sixty years or more may be living apart for the first time. Some of the issues that arise may include an overwhelming fear of being alone (for both parents), relocation anxiety (for the nursing home parent), guilt (both), sadness, or loss. When one of your parents must move to a nursing home, both of your parents may feel better about the move if:

- They make the decision together. The worst situation is if one of your parents feels as though he or she has to make the decision without the other's approval. In circumstances where it is absolutely not possible for them to decide together, try and reassure your parents that the move is the right decision for them both.
- They arrange for frequent visits, if possible.

▶ **CHOOSING IN A HURRY**

Often a nursing home is chosen in a hurry, as when families are given twenty-four hours to move their parent or loved one from a hospital. In those cases, you may rely on the discharge planner at the hospital. Typically discharge planners are social workers found in hospital social service departments, case management offices, or utilization review offices.

The discharge planner assigned to your parent's case should have a good sense of the better homes in your area. If you have time, it may be helpful to follow several steps. Once you receive the names of the better homes in your area from the discharge planner, go and visit them. Try to obtain a report on the state evaluations of these homes. Your local nursing home ombudsmen may also prove to be a good source of information. Representatives from these offices visit facilities and receive complaints from nursing home residents and their families.

It is important to remember that virtually every facility, even the very best, will have some problems. You should be on the lookout for facilities that have demonstrated serious or repeated deficiencies.

- The community parent is engaged in the decision-making process regarding the nursing home parent's care. This helps to prevent either parent from feeling that the community parent has given up on his or her spouse.

  Neither you nor your community parent should forget that the nursing home parent may have relocation stress. Moving from a familiar setting may worsen any anxiety or stress that your nursing home parent already experiences. This reaction can be difficult on both your community parent and you, and may increase any existing feelings of guilt. Both parents should recognize that this type of move often requires an adjustment phase. Try to move some familiar items with your nursing home parent in order to ease the transition.

  Guilt may play a large role in either parent's reaction to the move. Your community parent may feel that he or she has failed his or her spouse, and your nursing home parent may also feel as though he or she is abandoning your other parent. They may both feel loss and sadness. This is expected, and these feelings should not be ignored or undermined. Many older adults have amazing resilience and make the adjustments necessary for them to accept such major changes. However, each parent may need the opportunity to express his or her feelings about the changing situation. A clinical social worker can be an invaluable resource for helping your family navigate such feelings of anxiety, depression, loneliness, or fear.

Sometimes your community parent may actually feel relief. For instance, if one of your parents has experienced long periods of agitation, aggression, or psychosis due to dementia or another disorder, then your other parent may actually be frightened or worried about the two of them continuing to live together. The community parent may realize that he or she can no longer care for the nursing home parent in a safe way, and may thus view the move to a nursing home as a positive step.

Q. Where will my dad live after my mom moves out?

A. This will totally depend on your dad's health and ability to function on his own. He may decide to stay in the residence he shared with your mom, or he may decide he would prefer a facility that provides various levels of care. Some facilities, such as

▶ **LINGO**

If one of your parents plans to move into a nursing home and the other does not, the nursing home staff and various government agencies will likely use special terms to refer to them. Your parent who stays out of the nursing home will usually be referred to as the community spouse, and the parent who moves into the nursing home will be referred to as the nursing home parent.

CCRCs, have assisted-living floors as well as nursing floors; this might allow your parents to move into the same facility, but on different floors, which could make it much easier for them to visit one another.

If your dad turns to you for help, the best way to start is to work with him to determine his options. You may want to consult

▶ **PETS**

If you are a pet lover, you know how important a furry friend may be to your parent. However, if your parent is preparing for a move into a nursing home, your family may face some tough decisions about your parent's pet. Most nursing homes do not allow pets to live with residents. If this is the case with the facility your family is considering, you may be able to work with the staff to determine a way for your parent and the pet to have regular visits. If you are able to find another family member or friend who can take in the animal and help with these regular visits, then your parent will be able to maintain his or her relationship with the pet, and hopefully experience an easier adjustment to the move.

Some facilities are beginning to recognize the important role a pet can play in an individual's life and, as such, are beginning to use pets during therapy sessions. Some facilities even allow certain residents to own pets. If your parent is able to find such a facility, there will likely be some restrictions on his or her ability to bring in an animal: your parent may have to be able to care for the animal on his or her own, the animal may have to be under a certain size, and your parent will likely be responsible for any vet and food bills. Talk to your local area agency on aging or long-term care ombudsmen to determine if your parent is eligible for admission to any such facilities in your area.

If none of these options is available, talk to your local humane society as early as possible to identify any foster care programs in the area that may be able to provide a home for your parent's pet. Knowing that a plan is in place to provide a good home for your parent's pet will go a long way toward helping him or her adjust to the move.

with a geriatric care manager or the staff at the nursing home to determine what options are available in the area. You and your father will also need to make an honest assessment of his skills, abilities, and income.

Q. What should we expect from the nursing home itself?

A. First, you should expect that the staff knows your parent's name and not just the number of his or her room. The staff should be trained and expected to interact with your parent. Second, you should not expect that the staff has specialized medical training needed to care for your parent. The majority of the day-to-day care in nursing home facilities is custodial (meaning help with eating, dressing, bathing, using the toilet, and moving about), and is provided by certified nursing assistants, not skilled professionals. While most nursing assistants provide quality care, there may be a problem in some nursing homes if your parent requires specialized medical assistance. In some cases, staff may be under-trained for the jobs they are asked to perform.

As to whether you should expect to see any progress or positive changes in your parent's abilities, this will depend on whether the nursing home is therapeutic or compensatory and, of course, on your parent's specific circumstances. If the facility is expected to provide therapeutic services, you should expect to see your parent make progress and improvements in his or her health. Services like rehabilitation should be of high quality and an important part of the day-to-day routine. If the home is expected to provide compensation for lost functions to your parent, then you should expect to see your parent clean, well fed, and receiving reasonable attention to his or her personal needs, such as using the bathroom.

Q. What is my role after my parents move into a nursing home?

A. You should try to visit your parents often. Not only will this be good for you and your parents, mentally and emotionally, but it will also help you to ensure your parents' safety. When you visit, be alert to your parents' cleanliness, skin condition, weight, and overall health and safety.

If possible, try to take your parents out of the home during visits (assuming you can safely move your parents). Nursing homes aren't prisons. You should feel as though you can, and should, take your parents on day trips—a trip to the movies or lunch at a restaurant with grandchildren will do wonders for your parents.

Regulations and Complaints

Q. Who regulates nursing homes?

A. Except for a small number of completely private nursing homes, most nursing homes are regulated at both the federal level—because they receive Medicare and Medicaid—and also at the state level. Many states have more stringent protections for residents than those required by federal law. Each state has an ombudsman's office charged with watching out for long-term-care residents. The ombudsman is responsible for advocating on behalf of residents of nursing homes, assisted-living facilities, board-and-care facilities, and other long-term-care facilities. To find your state's long-term-care ombudsman and information on your state's law, visit *www.nccnhr.org/*.

Q. Can the nursing home ask me to sign a contract holding me responsible for the monthly fee if my mother does not qualify for Medicaid and cannot otherwise make her payments?

A. If the nursing home receives Medicare or Medicaid funds, it cannot require a third party (in this case, you) to guarantee payment as a condition of admission. However, not every home follows this mandate. Read any contracts very carefully. This is especially true if you are your parent's guardian or agent. If you are, and if your parent no longer has the ability to enter into a contract, then you may be asked to sign an admissions contract on behalf of your parent. If you do, make sure that you indicate next to your name that you are signing as your parent's agent or guardian. The sidebar below outlines the language you should try to use.

If the facility does not accept Medicare or Medicaid funds, then it can require you or another party to cover expenses. This is why it is important whenever possible to work with your parent *before* he or she gets to this point to make sure such costs can be covered.

Q. Can the nursing home ask my mother to pay an entrance fee or make a donation?

A. Not if your mother is paying by Medicare or Medicaid. If your mother is entering as a private-pay patient or using long-term-care insurance, then the nursing home can ask for such a deposit or donation.

Q. My mom has asked me to review her nursing home contract. What should I look out for?

A. Some nursing home contracts attempt to limit the facility's liability if the resident is injured. Such provisions may or may not

▶ **SIGNING NURSING HOME DOCUMENTS**

If you are signing a nursing home document as your parent's agent or guardian, make sure it is clear on the face of the document that you are signing on behalf of your parent. Otherwise, a court reading the document may find that you were taking personal responsibility for the contract.

Correct Form of Signing	Incorrect Form of Signing
Mary Doe, as agent (or guardian) for John Doe	Mary Doe
John Doe, by his agent (or guardian) Mary Doe	John Doe by Mary Doe

be legal in your state. Generally, these contracts are regulated by state contract law and can vary greatly depending on where the nursing home is located. Check with your state Long-Term Care Ombudsman Program and your area agency on aging for information about the laws in your state relating to such contracts.

Q. What should I do if the nursing home asks me or my mother to sign something that we think is illegal or to which we object?

A. Explain your concerns to the nursing home administrator and tell him or her how you would like to change the contract. If the nursing home will not accept these changes and if there is no other nursing home that you feel would be acceptable for your mother, consult with an elder law attorney regarding the provisions that concern you.

Q. The nursing home has filled out my mother's application for Medicaid and asked me to sign it the next time I come to visit. Should I go ahead and sign it even though I haven't had a chance to read it?

A. No. Nursing homes sometimes fill out Medicaid applications and ask family members to sign them without giving them the opportunity to review the information in the application. If you sign the application and the information in the application is incorrect, you will be liable for any errors and could face civil and even criminal penalties. Insist that the nursing home give you an opportunity to review the completed application and review it very carefully.

Q. Where can I file a complaint about a nursing home?

A. Every state has two agencies that handle complaints about nursing homes: the Long-Term Care Ombudsman Program and a state licensing agency (often part of the state department of health). Complaints can be filed with one or both agencies. The Long-Term Care Ombudsman Program is ideal for resolving less serious disputes when your parent still wishes to remain in the facility. More serious violations should be reported to the state agency that licenses, investigates, and prosecutes nursing home violations. In order to avoid the possibility of retaliation against your mother, you may want to move her to a new nursing home before filing a complaint with the state agency if possible.

Q. *My mother was hospitalized for two weeks. When it came time for her release, the nursing home where she had been living for over a year told us that they no longer had a bed for her. Can they do this?*

A. Possibly. The nursing home is required by federal law to have a bed-hold policy that notifies residents of how long the home will hold a bed when a patient is hospitalized. You should ask for a copy of the policy when your parent first moves into the facility. If your parent's hospital stay exceeds the length of time set forth in the bed-hold policy, then the nursing home may give your parent's bed to another patient. Some state Medicaid programs will pay for a bed while a Medicaid resident is hospitalized. However, this payment will not last indefinitely, and at some point Medicaid patients may also lose their beds. If your parent's absence exceeds the length of time specified in the bed-hold policy (or the length of time for which the state will pay, assuming your parent receives Medicaid), and if his or her bed is given away, then your parent must be given the next bed available.

Q. *When I went to visit my mother this morning, she was very disoriented and drowsy. The nurse told me they had given her medication to calm her down the night before because she had been yelling and wandering around. Is the nursing home allowed to do this without consulting me? I am her agent under a health-care power of attorney.*

A. Possibly. Federal law bars nursing homes from using physical or chemical restraints without prior authorization from a doctor. The only exception to this rule is where there is an emergency situation.

At this point, you should collect as much information as possible about the circumstances surrounding the decision to medicate your mother, and discuss them with her doctor to determine whether it was truly an emergency situation. Your mother's doctor may decide that chemical restraints are necessary under certain circumstances, and that the restraints will not conflict with her other medications. Regardless of the doctor's decision, have him or her put the decision in writing, include it in your mother's chart, and inform the nursing home staff so they know how to respond to future incidents. If the restraints were not appropriate, you can take the steps outlined earlier in this chapter for filing a complaint against a nursing home.

Q. A nurse's aide is being very rough with my mother when she moves and bathes her. My mother doesn't want me to say anything because she is afraid the nurse's aide will retaliate against her. What are my options?

A. This can be a very difficult situation. If your mother wants to stay in the facility and you report the aide against her wishes, your mother may be very demoralized and, in the worst case, could face retaliation. At the very least, document the incident and try to persuade your mother to talk to a long-term-care ombudsman, who will keep her report confidential if your mother wishes him or her to do so. The ombudsman should be able to suggest options for communicating with the aide in a non-adversarial manner. Also, the ombudsman can begin to monitor the aide to determine whether the same problem affects other residents. Depending on your mother's wishes and the severity of the harm, you may want to report her complaints to the nursing home staff and to the state agency that regulates nursing homes. Before taking these steps, however, you should carefully consider the potential for retaliation if your mother wishes to remain in that particular nursing home.

▶ PHYSICAL AND CHEMICAL RESTRAINTS

Physical restraints include:

- ties;
- chairs that restrain the resident; and
- vests.

Chemical restraints include:

- tranquilizers; and
- psychotropic drugs.

When a resident becomes agitated or wanders in such a way that could lead to a fall or other harm, nursing homes and family members may have to resort to physical or chemical restraints in an effort to prevent harm. In some cases, restraints are a necessary step to prevent harm to a resident or others. The nursing home staff should be able to use soft, safe restraints when they are necessary for your parent's safety and well-being.

It is important to note that in some cases, the stress caused by a restraint may ultimately cause more harm to a resident than agitation or wandering. Additionally, there are other methods that can be used to protect residents, including behavioral modification techniques and alarm systems (though admittedly such alarms cannot *prevent* falls).

Some nursing homes may choose not to pursue alternative methods of protecting a patient (e.g., alarms, behavior modification) because they are perceived as more costly or time-consuming than restraints. In many cases, the resident's family, in conjunction with his or her physician, will have to advocate for these alternative methods. Proper planning and open communication with the nursing home staff and your parent's medical providers can hopefully reduce the possibility of restraints being used unnecessarily.

Q. *My father fell the other night at his nursing home. Does this constitute neglect?*

A. Not necessarily. Nursing homes can only do so much to prevent an ambulatory patient from falling. As discussed earlier, chemical and physical restraints may cause more harm than good. Start by discussing the problem with the nursing home and your father's doctor. If your father's fall was an accident, work with the staff to determine what, if any, changes can be made to his care plan to prevent future accidents. If you do not feel that the nursing home is responsive to your concerns, follow the steps outlined earlier in this section for filing a complaint.

Q. *My mother, who has advanced dementia, told me that an aide forced her to have sex with him. What should I do?*

A. As hard as it is to believe, sexual assaults do occur in nursing homes. The first thing to do is bring your mother to a doctor who is not affiliated with the nursing home. If he or she finds physical evidence of sexual assault, **do not return your mother to the facility. Immediately call the police and the state agency that investigates nursing home complaints.** Do not notify the nursing home of the reason for the removal, as doing so may give the perpetrator an opportunity to destroy evidence and intimidate potential witnesses. For these reasons, the police should be the first ones to contact the nursing home about the incident as part of an official investigation. You may also want to contact a personal injury attorney who has expertise in nursing home abuse cases.

REMEMBER THIS

- A wide variety of housing and communities are available for older adults who require assistance, including assisted-living communities and continuing-care retirement communities.

- Carefully review all fee arrangements, especially ones that involve large entrance fees.

- If your parent is living in an assisted-living facility, he or she may be required to move if his or her needs change and if the facility is no longer able to safely meet those needs.

- Communities may legally restrict admission to people over a certain age, so long as they follow specific federal guidelines. Therefore, you and your parent should carefully review any contracts and make sure that the community you are interested in will be able to meet your family's needs, both now and in the future.

- If supportive housing is the right option for your parent, but he or she has limited means, subsidized housing might be an option. The availability of such housing is limited, so it is important that you don't rely exclusively on this option when planning with your parent.

- A nursing home may be the appropriate option for your family if your parent is no longer able to care independently for himself or herself; if your parent is about to be discharged from a hospital and needs temporary skilled nursing care; or if your parent can no longer live alone.

- Finding a good nursing home is critical. Review the state evaluations of homes you are considering, talk to your long-term-care ombudsman about various homes, and try to visit the home at various times throughout the day. No home is perfect, but you should try to find a home that hasn't had serious or repetitive problems.

- If one of your parents is moving into a nursing home and the other will remain in the community, be prepared for a period of adjustment. Both of your parents (and you!) will have to adjust to the changes and confront feelings of guilt, fear, and sadness.

- Your state Long-Term Care Ombudsman Program is a valuable ally for you and your parents. This is the office to call if you have questions about the laws regulating nursing homes in your state, or to voice a minor complaint about a specific home. More serious complaints should be reported to the agency that licenses nursing homes in your state.

• If your parent has been the victim of sexual assault in a nursing home, do not return your parent to the facility. Notify the police immediately and allow them to conduct an investigation and contact the facility.

CHAPTER 10

Transportation

When Driving Becomes Dangerous

Last year, Brian's mother, who is eighty-five years old, acciden-
tally stepped on the gas instead of the brake while trying to park
at the grocery store. Although she was not injured, she struck a
parked vehicle. Brian's mother was clearly shaken and contin-
ued to ruminate on "what if" scenarios, concerned that she
could have killed someone. However, she was still very reluctant
to give up driving. Three months later, she drove her car into a
tree. She was hospitalized with minor injuries. How can Brian
get his mom to stop driving? Can he simply take her keys away?
Will he then have to drive her everywhere?

For many older Americans, the ability to drive is essential to
their sense of autonomy and personal freedom. Having conversations about limiting driving or removing it from your parent's daily activities can be very difficult. However, having these
conversations and exploring the available options *before* an accident or other crisis occurs will go a long way toward ensuring that
the necessary transitions are not only safe, but also positive. This
chapter explores the signs and signals that it may be time for your
parents to stop driving, identifies alternative modes of transportation, and outlines your (somewhat limited) legal options
should your parent continue to drive after it is no longer safe.

DRIVING AND OLD AGE

Q. Will my parents have to stop driving at a certain point?

A. Not necessarily. No state has a pre-set age at which people
must stop driving. However, your parents—whether due to poor

vision, delayed cognitive ability, or some other factor—may have to limit or stop driving as they age. Many older drivers will self-monitor and begin to limit their driving as needed in order to remain safe. But for some families, the transition isn't always so easy, and you may need to work with your parent to assess his or her abilities and find alternatives.

Q. How do I know when my parents should stop driving?

A. There are many different warning signs. If your parent reports getting lost, running a stop sign, or confusing the gas and brake pedals, it is probably time to have a candid conversation. Some older adults may get lucky and not experience any noticeable problems with driving. But some of the changes associated with aging may naturally impair driving skills and may serve as warnings. Vision problems can cause older drivers to misjudge the distance between cars and the speed of oncoming traffic, and can affect their sensitivity to light (night driving usually declines before daytime driving). Certain types of hearing loss may prevent your parent from hearing emergency vehicles, railroad warnings, or even the honking horns of other drivers. If your parent's health insurance will cover eye refraction every two years (or more), or hearing tests with ear, nose, and throat specialists, encourage your parent to take advantage of these benefits and obtain regular checkups. Of course, confusion or possible dementia are also warning signs that it's time to evaluate your parent's driving ability.

Certain medications may increase drowsiness or slow your parent's response times. You may want to consider establishing a periodic review with your parent and his or her primary health-care provider to take inventory of all the medications your parent is taking, including over-the-counter drugs and vitamins. This review should assess how these medications may interact with each other and impact your parent's driving. Your parent's pharmacist may also be a helpful resource during these evaluations.

Q. What should I be alert to regarding my parent's driving?

A. There are a variety of signals that may indicate a need to evaluate your parent's driving ability, including:

- problems judging gaps in traffic;
- difficulty reading road signs or pavement markings;
- problems moving his or her foot from the gas to brake pedal, or confusing the two pedals;
- physical difficulties turning around to check over his or her shoulder while backing up or changing lanes;
- a number of "close calls";
- warnings or tickets from the police;
- dents or scrapes on the car or garage door;
- a tendency to drive dramatically slower than the flow of other traffic, especially when negotiating turns; or
- other drivers honking or yelling at your parent.

Q. What if I think that my mother probably shouldn't drive as much, but I don't think that she has to stop driving completely? Is there anything I can do?

A. Yes. There are many options that could both improve your mother's driving ability and help both of you to be alert to any further declines. These include:

- working with your parent to establish some limited restrictions on driving;
- asking your mother to drive only during the day and in familiar neighborhoods;
- working with an occupational therapist to determine whether your mom's car can be fitted with any assistive or safety features;
- exploring other transportation options such as mass transit and senior citizen shuttles; and
- looking for training options or "senior driving courses" for your mom. State affiliates of several organizations, such as the National Safety Council (*www.nsc.org*) and American

▶ **FINDING AN OCCUPATIONAL THERAPIST**

If you and your parent decide to work with an occupational therapist to outfit your parent's car for increased driving safety, make sure you use a therapist who is certified in dealing with driving skills. Not all occupational therapists are trained in this area. For more information on finding an appropriate occupational therapist in your area, contact the American Occupational Therapy Association (*www.aota.org*).

Automobile Association (*www.aaa.com*) offer such courses and in many cases, upon completion of the course, your parent may receive a 10-percent discount on his or her auto insurance. In addition, AARP offers driver's education programs for older adults.

Q. My mom has had three accidents in the past month, but she won't stop driving. What can I do?

A. You have several options. Do not just take away her keys. If possible, talk to her about your concerns, recognizing that sometimes she may not perceive the safety issues as clearly as you do. When having these discussions, you must be very patient and willing to talk about this issue over several sessions. You must be organized and persistent in any discussions that you have; rarely will the first discussion result in changed driving habits.

Try to have your mom evaluate her own driving skills on a regular basis and to recognize your safety concerns for other people. The American Automobile Association (AAA) offers an inexpensive computer program that will enable her to self-evaluate those changes that may impact driving. Self-evaluation will allow your mom to play an integral role in the transition away from driving, and may allow her to take ownership over the changes.

Research alternative modes of transportation in your mom's area. Be sure that she has alternative ways to get to her activities.

▶ **TIME TO MOVE?**

   If your parent is starting to have problems with driving, this may provide you with an opportunity to discuss other housing options. Continuing-care retirement communities and assisted-living communities may provide various services such as health care and meals, shops, and religious services within the community (all within a walkable distance). A move to such a community may allow your parent to continue to live independently without having to worry about driving. These types of housing options are discussed further in chapter 9.

This should help your mom to avoid feeling trapped or isolated. You also may want to consider putting the issue into economic terms. Together with your mom, look at the cost of insurance, gas, and upkeep of a car—depending on how much she drives, it may be less expensive for her to use a taxi or mass transit. Lastly, you may want to consider asking your mom's physician, a family attorney, or a local law enforcement officer to talk to her about driving and safety.

   If the problem persists, you may need to take other more formal actions. These are discussed later in this chapter.

Q. What alternatives are available to help my parent get where he or she needs to go?

A. Easily accessible alternatives to driving include:
   • ride-sharing programs (some communities offer transportation between major points within the community, and some community centers offer car pools for specific programs);
   • shuttle bus services;
   • public transportation (many communities provide free or low-cost passes to seniors);
   • rides provided by family and friends (who may create rotation schedules);
   • special bicycles or tricycles designed for older adults;

> ▶ **MORE INFORMATION**
>
> For more information on driving safety and alternative methods of transportation, visit *www.seniordrivers.org* or the website Alzheimer's, Dementia & Driving (*www.thehartford.com/alzheimers/*), which provides specific resources for families confronting dementia and driving. The American Medical Association and the National Highway Traffic Safety Association have developed a guide for doctors working with older drivers; it may be useful in preparing for any discussions and finding alternatives to driving (*www.ama-assn.org/ama/pub/category/10791.html*). The department or agency responsible for licensing drivers in your state will have information about the specific state rules, as does the Governors Highway Safety Association (*www.ghsa.org*). AARP's website also provides information on signing up for its driver's education programs.

- neighbors (help your parent connect with those individuals in the neighborhood who might provide rides to the grocery store or other places);
- taxis;
- paratransit programs, which provide transportation to people with limited mobility; and
- transportation programs provided by religious organizations (often available for bringing members to religious services).

If your parent plans to use public or mass transit, you may want to accompany him or her the first few times until he or she is comfortable and sure of the route.

LEGAL INTERVENTIONS

Q. Legally, when does someone have to stop driving?

A. State laws control who can drive and under what circumstances the state can take away a person's driver's license or

refuse to issue or renew a license. There are significant variations between states in this regard, but no state requires older
adults to give up their driver's licenses merely because they have
reached a certain age. Your area agency on aging can provide you
with information about the laws in your state. States ensure
oversight of older drivers (which may lead to restrictions on their
driving) in three ways:

1. **Reporting.** Some states require doctors to report patients
   whose driving may be impaired because of physical or
   mental conditions. Other states permit *anyone* to report a
   possibly unsafe driver.

2. **Shortened license renewal periods.** Some states shorten
   the period between driver's license renewals for people over
   a certain age. This means that as your parent ages, he or
   she will have to renew his or her license more frequently.

3. **Additional registration requirements.** Other states
   impose additional registration requirements for people over
   a certain age. For instance, a state may require someone
   who is over eighty years of age to register in person or take
   additional vision or road tests not normally required for
   renewal.

**Q. Are there more restrictive measures I can take?
I have tried numerous times to talk to my mom,
but she continues to drive and it is no longer safe.**

A. Unfortunately, if your mother still has decision-making capacity and hasn't caused an accident involving the police, there
isn't a whole lot you can do. If your mother is posing a safety risk
for herself or others, guardianship may be a possible step. In
some states, a court ordering guardianship can issue an order
stating that the ward (i.e., the person for whom the guardianship
is being sought) is no longer permitted to drive. While a problem
with driving should not, in and of itself, be a basis for seeking
guardianship, such a step may give you an important tool to en-

sure that your parent's safety (and that of other drivers and pedestrians) is not put at risk. Chapter 4 provides more information on guardianships. Guardianship is a very serious step and may have some unintentional consequences. If you are considering this step, it is important to consult with an attorney who is experienced in this area. An attorney may be able to outline whether a guardianship will be effective in your case and whether other options exist.

REMEMBER THIS

- No state has a pre-set age at which people must stop driving. However, many older adults—whether due to poor vision, delayed cognitive ability, or some other factors—may have to limit or stop driving as they age.

- There are many options for both improving your parent's driving ability and alerting you both to any further declines. These options include working with your parent to establish some limited restrictions on driving, asking your parent to drive only during the day and in familiar neighborhoods, or looking for training options or "senior driving courses" for your parent.

- States ensure oversight of older drivers (which may lead them to impose restrictions on driving) in three ways: reporting, shortened license renewal periods, and additional registration requirements. Your area agency on aging can provide you with information about the laws in your state.

CHAPTER 11

Protecting Your Parent

What You Need to Know
About Elder Abuse and Neglect,
Financial Exploitation,
and Consumer Fraud

Cynthia has worked tirelessly to develop a care plan for her mom and coordinate numerous service providers. She checked the references on every person coming into her mom's home, and made sure each person was properly licensed. However, lately she has noticed some strange marks on her mom's arms and legs. Her mom, whose decision-making capacity has declined substantially, has been talking about "the men who hit her." Cynthia can't believe that her mom would be the victim of abuse—it just doesn't happen in these circumstances, does it? Can Cynthia do anything to protect her mom's assets and well-being?

Most of us would prefer to trust the individuals who are caring for our parents, which may blind us to potentially abusive behavior. This is particularly true when we are already questioning the accuracy of our parent's perceptions. However, trust your instincts and what your parent is telling you. Elder abuse is a recognized social problem with legal, medical, and psychological implications. It can take place at home, in institutions, or within health-care systems. Perpetrators of abuse may be family members, hired caregivers, or those who provide various services to the elderly. In this chapter, we will discuss the current definitions of elder abuse, the prevalence of abuse in domestic and institutional settings, and the applicable legal concerns. We conclude by examining two specific types of nonviolent abuse: financial exploitation and consumer fraud.

SIGNS AND SIGNALS OF ELDER ABUSE

Q. What kinds of behaviors constitute elder abuse and neglect? What are the signs I should look for?

A. Elder abuse is any form of mistreatment that results in harm or loss to an older person. The broad categories include: physical, emotional, or sexual abuse; neglect or abandonment by caregivers (which can be either passive or active); and financial exploitation. (Strategies for protecting your parent from financial abuse are discussed in more detail below.)

SIGNS, SYMPTOMS, AND EXAMPLES OF ABUSE AND NEGLECT:

Physical abuse	• Unexplained bruises, welts, or burns • Fractures, sprains, or dislocations • Misuse of restraints • Forced feeding • Broken eyeglasses or frames • A caregiver trying to prevent you from seeing your parent
Emotional abuse	• Threatening language or behavior, intimidation or harassment (note that emotionally controlling behavior can be either verbal or nonverbal) • Your parent expressing fears about being alone with a caregiver (e.g., your parent saying that he or she is afraid to report problems or complaints, possibly fearing repercussions)
Sexual abuse	• Bruises around breasts or genitals • Unexplained genital infections • Unexplained vaginal or anal bleeding

	• Any nonconsensual sexual activity • Forced exposure to pornography
Passive Neglect	• Overlooking weight loss or bedsores • Assuming that your parent will eat when he or she is hungry and not actively providing meals at regular intervals • Failing to check in on your parent with enough frequency to notice changes in his or her health • Unintentional lapses in providing medication to your parent
Active Neglect	• Intentionally leaving your parent alone • Refusing to provide adequate food • Refusing to obtain needed medical care for your parent • Refusing to provide care that has been directed by a physician or geriatric care manager • Leaving your parent in an unsafe situation (for example, near fire hazards, or without access to a phone or running water)
Self Neglect	• Unsanitary or unclean living quarters • Dehydration, malnutrition or untreated wounds • Poor personal hygiene • Excessive clutter and hoarding of mail • Feces and urine from pets left on the floors or furniture • Food left out of the refrigerator • Medication bottles left unfilled or clearly unused as prescribed • A house in disrepair
Financial Exploitation	• Missing items of value • Depleted bank accounts

- Checks cashed with a forged signature
- Service contracts signed through use of deception or coercion
- Scams targeted at older people

These are limited examples of specific kinds of elder abuse. Some are intentional and malicious, while other forms (particularly passive neglect) may be due to a lack of knowledge, lack of resources, or insufficient help and support.

Q. What signs in a caregiver may indicate an increased likelihood that he or she could abuse my parent?

A. Certain signs may indicate the possibility of abuse and should be explored, but of course they are not by themselves definitive indications of abuse. Signs can include a caregiver making excuses for why you cannot see your parent at a given time, or refusing to allow you to see credit card bills or other receipts for expenses. You should also be alert to a caregiver who has started to complain increasingly about your parent's behavior, or who asks for more authority in banking or credit card use. Other potential signs may include a caregiver leaving your parent alone more often, not showing up on time, forgetting to take

▶ **MORE INFORMATION AND RESOURCES**

The National Center on Elder Abuse, which is administered by the federal Administration on Aging, provides a wealth of information and resources on elder abuse (*www.ncea.aoa.gov*). Its website outlines various resources state by state, and discusses additional warning signs of abuse and measures for preventing it.

your parent to doctor's appointments, or acting irritable or short-tempered. Other signs of potential abuse include a caregiver arguing with you about care, or refusing to take any time off or permit substitute caregivers. Lastly, be alert to a caregiver who makes unrealistic promises to care for your parent long-term.

PREVENTING ELDER ABUSE

Q. What can I do to protect my parent from abuse at the hands of a caregiver?

A. First, ask a lot of questions and be informed! As a family member, there are a number of specific steps you can follow:

- Make sure you maintain open and constant communication with your parent's caregivers.
- Don't leave your parent with a family member who has a history of substance abuse or aggression.
- Ask friends and family to visit your parent frequently.
- If your parent is in a nursing home, find out about the staff-to-resident ratio, the working conditions for the staff, and the staff's history of training and retraining. Look at the other residents and get a sense of the level of care. Make frequent and unannounced visits to the facility. Take note of how many doors to residents' rooms are left open. Closed doors could indicate that the staff is trying to ignore resident calls, or could indicate a lack of activity and social interaction among the residents.
- If your parent has a provider coming into his or her home, make sure that the caregiver is employed by a certified, bonded agency and provides excellent references. You should encourage your parent to review any changes in services or contract agreements with you or an attorney before signing them.
- Listen to what your parent tells you! Even if your parent has dementia and seems confused, he or she may still be able to communicate some aspects of a story that raise concern.
- Make sure your parent is aware of his or her rights. Most in-

stitutions provide a resident's bill of rights. Obtain a copy, and make sure your parent has one.

• Educate your parent about what to do in case of abuse. Sometimes older people are afraid to report misconduct. Encourage your parent to tell you or another trusted family member or friend about anything that does not seem right. If your parent seems unwilling to talk about these issues, encourage him or her to write about them and give you a note.

Q. How should I talk to my parent about the potential for elder abuse?

A. Talking to your parent about potential elder abuse or neglect is important to ensure that he or she can self-protect, and that he or she feels comfortable talking to you about what (if anything) is occurring when you aren't present. While it is important to ask open-ended questions so that your parent can speak freely and provide you with details, it is also important to direct his or her attention to particular areas of risk. It is important to be non-threatening and non-shaming. For example, if your parent's credit card bills seem a little high, you could ask your parent, "Can you tell me how your caregiver pays for the groceries he/she buys for you?" or "How do you limit the spending on your

▶ **IF YOU ARE THE CAREGIVER**

If you are providing care to your parent, it is important to take stock of your emotions to ensure that you don't take out any frustrations or worry on your parent. Take time off from caregiving whenever you can. Know your limits, and communicate them to your parent. Educate yourself about the resources in your community for caregivers, and educate yourself about respite care. You should also consider participating in a support group for caregivers. You don't have to—and shouldn't—perform all the caregiving on your own.

credit card?" These questions should work better than asking, "Did you give the caregiver your credit card?" A question that requires a simple "yes" or "no" answer may make your parent feel as though his or her actions were foolish or naïve.

Nevertheless, when you talk to your parent, it is important to be frank about the potential for elder abuse. Share stories that you have read in the newspaper or heard on the news. Try to be non-judgmental and supportive so that your parent will feel comfortable sharing his or her experiences. Things to ask about include:

- the details of your parent's relationship with caregivers;
- the details of your parent's day (e.g., what he or she did on a particular day, what the caregiver did);
- details about how the caregiver performs tasks like giving showers, getting your parent up and out of the room, etc.; and
- details about how your parent gets along with the caregiver.

Q. My parent is in a nursing home (or other institution). What are some signs of potential abuse I should look out for?

A. Most importantly, make sure your parent is in a facility with staff that you trust, and make sure you listen to your parent. Even if your parent has experienced cognitive decline, a single moment of lucidity could allow him or her to provide insight into

▶ **ABUSE OUTSIDE OF FACILITIES**

Although you may think your parent is safest outside of a facility such as a nursing home, in many cases, elder abuse occurs at the hands of a family or paid caregiver outside nursing homes. Regardless of where your parent resides, you and your family must be on the lookout for signs of abuse.

what happens when you aren't present. Signs that may indicate possible abuse include:

- unexplained injuries like fractures (pay particular attention to the area around your parent's mouth or bruises on his or her body);
- bedsores or a general decline in health beyond reasonable expectation;
- fear of particular staff members (or acting differently in the presence of certain staff members);
- a staff person's explanation of an injury that does not seem credible (e.g., a staff person maintaining your parent slipped and fell when your parent is wheelchair-bound);
- depression;
- a sudden desire to move to another facility; or
- a desire to change a power of attorney or will without reasonable explanation (this may be a sign that your parent has been coerced by a staff person).

These are not absolute indications of abuse, but are listed to raise your curiosity about changes you may observe in your parent. The remedies available to your parent as a resident of a nursing home are outlined in chapter 9. Chances are that if abuse is going on, the state Long-Term Care Ombudsman program will be a great resource for you and your family. These programs are discussed further in chapter 9.

WHAT TO DO IF YOUR PARENT IS BEING ABUSED OR NEGLECTED

Q. How does the law address elder abuse and neglect?

A. Each state has its own legal definitions of elder abuse and neglect. Some states do not include emotional or psychological abuse in their definitions; a few states do include unreasonable confinement. To make matters even more confusing, some states use one set of definitions in connection with their elder abuse

▶ **ABUSE IN THE HOME**

Abuse and neglect occur more often in the home or at the hands of family members or friends than most people assume. It may be difficult to believe that a family member or in-home caregiver would abuse your parent, but you must stay alert to such a possibility. The following are theoretical examples of elder abuse and neglect in the home:

- Your sister moves in with your mom and they are always fighting. You know your mom gives your sister money whenever she asks for it, and your mom has said that your sister hits her. Now when you ask, your mom denies that anything is wrong.

- You have hired a neighbor to help check in on your dad. The neighbor is supposed to make sure your dad takes his medicine and eats three times a day. Lately you have noticed that your dad is losing weight, and his medicine is piling up. Your dad says he hasn't seen the neighbor in at least a week.

- You have been caring for your mom for six months now (she is recovering from a broken hip). You are pretty much in charge of everything–not to mention your three kids and full-time job. Your mother has been complaining about everything lately, and refuses to thank you for anything that you are doing. Suddenly, before you realize it, you have smacked her.

and neglect programs, another for civil orders of protection, and yet another for criminal prosecution of abuse and neglect.

Q. Legally, what can I do if I think a caregiver is abusing my mother?

A. A number of legal interventions are possible in a case like this. The more common options are: reporting to the state agency that investigates elder abuse and neglect; obtaining an order of protection or a stay-away order; and criminal prosecution. However, the first step is to discuss the situation with your mother, find out what she would like to see happen, and determine whether she wishes to pursue any of the possible legal interventions.

Report to an Elder Abuse and Neglect Agency

Q. To whom do I report suspected elder abuse?

A. Every state has an agency that investigates elder abuse and neglect. Sometimes known as **adult protection services**, these agencies may handle cases involving disabled adults as well as the elderly. Your local area agency on aging can tell you how to file a report with the appropriate agency in your state.

Agencies vary from state to state as to how they handle reports of abuse and neglect. Some agencies focus more on identifying underlying conflicts and sources of stress and offering services to help resolve problems. Others are more likely to work directly with the police and use the criminal process to punish perpetrators. If the agency offers any services to address the abuse, the elderly person will have to consent to the services; the agency cannot force its services on an adult victim. In cases where the abused does not consent, and the agency feels that he or she lacks decision-making power, the agency may pursue guardianship. If the agency feels that the person is in immediate danger of substantial harm to him- or herself or others, the agency may pursue civil commitment or other state remedies to take the person into protective custody.

Q. What are the advantages of reporting to a state agency?

A. Of course, the specific advantages will depend on your exact family situation, but some advantages may include the following:
- the agency will help to obtain services for your parent and the abuser;
- the agency will keep the name of the reporter anonymous;
- there is no cost for the agency's services;
- the agency likely has strict time frames for responding to reports of abuse, and will respond on an emergency basis if necessary;

- the agency workers have received training in how to talk with older people about abuse and neglect; and
- the agency staff will analyze the situation and suggest legal remedies (which can be criminal or civil in nature).

Q. What are the disadvantages of reporting elder abuse to a state agency?

A. Again, this will depend on your individual family, but some general disadvantages may include the following:

- while the agency will talk to your entire family, the staff will work directly with your parent and may not share information with you without your parent's permission;
- the agency may report the matter to the police without your parent's permission or your agreement;
- the agency staff may be accompanied by a police officer when conducting the investigation;
- you may disagree with how the agency decides to handle the matter;
- your parent and your family may lose control over the matter; and
- the agency may initiate guardianship or civil commitment proceedings without your knowledge or agreement.

Orders of Protection or Stay-Away Orders

Q. What is an order of protection?

A. The exact name for this type of order varies from state to state. Originally developed for victims of spousal abuse, orders of protection have been expanded to include violence among family members and, in some states, abuse or neglect of the elderly. An **order of protection** can require that the alleged perpetrator do one or more of the following:

- stop abusing, neglecting, or threatening the alleged victim;
- stay away from the alleged victim;
- not contact the alleged victim by telephone;
- move out of the alleged victim's home;

- repay money owed the alleged victim;
- return property taken from the alleged victim; or
- attend Alcoholics Anonymous meetings, Narcotics Anonymous meetings, or counseling.

Q. How can I obtain an order of protection for my parent?

A. There is normally a two-step process for obtaining such an order. As a first step, it may be possible to obtain an immediate order *ex parte* (meaning without the alleged perpetrator being present). This order will only last for a short period of time. The order will be given (served) to the alleged perpetrator, along with notice of a second hearing. At the second hearing, the alleged perpetrator will be given the option of agreeing to the order (without admitting guilt) or contesting it. If the alleged perpetrator contests the order, there will be a full hearing at which both sides will present evidence and testimony.

Q. If there has to be a second hearing, won't this mean that my parent has to be in the same room as the abuser?

A. Unfortunately, yes—both your parent and the alleged abuser will have the right to be present at the second hearing. However, this hearing will be in a courtroom in the presence of sheriffs and other court personnel. If you are particularly worried about your parent's safety prior to such a hearing, call the courthouse beforehand in order to ensure that proper protection will be present.

Q. What are the advantages of orders of protection?

A. There can be many advantages. For example:
- Getting an order of protection is a private process, and your parent will control all phases and can choose to stop the process at any time.
- This is a civil remedy that will not affect the alleged perpetrator's employment options as a criminal case might.
- Most courts are set up to allow people to pursue this option *pro se* (i.e., without an attorney).

- The alleged perpetrator may not even show up at the second-phase hearing. If he or she was given proper notice of the hearing and still fails to show up, then an order can be entered by default (meaning that a full order will be entered without the alleged perpetrator being present).
- The alleged perpetrator may show up at the second hearing, but simply agree to the order.
- If the case goes to trial, a lower standard of proof is required than there would be in a criminal case.
- Violation of the order is punishable by contempt (which could involve jail time), and may constitute a separate crime which can be prosecuted by the state.

Q. What are some of the disadvantages of orders of protection?

A. It is important to recognize that orders of protection are legal interventions and can have some serious disadvantages. For example, your parent and any other witnesses to the abuse will have to go to court and may have to testify in public. Moreover, at the end of the day, the order is only a piece of paper. If your parent has not been adjudicated incompetent and chooses to allow the alleged perpetrator back into his or her home, there is probably nothing that you will be to do about it (the prosecutors' office may view this action as a violation of the order, but you will likely have no say in the decision). Additionally, an order doesn't guarantee that a perpetrator will stop abusing your parent. However, it can ensure that if the behavior continues, the perpetrator can face fines or even jail time.

Criminal Prosecution

Q. How does criminal prosecution work in cases of elder abuse?

A. Elder abuse and neglect can be crimes. To initiate a criminal prosecution, you or your parent should call the police and make a report. Make sure that you get a report number. The police will in vestigate and make a decision as to whether or not there is enough evidence to prosecute. The prosecutor, often known as the assistant district attorney or assistant state's attorney, is a lawyer employed by the state or county to prosecute crimes for the benefit of society. In a criminal prosecution, your parent will not be the prosecutor's client, but instead will be a witness in the case. The prosecutor's office will make the decision whether to go forward and take the case to trial, or to accept a plea bargain and settle the case. Your parent probably won't be consulted in this decision.

Q. What are the advantages of criminal prosecution?

A. During a criminal prosecution, the government has its own lawyer and legal office to prosecute the case, so there is no cost to your parent (unless he or she has to miss work to testify). Criminal prosecution can also result in jail time, and therefore can make a greater statement to the perpetrator that what he or she has done is wrong. This could possibly stop the perpetrator from abusing your parent or another older person in the future. Criminal prosecution may also empower the victim by sending the message that the state—and society—see the abuse or neglect as wrong. Lastly, the perpetrator may be able to get needed drug, alcohol, or other counseling while incarcerated.

Q. What are the disadvantages of criminal prosecution?

A. Criminal prosecution is a very serious step, and may have lasting and unintended consequences. Your parent will likely have no control over the case; the prosecutor may settle the case against his or her wishes, and once a criminal case is initiated, your parent cannot change his or her mind and decide not to go forward with it (although he or she could refuse to testify about the abuse). A criminal prosecution can take a long time, and in some cases can be dehumanizing for the victim, who is treated as a mere witness and can be expected to testify about very personal issues. Elder abuse and neglect can also be very difficult to prove. There is a higher standard of proof in criminal cases than there is when obtaining orders of protection: the prosecutor must demonstrate that the abuse or neglect occurred "beyond a reasonable doubt."

Lastly, criminal prosecution can ruin an alleged perpetrator's life—he or she may end up in jail or with a criminal record that could impact future employment or eligibility for government benefits. Your parent may want the abuse to stop, but may also be upset at the thought of a loved one going to jail.

Q. If I think my parent is being abused, how do we choose the proper legal intervention?

A. First, you should talk to your parent about the abuse and possible remedies. If your parent has decision-making capacity, the choice of intervention is his or hers to make. Even if your parent lacks decision-making capacity, pursuing the intervention that makes your parent most comfortable can greatly increase the chance that the abuse will stop and that your parent will feel empowered. You can choose to pursue one, two, or all three of the legal interventions described in this section. You can pursue them at the same time, or try one and then (if it doesn't work) try another. It's important to be aware, however, that the longer you wait to pursue a remedy in court (either civil or criminal), the harder the case may be to prove.

The major difference between the three remedies is that the first (reporting to an agency) and the third (criminal prosecution) may result in a loss of control for the victim. Since in elder abuse cases there is often a close relationship between the victim and the perpetrator, the victim may wish to end the abuse with as little harm to the perpetrator as possible. Additionally, your parent may be worried about what will happen to him or her if the perpetrator leaves. For example, if the abuser is a live-in caregiver, your parent may fear that, without the abuser, he or she will have to move into a nursing home.

Q. I just don't understand why my parent doesn't want to see the abuser put behind bars. What can I do?

A. As a loved one helping a parent, it can be very painful to watch this type of situation unfold if the perpetrator is clearly in the wrong and you believe he or she should be punished regardless of the consequences. First, you should try to talk to your parent about your fears and concerns. Don't press your parent if he or she is unwilling to talk about the abuse, but be honest about your worries. You may want to work with your parent to obtain a civil order of protection. Explain to your parent that orders of protection are a remedy developed for domestic violence cases involving spouses who, like your parent, may still have a relationship with the perpetrator. This remedy allows the victim the greatest degree of control over the proceedings. Since the victim may feel a greater sense of control and empowerment, he or she may be more likely to follow through with the process and testify as needed.

If your parent has full mental capacity, you won't be able to force him or her to cooperate with a legal intervention. Because elder abuse and neglect occur behind closed doors, the victim's testimony is crucial to a successful resolution of the case. If your parent resents your intrusion, or that of the agency or prosecutor, he or she may refuse to cooperate. This is particularly true in families with a long-standing mistrust of government intrusion in their affairs. Without your parent's cooperation, you will likely be no better off than when you started to intervene.

Q. *Last month my mom said that her caregiver was hitting her. But now she claims nothing is wrong. I don't think my mom would have made up such a story. What can I do?*

A. The answer to this question depends on whether your mother is suffering from any deficits in her decision-making capacity. If your mother is fully aware of what is going on and choosing not to take steps to end the abuse, you may report the abuse for investigation, attempt to get an order of protection on your mother's behalf, and even pursue criminal prosecution without your mother's cooperation. However, this may cause permanent damage to your relationship with your mother (and with the abuser). In addition, as discussed earlier, it may be impossible to investigate or obtain legal remedies if your mother, the only witness, refuses to cooperate. In this situation, you are strongly advised to consult a counselor knowledgeable about aging and elder abuse for guidance on how to talk to your mother about taking action against the abuser. In some cases, families stage interventions similar to those for alcoholics or drug abusers.

If your mother is not able to make reasonable decisions because of dementia or other mental decline, you should consider the legal interventions described in chapters 3 and 4. These options may allow you to step in and remove your mother from a dangerous situation or fire an abusive caregiver. However, even where your mother lacks decision-making capacity, the first step should always be to talk with her and, if possible, determine how she would like to proceed.

Q. The agency for elder abuse is investigating my family. The investigators say that they received a report that my mother is being abused. Is this possible? Who would make such a report?

A. Yes, this is possible. All states have agencies that investigate suspected cases of abuse. Reports to such agencies can be anonymous and can come from either mandated or non-mandated reporters.

In many states, certain individuals, because of their profession, are **mandated reporters** under state law. These individuals must report suspected or actual incidents of abuse to the elder abuse offices in their respective states within a prescribed twenty-four- or forty-eight-hour period after the incident. A report will result in an investigation of the situation. Mandated reporters may include social workers, doctors, teachers, police officers, and other employees of social, health, and law enforcement agencies. Employees of long-term and residential care facilities are mandated reporters.

Non-mandated reporters are also encouraged to report incidents of suspected or actual elder abuse. A non-mandated reporter can be a family member, a friend, or a neighbor who sees

▶ **UNDERSTANDING ELDER ABUSE**

While the motives for elder abuse may be complex and varied, there are some general trends. Surprisingly, most abusers are family members. In some cases, the perpetrator may be an individual with personal problems such as mental illness or substance abuse. The perpetrator may be unemployed and dependent on the victim for money and housing. In other cases, a family caregiver may be experiencing overwhelming stress related to caring for the victim. The family member may also be dealing with feelings of resentment or frustration. If there is no option for respite care or time off, a family caregiver may end up taking out such feelings on the older person.

Some elder abusers (regardless of whether they are family or non-family members) simply do not have the necessary knowledge or training to provide adequate care. Other caregivers (particularly family or friends) may be socially isolated, and may not have access to sufficient support. Lastly, an adult providing care to his or her aging parent may have been abused by the parent as a child, resulting in feelings of anger and resentment that have gone unaddressed.

By no means do these reasons justify abuse or neglect. But understanding the "why" can possibly help stop the abuse. Elder abuse is an underreported problem, partly because of the social isolation of abused elders, and partly due to fear of the consequences associated with reporting. Individuals may be concerned about court appearances, retribution from employers, and loss of their own jobs. Victims may be afraid of retribution from the abuser, losing a close relative or friend, or the shame and embarrassment of being in such a situation.

something that raises suspicion. These reports can often be anonymous and, in many locations, reporters who make a report in good faith are protected from later legal action by the alleged perpetrator. Good-faith reports are those that are made with the honest and reasonable belief that abuse is occurring.

FINANCIAL EXPLOITATION

Q. My dad never seems to have as much money as he thinks he should have. Is he just forgetful, or would someone really steal from an elderly person?

A. Either option is possible. Your father could simply be forgetful or not totally aware of how much money he has. But as much as you may not want to believe it, there are individuals out there who will steal from or financially take advantage of the elderly. If this is a recurring problem, you may want to determine whether your father is a victim of financial exploitation.

Q. What is financial exploitation?

A. **Financial exploitation**, also known as **financial mistreatment**, is one of the most common forms of elder abuse. State elder abuse and neglect statutes include financial exploitation as a type of abuse. Definitions of financial exploitation vary but, in general, require some misuse of an older person's funds or property. In some states, it is not necessary for the misuse to be intentional. Some of the legal terms describing the misuse of funds are described later in this section. Financial exploitation of an aging parent could include stealing from an elderly person; pressuring an elderly person into altering a will, power of attorney, or trust documents; coercing an elderly person into signing or drafting a contract he or she normally wouldn't sign; or forging an elderly person's signature.

Q. What are some of the signs of financial exploitation?

A. Financial exploitation can take many forms, but some general signs to look for include:
- a caregiver using your parent's funds for personal use;
- significant withdrawals from your parent's accounts;

- sudden changes in your parent's financial condition;
- your parent saying he or she is missing personal items or cash;
- unanticipated or unexplained changes to your parent's will, powers of attorney, titles, or insurance policies; or
- new credit cards in your parent's name.

Q. My brother lives with my mother rent-free, and is taking all of her pension payments and spending them on himself. What can I do?

A. In order to begin to answer this question, you must first determine whether your mother has the capacity to know what is going on and, if so, whether she approves of your brother's actions. If your mother has decision-making capacity and she does want the situation to change, you can tell her about her legal options and help her find an attorney. As outlined later in this section, the remedies and procedures available will vary depending your mother's capacity and the type of conduct.

Q. What are the legal interventions available if my parent is being financially exploited?

A. A variety of options are available depending on your parent's relationship with the abuser, your parent's current cognitive capacity and legal status (for example, whether your parent has a guardian), and whether the abuser's actions meet the requirements for a civil or criminal case.

Many of the legal interventions available to victims of other types of elder abuse or neglect (e.g., making a report to an agency) are also available to the victims of financial exploitation. Your parent may also be able to bring a civil or criminal complaint. (Criminal cases are actually brought by local prosecutors, but your parent can make a complaint to start the proceedings.) Civil remedies and/or criminal penalties may apply in cases of:

- **incapacity**—i.e., where the older person did not have decision-making capacity at the time of the transaction;
- **theft/conversion**—the taking of the older person's property without their permission;

- **fraud**—intentionally deceiving or tricking the older person into handing over property based on false or misleading statements;
- **undue influence**—using influence over the older person to get him or her to hand over property (such influence can derive from a relationship with the older person, authority over the older person, or the older person's cognitive deficits); or
- **breach of fiduciary duty**—where a person has a fiduciary duty to an older person (through a power of attorney for property, guardianship of the estate, trust, or simply by being more powerful in the relationship) and that person's action or failure to act results in the loss of the older person's property. The actions do not necessarily have to be intentional or purposeful (although if they aren't, then the action will likely be for negligent conversion rather than breach of fiduciary duty).

Q. My parent has limited cognitive ability and is being financially abused by a caregiver. What can my family do?

A. If your parent currently lacks decision-making capacity and has no guardian or agent, you will first have to petition a court for guardianship in order to bring suit on your parent's behalf. Then, as the newly appointed guardian, you can pursue the recovery of any property on behalf of your parent.

Q. What if my mother already has a guardian of the estate or an agent under a valid power of attorney?

A. If your parent already has a guardian or valid agent, that person will bring any court actions on behalf of your parent. It is vital that the guardian or agent attempt to determine how your mother wants to proceed, regardless of her decision-making capacity. If your mother disagrees with the actions an agent takes, she may be able to revoke the power of attorney.

Q. What if a guardian or agent is financially exploiting my mother?

A. If it is a guardian who is financially exploiting your mother, you (or another interested friend or family member) can petition the court to have the guardian removed and your mother's property returned. If the court agrees with you, it will remove the guardian and appoint a successor or alternative guardian. The court may also order that the financial abuser return any property that was taken.

If the abuser is an agent under a power of attorney, and if your parent retains decision-making capacity, then your parent can revoke the power of attorney and pursue recovery of his or her own assets. If your parent currently lacks decision-making capacity, you (or someone else) can petition the court to have a guardian appointed and the power of attorney terminated.

Q. Will we need an attorney to pursue these options?

A. Yes. These are complicated situations and a great deal will depend on the exact actions of the abuser, his or her relationship with your parent, and your parent's mental capacity, both at the time of the exploitation and at present. For this reason, you will need the help of an attorney who is familiar with this sort of case. If your parent has decision-making power, then the attorney will represent your parent. Otherwise, the attorney can represent the guardian or the agent who is acting on behalf of your parent (or, in a case where a guardian or agent has financially exploited your parent, the attorney can represent anyone else seeking to intervene).

Q. Is it difficult to prove financial exploitation?

A. As the questions later in this section demonstrate, it can be especially difficult where the person committing the financial exploitation has a close personal relationship with the older person. The relationship between the exploiter and the victim may make it difficult to counter the exploiter's claim that a transfer of money or property was voluntary. This is especially true in cases

▶ POTENTIAL SIGNS OF FINANCIAL EXPLOITATION BY SERVICE PROVIDERS

Even if you have done everything possible to ensure the quality and integrity of people coming into your parents' home to help care for them, there is no guarantee that they won't steal from or otherwise financially exploit your parents. However, there are some signs that may indicate something is wrong, including:

- your parent complaining of items that are lost, and the service provider insisting that your parent gave the items to him or her;

- the service provider keeping your parent away from you and claiming that your parent does not want to visit with you;

- the service provider speaking for your parent, and your parent becoming unable to give his or her dissenting opinion; and

- your parent suddenly giving the service provider the power to make financial decisions.

If you think that your parent is, or might be, a victim of financial exploitation at the hands of a service provider, there are some steps you can take, including:

- keeping an inventory of your parent's possessions;

- asking your parent if you can look at any contracts with the service provider;

- asking your parent for copies of important documents, or making sure these documents are in a locked box;

- maintaining a regular visiting schedule with your parent and questioning any need to change it; and

- suggesting to your parent that he or she consult with you before changing any financial arrangements.

involving adult children. It is not uncommon for fully competent adults to give or lend their children property or agree to transfer a property in exchange for help—especially if the help allows the older person to avoid nursing home placement. For this reason, before taking any action, it is vital to ensure that you are doing what your parent wants—or, if he or she lacks decision-making capacity, what he or she would have wanted when competent.

Q. I just learned that my mother transferred her house to my sister three years ago. My mother would never do this willingly–our entire adult lives she has said that she would never give my sister the house. What can I do?

A. Once again, this depends on your mother's current decision-making capacity. If she lacks such capacity, you will have to take some legal action (such as obtaining guardianship) in order to contest the transfer. If your mother has decision-making capacity, she should find an attorney to help her void (meaning cancel) the transfer. Her decision-making capacity at the time of the transfer is relevant. If it can be demonstrated that she lacked decision-making capacity at that time, that may be enough to void the transfer. Otherwise, she (or you) will have to prove undue influence or fraud.

Q. My mother has been paying her neighbor a ridiculous amount of money to help her with small things around the house. What can I do?

A. If your mother has decision-making capacity and your mother is happy with the situation, unfortunately there is nothing that you can do. If your mother lacks decision-making capacity, or if she is unhappy with the situation and would like it to stop, you and your mother can work with a private attorney to change the situation and possibly get the money back. You may also want to report this to your local elder abuse and neglect agency.

Q. Is there anything my parent or I can do to prevent financial exploitation?

A. Yes–lots! Education is one of the most important safeguards. Your local library or area agency on aging may have pamphlets and brochures to teach your parent how to be careful and to recognize early signs of financial abuse.

You can also help your parent create an inventory of important possessions. You and your parent can use this to keep track of his or her possessions, and also to determine whether any additional precautions could be taken. For example, if your mom keeps her wedding ring in a jar on the kitchen counter, perhaps she could place it in a locked box in her room instead.

Also, make sure that hired caregivers or service providers are certified and provide good references. Before a caregiver is hired, someone should actually call the caregiver's references. Finally, if your parent has a geriatric care manager, find out if a money manager is available to talk with your parent about everything from bill payment to making personal loans. Again, education about financial exploitation is the best protection against it.

CONSUMER FRAUD

Q. My parents frequently receive junk mail telling them it is necessary to purchase additional health insurance. Should we consider doing so?

A. This kind of mail should make you wary, because it represents a type of consumer fraud that frequently targets older Americans. Anyone at any age can be a victim of consumer fraud. However, some of the conditions that may correlate with aging, such as isolation or impaired vision, may weaken an older consumer's defenses against this type of fraud. There is also evidence that perpetrators of consumer fraud target the elderly in part because they have disposable income and are often home during the day.

▶ **IDENTITY THEFT**

There are steps that your parents (and you!) can take to avoid becoming a victim of identity theft. Talk to your parents about:

- Being careful to whom they reveal personally identifiable information such as their full names, dates of birth, address, or Social Security numbers. Your parents should not give out this kind of information over the phone or online unless they know the person with whom they are dealing.

- Not using easily obtainable passwords for bank and credit card accounts, such as mother's maiden name or the name of a spouse or child.

- When writing checks to pay on credit card accounts, tell your parents not to put complete account numbers on the checks. The last four digits are sufficient, and will not expose the full account number.

- If your parent's wallet goes missing, he or she should call the three national credit-reporting organizations immediately to place a fraud alert on his or her name and Social Security number.

- If your parent does not receive a bill from a regular creditor, he or she should contact the creditor to make sure that it still has a current address. A thief may have changed the billing address.

- Many states have passed identity theft laws. Contact a local consumer protection agency or attorney general's office to learn more about applicable laws.

- Protecting credit cards:
  - Your parents should sign new credit cards as soon as they arrive. Old or expired cards should be cut up and thrown away and all unused preapproved credit applications should be destroyed.
  - Help your parents maintain a list of current credit card numbers, expiration dates, and the toll-free telephone number of each card issuer. This list should be kept in a safe place, so that your par-

ents can report missing or stolen credit cards and possible billing errors.

- Your parents should never lay their credit cards down on a counter or table. If possible, your parents should hand cards directly to the clerk or waiter.

- Make sure that your parents never leave a credit card or car rental agreement in the glove compartment of a car. Furthermore, they should never leave a credit card in an unlocked desk drawer, grocery cart, or hotel room.

- Talk to your parents about opening all credit card bills promptly, and comparing them with their receipts to check for unauthorized charges and billing errors.

- Your parents should never provide their credit card or checking account numbers over the telephone, unless they have placed the call themselves. They should never write their credit card numbers on a postcard or on the outside of an envelope.

Q. What are some examples of consumer fraud?

A. There is a vast array of very sophisticated scams. New ones keep popping up every day. People who engage in consumer fraud aren't just pushy salespeople to whom you can't say no, they are skilled professional criminals who prey on the vulnerable members of our society. The list below enumerates some of the more common examples of consumer fraud. If your parent indicates that he or she is involved with any of the following, you should definitely explore the matter further.

- **Lottery or sweepstakes fraud.** In these scams, the victim usually receives something in the mail indicating that he or she has won a prize, but must first pay shipping and handling fees to receive it. The victim sends the fees, which can be substantial, but never receives the prize.

- **Home repair fraud.** A contractor comes to the home, often unsolicited, and offers to fix something. The price may be too high, the work may not be needed, or the work may never be completed. In some cases, the contractor offers to help the victim obtain financing, which often results in some form of mortgage fraud.

- **Mortgage fraud/predatory lending.** This type of consumer fraud involves the victim being offered the opportunity to refinance a home loan at an exorbitant interest rate. Sometimes the arrangement may involve balloon payments, which means that after just a few years of low monthly payments, the victim will be required either to pay off the balance of the loan in one large payment or refinance at a much higher interest rate.

- **Health insurance/health-care fraud.** Fraud involving health insurance or health care usually involves the victim being sold medical care or services that he or she does not need. This is becoming more frequent in connection with the sale of Medicare Part D prescription drug plans.

- **Funeral industry fraud.** Because of the nature of the purchase, fraud relating to funerals can be particularly devastating. Often the victim is sold an expensive funeral, usually with financing provided. But when it comes time for the victim's family to use the services, a funeral is not provided, or what is provided is much less than what was purchased.

- **Financial services fraud/investment fraud.** This type of fraud usually involves sales at exorbitant rates, and/or sales of products that do not exist or that the purchaser doesn't need. These scams frequently involve penny stocks, oil and gas leases, coins, and precious metals. There is also a particular problem with the sale of annuities and trusts by unscrupulous and unqualified sellers.

- **Charity fraud.** Charity fraud involves donations that are solicited for charities either that do not exist or that only direct a very small portion of the money received to the charitable cause.

- **Identity theft.** Here, the victim's personal information is used to access his or her assets. With such information, the thief can apply for loans and credit cards in the victim's name and completely destroy the victim's credit rating.

> ### ▶ INTERNET SCAMS
>
> Many of us who use e-mail frequently are used to ignoring or blocking spam e-mail, but if your parent is new to the Internet, you may want to talk to him or her about Internet scams and about general Internet safety. For more tips and information on Internet safety, visit WiredSafety at *www.wiredsafety.org*.

Q. My mother is careful about whom she talks to. She rarely goes out of the house these days. How could a scammer possibly reach her?

A. There are many ways, including television and print ads, telephone, mail, the Internet, or e-mail. Your parents may also be susceptible to phishing tactics. **Phishing** involves e-mails that appear to come from established organizations (such as a bank, credit union, or online auction company) and ask the recipient to verify personal information or warn the victim about the unauthorized use of an account. These e-mails may contain logos and personal information that make them appear authentic. When a recipient responds, he or she may innocently provide the information the scammer needs to access bank accounts or possibly steal the recipient's identity.

Perpetrators of consumer fraud may also use presentations and free seminars to reach your parent. These are usually advertised in newspapers for seniors and frequently have to do with financial services and products, such as trusts and annuities. Sometimes a meal or gift is provided to attendees.

Prevention

Q. Is there anything my parent can do to avoid becoming the victim of consumer fraud?

A. Yes. There are a variety of steps your parent can take, including:

- putting his or her name on the National Do Not Call Registry. (To do this, your parent can call 1–888–382–1222 (or for TYY, 1–866–290–4236) or visit *www.donotcall.gov*. Telemarketers should stop calling within three months of your parent registering. If telemarketers continue to call, tell your parent to get their names and telephone numbers and report them to the Federal Trade Commission and the state attorney general.)
- not providing personal information to anyone who calls unsolicited;
- not responding to letters indicating that he or she has received a prize;
- shredding his or her mail and other documents containing identifying information;
- never allowing a door-to-door salesperson into his or her home;
- periodically reviewing his or her credit reports by visiting *www.annualcreditreport.com* (where any individual can get one copy of his or her credit report per year for free);
- routinely checking bank statements and credit card bills;
- being skeptical (if something sounds too good to be true, it probably is); and
- not making any major purchases on the spur of the moment.

Above all, help your parent to understand his or her rights. Some older people may feel uneasy about simply hanging up the phone or throwing out a letter; they may fear that it comes across as rude or impolite. Criminals engaged in consumer fraud know this, and will use their victims' desire to be courteous to their advantage. Empower your parent to feel comfortable hanging up or saying no.

Legal Interventions

Q. Are there any legal remedies if my parent is a victim of consumer fraud?

A. Yes. You and your parent should consider contacting the Federal Trade Commission (*www.ftc.gov*) and your state attorney general's office. You can find your state attorney general's contact information by visiting the website of the National Association of Attorney Generals at *www.naag.org*. These offices prosecute deceptive advertising and sales practices. However, they are only able to get involved in a very small number of cases, and may not always be responsive in a particular case. Nevertheless, you should make a report; if these offices notice a trend (i.e., a pattern of reports implicating the same perpetrator), they may act sooner. In addition, a private attorney knowledgeable about state consumer laws might be able to have a fraudulent transaction voided. If the attorney can demonstrate that your parent suffered from incapacity or undue influence, was defrauded, or that he or she has a remedy under state or federal consumer protection law, then the funds from the fraudulent transaction may be returned. In addition, an attorney can raise these arguments to defend against a scammer's effort to collect money from your parents.

Q. My mom has been the victim of identity theft. Can she make sure that no information relating to the theft is connected to her credit report?

A. Yes. If your mom has already been a victim of identity theft, federal laws will help her block consumer reporting agencies from providing information that can be attributed to the theft. This will allow her to limit the damage caused by identity theft. Federal fraud alerts are discussed earlier in this section.

State laws have supplemented these federal tools with an important self-help tool of their own: credit freezes. **Credit-freeze laws**, effective in a majority of states, enable consumers to prohibit consumer reporting agencies from providing information from their files to companies requesting credit reports. This is a more powerful anti-identity-theft weapon than the federal fraud alert. However, some consumers may find this option inconvenient because it can interfere with or delay their ability to enter into a legitimate credit transaction.

If your parent has a problem with a particular item on his or her credit report (or on a bill that a creditor is trying to collect), and if the problem is due to identity theft, then he or she should file an identity theft report. The first step is to file a report with a law enforcement agency, under oath, explaining what happened. Your parent should then get a copy of that report and send it to the creditor involved and to any credit bureau who reports the fraudulent debt in his or her name. The credit bureaus and the creditor must stop reporting that debt when they receive this report. If your parent is contacted by a debt collector about the fraudulent debt, your parent can send the collector a copy of the report. The debt collector must consult the creditor and, in most cases, must stop trying to collect. An identity theft report is a powerful tool.

Q. My mom is talking about purchasing credit monitoring services. Is this a scam?

A. Credit monitoring services are consumer tools that can help prevent identity theft. These services keep a close watch on a subscriber's credit report and alert the subscriber whenever a potential creditor has requested information from that report. This allows the subscriber to learn of possible credit transactions involving their file, and to stop unauthorized transactions before they occur. These services are usually offered in exchange for a monthly or annual fee, and some allow subscribers access to their files and credit score.

Q. Where can I get more information about consumer fraud and protecting my parents from scams?

A. For general information on consumer protections and information on how to contact your state consumer protection agency, visit *www.consumeraction.gov*.

The National Fraud Information Center can answer questions relating to consumer fraud and tell you where to report fraud and file complaints (*www.fraud.org*). The National Consumers League runs a variety of programs aimed at eliminating fraud from consumer projects and the Internet. Their programs can be accessed through their website at *www.nclnet.org*. Lastly,

the Identity Theft Resource Center (*www.idtheftcenter.org.*) outlines the steps you can take to prevent identity theft and what to
do if your parent is a victim.

REMEMBER THIS

- Victims of elder abuse can come from any educational background, ethnic background, or economic class. Abuse can occur
  in any number of locations and at the hands of family, friends,
  volunteers, or paid service providers.

- Elder abuse can come in a number of forms, including: physical, emotional, or sexual abuse; neglect or abandonment by
  caregivers, which can be either passive or active; and financial
  exploitation.

- If your parent is the victim of elder abuse, first talk to your parent about what options and remedies he or she would like to
  pursue. A variety of legal options may be available, including
  making a report to the agency on elder abuse and neglect, obtaining orders of protection and stay-away orders, or criminal
  prosecution.

- Consumer fraud is more than just pushy salespeople; perpetrators of consumer fraud are skilled professional criminals who
  prey on vulnerable individuals.

- Perpetrators of consumer fraud can reach your parents even
  if you think they are safe. Common tools include television
  and print ads, telephone or mail, and free presentations and
  seminars.

- Your parents can protect themselves from identity theft by
  being careful about revealing personally identifiable information, not using easily obtainable passwords, and immediately
  notifying the three national credit-reporting agencies if their
  wallets go missing.

CHAPTER 12
Mental Health Issues

Helping Your Parent Deal
with a Changing Lifestyle

*I don't understand what has happened to my dad. He used to
take such pride in his appearance. But lately he refuses to
shower, he wears the same clothes for weeks without washing
them, and his mail is piled high to the ceiling. He has also
stopped taking his medications. His teeth look terrible and he
says they "hurt," but he refuses to go to the dentist. It isn't like
he doesn't have the money to care for himself; it's almost as if he
has just stopped caring. He says he is not depressed. What is
causing this?*

Changes in the mental health of an aging parent can be a
very serious and confusing situation. Your parent may have
lost the motivation or the capacity to provide care for him or herself. Often these changes can be due to depression, dementia, or
certain medical conditions that coexist with mental health problems. In many cases, a serious mental issue can result in self-
neglect. This chapter looks at common mental health problems
that may be affecting your parent, as well as potential indicators
of self-neglect and legal options that can help you deal with your
parent's changing condition.

Q. What sort of mental health issues impact
individuals as they age?

A. Depression and anxiety are among the most common mental health concerns to affect older people, and they often may be
overlooked. Symptoms of depression and anxiety often occur together. Other more common concerns include dementia and
delirium. If your parent experiences changes that result in sad-

> ### ▶ ANXIETY?
>
> You may be surprised to learn that your retired parent or a person living in a facility is at risk for experiencing anxiety. Anxiety is becoming an increasing problem for older adults, and must be dealt with by professionals in order to be treated correctly and to avoid further complications. If left untreated, anxiety may, among other things, result in your parent becoming frightened or engaging in unsafe activities, such as leaving home without supervision.

ness, irritability, confusion, lack of energy, poor concentration, loss of appetite, inability to sleep, or reduced interest in activities or social relationships, have him or her evaluated by a physician, clinical social worker, or psychologist.

Q. My mother has never been depressed and now, at the age of eighty-five, the doctor says she is depressed. Is this a normal part of aging?

A. Depression is not a "normal" part of aging. However, many older people have symptoms of depression, and these symptoms often remain under the radar and don't receive treatment or medical attention. This underdiagnosis of depression is often due to the common impression that "everyone feels that way" when they are old. For others, there is still shame or a stigma attached to receiving treatment for depression. Many believe it to be one of the most underdiagnosed and underreported conditions of older adults.

It is important to consider the difference between a serious clinical depression, which is a persistent and recurrent condition, and milder forms of depression and depressive symptoms. These milder forms can persist for years and represent a lifetime pattern for many older adults.

Nevertheless, depression may not necessarily impair the quality of life to the extent of other major mental health disor-

▶ **PROPER DIAGNOSIS IS IMPORTANT!**

If you think your parent might be suffering from a mental health issue, do not attempt to self-diagnose, and do not delay in getting a professional evaluation. A proper diagnosis will result in proper treatment, which may lessen the impact of the illness. Left unchecked, many mental health issues in older adults may increase the chances of other, more serious medical concerns.

ders. Most often, older adults have temporary responses to particular life situations or specific events that result in behaviors and attitudes that appear to be depressive. Examples may include a significant loss (e.g., the death of a loved one), a major change in residence, a health crisis, or even retirement, all of which can trigger difficulties in adjustment accompanied by feelings of depression.

Q. Why should I be worried about my dad's mental health? There is so much else to be worried about for him right now; I really can't see how his mental health is a priority.

A. Mental health is just as important as physical health. For one thing, mental health issues and medical issues may coexist: mental health changes may be the first indication that a medical condition is present, or vice versa.

The risk of not treating depression and other mental health issues is very significant. Not only does a lack of treatment lower the quality of life for those suffering from mental health issues, but it also makes them more likely to suffer physical pain. The higher rate of suicide in older adults may be in part due to untreated depressions.

Q. What are some signs that my parent's mental health issues need to be addressed?

A. Any significant changes in your parent's behavior or mood can indicate a need for assessment or evaluation. More specifically, older adults with major depressive disorders can look vegetative, listless, withdrawn, or profoundly sad. Signs that you may want to seek help include: your parent giving things away; making unusual changes in his or her routines; becoming less interested in talking to you or visiting with friends; having more difficulty sleeping; losing weight; having no appetite; seeming very nervous or frightened to go out of the house; talking about life not being worth living; or even seeming confused or having other changes in cognitive function. Certainly if your parent seems to stop caring for him or herself (self-caring), consult a professional. (Self-neglect is discussed in further detail later in this chapter.)

Q. Does depression in older adults always manifest itself in the same ways it would manifest itself in someone younger?

A. Not necessarily. If your parent is depressed, symptoms may involve fewer mood changes than with a younger person. Instead, depression might significantly impair your parent's ability to perform activities. This is an important distinction and can often result in missed signals or missed diagnosis.

Q. My mom refuses to address her depression or even talk to me about it. Do I have any legal remedies?

A. This depends on the degree to which the depression impairs your mom's judgment. You cannot force your parent to talk about the suspected depression, nor can you force your parent to take psychotropic medications. See if your mother will allow you to talk to her doctor. If you feel that your mom's depression is preventing her from making important decisions or taking care of herself to the point where she might suffer serious physical or financial harm, you could, as a last resort, consider guardianship, which is discussed further in chapter 3.

Q. What is self-neglect?

A. Professionals frequently disagree over what exactly constitutes **self-neglect**. Most common definitions focus on the adult's inability to provide adequate self-care due to physical or mental impairment or diminished capacity. **Self-care** includes performing essential self-tasks such as:

- obtaining essential food, clothing, and shelter;
- accessing available medical care;
- obtaining goods and services necessary to maintain physical health, mental health, and emotional well-being;
- ensuring general safety; and
- managing financial affairs.

Sometimes self-neglect is caused by financial, situational, or physical stresses. For example, older adults may decide that saving money to leave to their grandchildren is more important than paying for their own medications. Other older adults who are afflicted with physically debilitating illnesses may not want to burden their families, and may refuse to allow needed help to clean their homes or help them with hygiene. This can be extremely frustrating for families and loved ones.

Some people may feel that if an adult is not endangering his or her health or anybody else, he or she should be left alone to make decisions and live with any eccentricities. However, it is important to recognize that in some cases, these behaviors can lead to serious health risks. This chapter looks at some of the symptoms of self-neglect and its legal implications.

Q. What types of people neglect themselves?

A. A self-neglecting adult can come from any economic, social, or educational background. Most self-neglecting individuals tend to be:

- individuals living alone;
- older people who are frail;
- older people who are depressed, confused, or have dementia;
- individuals with other mental disorders;
- older people with alcohol or drug problems; or

- older people with a history of poor self-care, such as poor hygiene.

Q. Why would my parent self-neglect?

A. The specific causes of self-neglect are unclear. Certainly some people have spent a lifetime engaged in patterns of self-neglect. Others deprive themselves over time, not wanting to spend money on food or medicine for fear of depleting their savings. Some simply lose perspective, motivation, energy, or the ability to provide self-care. They may be suffering from mental illness or substance abuse. Thus, some conditions that may be associated with an increased risk of self-neglect include the presence of a personality disorder, dementia, depression, substance abuse, severe physical illness, overmedication, malnutrition, or poverty.

Q. Can one's environment contribute to self-neglect?

A. An environment that promotes isolation of older people puts them at risk for self-neglect. As an older person begins to withdraw from the community, he or she may reduce the chances of engaging services and caregivers, or of interacting on a regular basis with people who may notice signs of neglect. If your parent is starting to reduce his or her social network, consider working with him or her to identify some community-based programs and senior centers that interest him or her and could help him or her remain engaged.

Q. How might an environment promote isolation?

A. Perhaps unintentionally. As neighborhoods change, there may be fewer neighbors who know your parent well enough to want to visit. Sometimes an older person may feel physically vulnerable, and choose to stay inside for safety. Even new construction in a neighborhood can make it seem less safe and unfamiliar to the older adult. The usual landmarks and guideposts your parent has traditionally used to find his or her way around may have

> ### ▶ POVERTY VS SELF-NEGLECT
>
> Poverty should not be confused with self-neglect. If people lack the resources to secure medical or dental care or to buy food, you should not automatically assume they are engaging in self-neglecting behavior. A proper diagnosis of self-neglect can help you and your family rule out other possible causes of such behavior that could be addressed through various supports and services such as Medicaid or Social Security.

changed or disappeared. Younger families often ignore the older person next door who usually stays indoors.

If a person is upset or depressed because of changes in his or her life that interfere with independent activity, he or she may be more prone to self-neglect. For example, if your parent is no longer able to drive, he or she may begin to retreat and become more isolated. These behaviors may increase the chances that your parent may begin to self-neglect.

Personal environments, like homes, can also create risks for self-neglect. If your parent lives in a three-story home and cannot manage the stairs, he or she may have to significantly limit the use of bath facilities. If he or she cannot open the cabinets in a kitchen, then he or she may stop eating. Sometimes older adults will hesitate to speak about limitations imposed by their environment for fear of losing their independence.

Q. What are the signs of self-neglect?

A. Signs in a person's home environment that could signal self-neglect include:

- a dirty home;
- the presence of pet feces and urine;
- more pets than the older person can properly care for;
- hoarding of mail or other material items;
- rodents; and
- a house in disrepair.

> ### ▶ MEDICAL CONCERNS
>
> Because self-neglect may actually be a symptom of other serious health concerns, don't ignore the signs if your parent starts exhibiting them. Self-neglect symptoms may be a signal that your parent needs to seek medical help. An early diagnosis could help with effective treatment; consequently, don't let such symptoms go unattended.

A person suffering from self-neglect may exhibit skin ulcers or rashes, malnourishment, be inappropriately dressed for the given weather conditions, or suffer from untreated medical or mental health conditions. A person who is self-neglecting may demonstrate disorientation, confusion, hallucinations, delusions, extreme isolation, or a lack of concern about the future.

Q. Is hoarding always a sign of self-neglect? My parent has always hung onto stuff.

A. Extreme hoarding is often associated with self-neglect, but it is not necessarily a health threat and often does not harm anyone. However, there is a difference between being a pack rat and engaging in hoarding associated with self-neglect, which can put a person at risk. If your parent is hoarding and it creates a fire hazard or in some other way puts your parent's health or safety at risk, it likely has risen to the level of self-neglect that should be addressed.

Q. If I think my parent is self-neglecting, what should I do?

A. There are several avenues to pursue. An important one is to help your parent get treatment for the causes and consequences of the self-neglect. Helping your parent get treatment for depression or another untreated medical condition may in fact treat the self-neglect. The best course of action is likely to work with your parent to find a mental health professional who can help address the underlying causes of the self-neglect and identify the services and supports in your parent's community that can help your parent take better care of him or herself.

If your parent's self-neglect is posing an immediate threat to his or her (or another person's) health or safety, you may need to contact your local agency that investigates elder abuse and neglect as discussed below. They may be able to help you assess the situation and determine appropriate interventions. They may also recommend social work services or some of the legal options discussed at the end of this chapter.

Q. When should I address my parent's self-neglect? I don't want to overreact to a simple phase that may pass.

A. It is difficult to know when to intervene. Making a reasonable decision based on issues of safety is a good standard to follow. As with other types of elder abuse and neglect, the self-neglecting person may try to hide the symptoms out of shame or fear. As such, you should realize that if you are starting to notice some changes that raise concern, there may be additional signs that you don't see. Therefore, it is important to work with your local area agency on aging and other service agencies to learn about such issues and to become aware of the services and supports available in your parent's area.

Q. Does the law address self-neglect?

A. As with elder abuse and neglect, definitions of self-neglect are based in state law and vary from state to state. Some states define self-neglect as a type of elder abuse and neglect.

Q. Legally, what can we do if my dad is self-neglecting, but won't address the issue or get help?

A. In states where self-neglect is included in the definition of abuse and neglect, it can be investigated by the same agency that handles elder abuse and neglect. Your area agency on aging can tell you which agency handles self-neglect cases in your state, and what to do if you think you should make a report. It is important to realize that making a report to such an agency is a serious step. Many of the advantages and disadvantages associated with making a report of abuse or neglect at the hands of another party apply to self-neglect cases as well. (See chapter 11 for a discussion on the advantages and disadvantages of making an abuse report.) In particular, the family and the elderly person may lose control over which legal interventions are pursued. On the other hand, if you do make a report and the agency decides to investigate, your parent may be offered much-needed services.

If the appropriate state law doesn't address self-neglect, there are some other options available, described below. However, a note of caution: *These options can have very serious disadvantages and consequences for your parent and family. Before pursuing any of these legal options, you should consult with an experienced elder law attorney or health-care professional to see if other, nonlegal options are available.*

Available legal options include:

- **Reporting code violations to the appropriate agency.** You could report any possible code violations to the appropriate agency. For example, if there is a rodent or insect infestation in your parent's home, you could make a report to the local department of health. Or, if your parent is warming his or her home by turning on the oven and leaving the door open, you could report this to the fire department. This will force your parent to deal with the truly dangerous conditions created by his or her self-neglect. However, this might also lead to your parent facing fines or legal proceedings, or possibly even losing his or her home. The possible consequences of reporting a code violation should be carefully considered before any action is taken.
- **Guardianship.** If a decline in mental capacity accompanies the self-neglect, guardianship may allow you to intervene and obtain services on your parent's behalf. Guardianships do require court orders and are not easily obtained. Many

people who are self-neglecting have full decision-making or cognitive capacity, and in these cases, guardianship is not an option. (Guardianship is discussed in chapter 4.)

• **Civil commitment.** If the self-neglect is accompanied by a serious mental health problem and your parent is in imminent danger of seriously harming himself, herself, or others, civil commitment may be an option. It is important to note that civil commitment is a very extreme remedy that is only temporary and can have very serious consequences. Civil commitment should only be pursued if all other options have failed and your parent poses a *serious* threat to himself, herself, or another person. By having your parent involuntarily committed, you are likely to lose any chance of having him or her trust you in the future. (The advantages and disadvantages of civil commitment are discussed in chapter 4.)

REMEMBER THIS

• Mental health issues are a serious concern for aging adults. If you think your parent might be suffering from a mental health problem, seek a consultation immediately. If left untreated, such a problem can seriously jeopardize your parent's mental and medical health.

• Self-neglect may create serious health and safety risks. If your parent is self-neglecting, do not let the symptoms go unattended.

• Self-neglect can include failure to provide oneself with essential food, clothing, and shelter; failure to obtain necessary medical care; and failure to attend to basic personal hygiene.

• If your parent is self-neglecting, you should try to work with him or her to address the underlying cause of the behaviors. Legal interventions in these cases are very limited, and should only be used in extreme situations when everything else has failed.

CHAPTER 13

Taking Time
for Yourself

The Physical and Emotional
Impact of Caring for
Your Aging Parent

Jim's dad lives in a nursing home and his mom was recently moved into hospice. Jim works full-time and has two kids, but these days it seems like most of his time and energy are focused on his parents: helping with Medicaid forms, talking to doctors, trying to sell their old house. Lately, Jim has been having problems sleeping. Could these circumstances be connected? Is the stress he feels normal? Jim feels like he is on the verge of a nervous breakdown. What can he do?

To effectively take care of your parents, you need to first take care of yourself. For any adult, taking care of aging parents can be a very stressful process. This chapter looks at the signs and signals that your own physical and emotional well-being may be at risk, the problems that can arise if you don't properly address these issues, and some tips on how to best handle the situation.

Q. Is it normal to feel burdened by the responsibility of caring for my parent?

A. It is perfectly normal. It can be difficult to balance personal responsibilities like work or caring for your own children while simultaneously caring for your parents. Many times, your responses will be impacted by your own feelings, such as guilt, remorse, or anger.

Much frustration in these interactions comes from the disparity between your assessment of your parent and your parent's perceptions of him or herself. Some aging parents are not comfortable with their children taking on caregiving responsibilities. The important thing to remember is that any such incongruent opinions are often a signal that something has changed in the parent's health, and they should not be ignored.

Q. I am always tired and anxious. I was never this way before I started to care for my parent. Can being burned-out like this result in physical symptoms?

A. **Compassion fatigue** is a state of tension that results from caring so much for a victim or victims of suffering that you lose yourself to the other person. Signs that you are suffering from compassion fatigue may include feeling numb to the experiences of the person you are caring for, or, in the alternative, feeling as if you cannot stop thinking about his or her problems.

On the other hand, **burnout** results from dealing with the daily frustrations and hassles of caregiving. It may be caused by feelings of resentment, a sense you are not being appreciated or valued enough, depression, or frustration with your role. You may also have physical symptoms in response to the stress. It is not uncommon for overburdened caregivers to have headaches, stomach problems, and increased aches and pains. Stress has been shown to have effects on the immune system, so you must find the time to take care of yourself!

Q. I think it will be easier just to accept the situation and tolerate the frustrations and burden. My fatigue won't impact my parent, will it?

A. It could! Your fatigue could have a serious effect on both you and your parent. You could end up with lower morale, less energy, or less interest in helping your parent. You may also find yourself making mistakes or forgetting details necessary for your parent's care—for example, by forgetting to pick up him or her at an adult day center, or forgetting to take him or her to the doctor. Remember: allowing yourself to experience fatigue and/or burnout may not only make your life more difficult and stressful, but may also create serious problems for the parent for whom you are caring.

Q. What can I do to manage compassion fatigue or burnout?

A. Both conditions can be avoided by making sure you take care of yourself, and by using coping strategies such as making time for yourself, dealing with your own issues, and being proactive. You should try to set aside a certain amount of time each day that is exclusively for you. Give yourself some time off. It may take just a few hours, or you may need a longer vacation. Regardless, you must know that time off is available. Even if all of your caregiving chores don't get done, it is important to abide by reasonable limits on your time.

Don't forget your own problems, and make time to deal with your own issues. If your caregiving precludes you from managing your own life, then your own issues are likely to grow, and may eventually interfere with your ability to care for someone else properly.

You should also be on the lookout for signs of increasing stress or depression in yourself. These signs can include changes in your mood, appetite, energy level, ability to sleep, or level of interest in other activities or people. You may want to talk with a mental health professional if these symptoms arise.

And most importantly, forgive yourself if everything does not go perfectly! You can only do the best that you can with the time and energy you have available.

Q. How can I make sure I am taking care of myself?

A. Several self-administered tests are available to monitor caregiver distress. The National Alliance for Caregiving is an excellent resource for caregivers (*www.caregiving.org*). Another resource is the National Family Caregivers Association, created to educate, support and advocate for caregivers of the chronically ill and older adults (*www.thefamilycaregiver.org*). You can also visit

▶ **TAKING CARE OF YOURSELF**

If you don't take care of yourself, you can't possibly take care of another person. Remember to take some time for you!

- Get regular exercise. This will enhance your physical and mental well-being, as well as help you to manage stress.

- Get enough sleep. Rest enables you to maintain the energy needed to provide care for yourself and your care recipient.

- Eat a nutritious diet.

- Talk to other people who may be in the same situation. You may want to consider joining a support group. Sharing your experiences with others who are in the same situation can be helpful, and can provide you with valuable support and advice.

Aplaceformom.com (*www.aplaceformom.com*), which provides resources, information on support groups, and stories from other families in similar situations. Local offices of your area agency on aging may also offer caregiver support groups and respite services. You can find one in your community by calling the Elder Locator at 1–800–677–1116.

One helpful reminder is that you should try not to personalize any of your parent's behaviors, or the stressful nature of your relationship with him or her. These changes are part of complex physical, psychological, and social processes in your parent; they are not about you. It is easy for us to say "be patient," but these changes can be very disconcerting both to you and your parent. Don't be afraid to get help or ask questions. You shouldn't have to go through this process on your own.

Q. Should I talk to my parent about my fatigue?

A. Yes! You should talk to your parent about your limits and stresses. It is important for your parent to recognize that you need some help providing the kind of care you both think is warranted. Your parent may not be aware that your stress level is as high as it may be. If you have begun to express resentment, your parent may misinterpret this as anger at him or her rather than as your own exhaustion.

Q. Who else could I talk to? I really don't want to burden my spouse or other family members.

A. This would be a perfect opportunity to speak with a geriatric social worker who has experience with families and their older parents. The worker will be able to help relieve any feelings of guilt, define your limits, sort out strategies to reduce your stress, and provide referrals to help manage the challenges of your parent's needs over the long term.

▶ **CIVIL COMMITMENT: A LAST STEP**

Involuntary civil commitment is a very serious step that, for a few families, may be the only option after all other legal avenues have been exhausted. Through an involuntary civil commitment procedure, a state can confine an individual to a hospital or nursing home and/or require him or her to take medications or participate in other treatment options on an outpatient basis against that person's will and even though he or she has not committed a crime. This process requires a court hearing to balance an individual's constitutional right to liberty against society's right to protect itself from those who pose a danger to themselves or others.

Civil commitment is very different from guardianship. In a guardianship case, the court takes certain rights away from an individual and appoints a surrogate decision maker called a guardian to make decisions on behalf of that person. The guardian is authorized to act on behalf of the elderly person from that point on, unless and until the court orders otherwise. While the guardian may have the power to control funds, or make medical decisions, the police cannot use physical force to make the elderly person comply with the guardian's wishes.

In contrast, through involuntary civil commitment, the police may forcibly place an individual in a mental institution or nursing home. Unlike guardianship, civil commitment is not for an indefinite period of time. A court must evaluate the basis for civil commitment within a few days of the initial placement. The civil commitment process also does not result in the appointment of a surrogate decision maker. That is, unlike a guardianship, no one is authorized to obtain information or make decisions on behalf of the committed person after an involuntary civil commitment.

Every state has a specific procedure for involuntarily committing a person who is in immediate danger of harming himself or others because of a mental illness. Some states specifically exclude Alzheimer's or other forms of dementia from their definition of mental illness. In these states, involuntary civil commitment is not an option for those suffering from dementia unless there is also evidence of mental illness, such as schizophrenia or severe depression. The relevant state law will list those circumstances under which a person may be involuntarily civilly committed.

In an emergency you can call the police if the person is in immediate danger of harming herself or someone else. In non-emergency situations, you must identify the state agency that handles petitions for civil commitment. In some states, this will be the Department of Mental Health and in others, it may be the Office of the State's Attorney. You should call your local area agency on aging (AAA) or an elder law attorney before trying to begin commitment proceedings. If you address issues early enough, you may not need to take such a drastic step.

If you nonetheless determine that involuntary civil commitment is your only option, you will need to determine the specifics of the law in the state where your parent resides, including:

- What terminology does the state use for the options described above?
- Which agency or agencies will initiate the proceedings?
- What is the legal standard for civil commitment?
- Can the state order participation in outpatient services as well as place someone in an institution?

- How long will the commitment order last before there must be another hearing?

- Will your parent lose any rights permanently as a result of being involuntarily committed?

- What, if any information can you obtain about your parent once the involuntary civil commitment proceeding has been initiated?

For more information on civil commitment and how to advocate for loved ones with mental illness, go to the website for the National Alliance for the Mentally Ill (NAMI) at *www.nami.org.*

REMEMBER THIS

- If you are taking on caregiving responsibilities for your parents, it is normal to feel stressed and overwhelmed. However, you must deal with these feelings and frustrations.

- If you allow your fatigue or burnout to go unchecked, it could end up impacting your parent. Missing an appointment or making a mistake could have a serious effect on your parent's health or day-to-day well-being.

- There are a variety of resources available to help you, including: friends, family, neighbors, the National Alliance for Caregiving, the National Family Caregivers Association, and your local area agency on aging. You don't have to take on these worries alone!

APPENDIX A

Where to Go for More Information

Throughout this book, we've provided you with resources for finding more information on a variety of topics associated with issues facing adult children caring for aging parents. You can build on your knowledge by checking out websites, books, and other helpful suggestions we offer here. Some of these resources may be mentioned throughout the book, and we still think they're the best place for you to start. This section starts by outlining general resources, and then moves on to options for specific issues and situations.

OVERALL RESOURCES

These websites, agencies, and books are good places to start for information on a variety of issues and concerns regarding aging.

- **Area Agency on Aging—Eldercare Locator.** One important advocate on behalf of elder Americans is the nationwide network of area agencies on aging (AAAs). Today, every area of the country is served by either an AAA or a state unit on aging. These agencies help local communities develop services specifically for older residents. AAAs also offer referral services and provide assistance to designated service agencies in the local communities.

  AAAs also provide funding and programming for local senior-citizen centers. Programs include recreation, socialization, meals, and educational programs. Additional funds are generally provided by local and state governments, as well as by organizations such as the United Way, private foundations, corporations, and individual donors.

  You can find your local AAA by calling the Eldercare Locator at 1–800–677–1116 or visiting *www.eldercare.gov*.

- The ABA publishes a Legal Guide for Americans Over 50 that can be purchased from the ABA Web Store (*www.abanet.org/abastore*), Product Code 2350226. It is also available in bookstores across the country.
- **FirstGov for Seniors** (*www.usa.gov/Topics/Seniors.shtml*). This government portal site features information on a variety of topics, including Social Security, the foster grandparents program, veterans, health care, retirement, leisure, and much more. It also features links to other government sites, including those of the Department of Health and Human Services and the Department of Housing and Urban Development.
- **AARP**, formerly the **American Association of Retired Persons**. The AARP's website (*www.aarp.org*) provides information on many topics and issues affecting older Americans, including health care, discrimination, estate planning, and reverse mortgages, just to name a few.
- **Nolo.com** (*www.nolo.com*) offers information on topics such as health-care and elder law, wills and estates, powers of attorney, and other issues of interest.
- The **National Council on Aging** can be contacted at 1901 L Street NW, Washington, DC 20036 (telephone: 1–800–479–1200; website: *www.ncoa.org*).
- The U.S. **Administration on Aging (AoA)** provides information on various federal and state programs for the elderly. To find such programs, visit *http://www.aoa.gov/*.
- **Older Women's League** (*www.owl-national.org*).
- **Alliance of Retired Americans** (*www.retiredamericans.org*).
- The **Department of Veterans Affairs** (*www.va.gov*).

FINDING ELDER LAW ATTORNEYS AND OTHER LEGAL HELP

- Your state or local agency on aging can refer you to publicly funded legal programs. These programs, along with other possible sources of legal assistance, are listed on the website of the American Bar Association's Commission on Law and Aging, at *www.abanet.org/aging* (click on "Resources," then "Law and Aging Resource Guide," and then select your state).

• If you need help finding a lawyer who specializes in elder law, the National Academy of Elder Law Attorneys' website includes a geographical directory of its members and specifies those who are certified elder law lawyers. In addition, NAELA can provide consumer information about what questions to ask a lawyer to make sure he or she can meet your legal needs. You can contact NAELA through its website at *www.naela.org*.

RESOURCES FOR CAREGIVERS

• Local offices of your area agency on aging may offer caregiver support groups and respite services. You can find one in your community by calling the Elder Locator at 1–800–677–1116.
• The National Alliance for Caregiving is an excellent resource for family caregivers (*www.caregiving.org*). It provides online information about how to deal with the challenges of caregiving.
• The National Family Caregivers Association was created to educate, support, and advocate for family caregivers of the chronically ill and older adults (*www.thefamilycaregiver.org*).
• The National Family Caregivers Association (*www.nfcacares .org*) provides resources, information on support groups, and stories from other families in similar situations.

PREPARING FOR RETIREMENT

• An online retirement planner can be found at *www.money .cnn.com/retirement*.
• Social Security offers a **Retirement Planner**, located at *www.ssa.gov/retire2*, which includes an online calculator that allows you to estimate retirement benefits.

UNDERSTANDING MENTAL HEALTH AND COGNITIVE DECLINE

- The **National Institute on Aging** (*www.nia.nih.gov*).
- **Health Line** (*www.healthline.com*).
- The **Alzheimer's Association** (*www.alz.org*).
- The **National Alliance for the Mentally Ill (NAMI)** (*www.nami.org*) provides information on caring and advocating for a mentally ill loved one.

PLANNING FOR INCAPACITY, POWERS OF ATTORNEY, AND OTHER SURROGATE DECISION MAKERS

- Information about advance directives for health care is available from most state area agencies on aging and from many state bar associations and medical societies.
- State-specific information and forms are also available from National Hospice and Palliative Care Organization (formerly Partnership in Dying), an organization concerned with excellent end-of-life care, at *www.caringinfo.org*.
- **Americans for Better Care of the Dying** (*www.abcd-caring.org*) publishes "Handbook for Mortals," an excellent guide for dealing with serious and eventually fatal illness.
- **Last Acts** provides a wealth of similar information on its website at *www.lastacts.org*.
- You may want to provide your parent with a copy of The **"Values History Form Packet"** created by the University of New Mexico Health Sciences Center Institute for Ethics, available online at *http://hscwebdev.unm.edu/SOM/ethics/adVdir/vhform_eng.shtml*. This tool will help your parent articulate how he or she wants his or her medical future to play out.
- The **National Association of Professional Geriatric Care Managers** (*www.caremanager.org*) and the **National Academy of Certified Care Managers** (*www.naccm.net*) can

provide information on finding a geriatric care manager in your parent's community.

- The **National Guardianship Association** (*www.guardianship .org*) provides information and resources for guardians, as well as questions and answers about the basics of setting up a guardianship and the various terminology that applies across the country.

PENSIONS AND INCOME OPTIONS

- The **Pension Rights Center** (*www.pensionrights.org*) offers information regarding retirement plans and your rights under ERISA, as well as contact information for legal organizations and lawyers with expertise in legal issues relating to pension claims.
- The **Department of Labor** website (*www.dol.gov*) is another valuable resource for information on pension rights.
- The **Pension Benefit Guarantee Corporation** (*www.pbgc .gov*) is the organization that insures defined-benefit plans in the event the pension funds are mismanaged, so that beneficiaries are still guaranteed payments upon retirement.
- For information on licensed brokers in your parent's state, consult with the **North American Securities Administrators Association** (*www.nasaa.org*).

SOCIAL SECURITY AND OTHER BENEFITS

- Contact your local office of the **Social Security Administration** (SSA) for literature about Social Security benefits, or to ask specific questions about your own case (*www.ssa.gov*).
- The **National Organization of Social Security Claims Representatives** (NOSSCR) is an association of more than 3,300 attorneys and paralegals who represent Social Security claimants. Its website at *www.nosscr.org* contains information about Social Security benefits, federal policy issues,

and legal resources for claimants. Its telephone lawyer referral number is 1–800–431–2804.

HEALTH-CARE INSURANCE, MEDICAID, AND MEDICARE

- The ABA's **Commission on Law and Aging** has a consumer tool kit for health-care advance planning available at *www.abanet.org/aging*.
- The **Centers for Medicare and Medicaid Services** maintains a website at *www.cms.gov* that contains comprehensive information regarding Medicare and Medicaid. The website includes features such as detailed explanations of coverage under the two programs, frequently asked questions, and a list of publications, many of which can be accessed online.
- **Medicare** also maintains a consumer website at *www.medicare.gov*, which provides a wealth of information about Medicare, Medigap, Medicaid, and nursing homes. The website also has a "Medigap Compare" feature. This is an interactive tool for Medicare beneficiaries to help find the insurance companies in each state that sell Medigap plans. You can also contact Medicare by calling 1–800–MEDICARE.
- Visit the website of the **National Clearinghouse for Long-Term Care Information** at *www.longtermcare.gov*. The U.S. Department of Health and Human Services developed this site to provide information on both public and private resources available to help plan and pay for future long-term-care needs.
- The **Federal Long Term Care Insurance Program**'s website (*www.ltcfeds.com*) offers helpful information about general long-term-care insurance programs and features.
- **America's Health Insurance Plans** offers a guide to long-term-care insurance, which can be found by visiting their website at *www.ahip.org*.

HOUSING OPTIONS AND COMMUNITY-BASED SERVICES

- The **National Citizens' Coalition for Nursing Home Reform** provides information regarding the rights of nursing home residents, including how to contact the state long-term-care ombudsman. It also publishes an excellent resource to help you with the care-planning process entitled *Nursing Homes: Getting Good Care There.* It is available by writing to the organization at 1424 Sixteenth Street NW, Suite 202, Washington, DC 20036, by calling 202–332–2275, or by visiting its website at *www.nccnhr.org.* The NCCNHR also provides information on the federal Residents' Bill of Rights.

- State or local agencies on aging frequently prepare directories or guides on housing options for older persons and persons with disabilities. You can find your local agency's number in your local telephone book.

- The **American Association of Homes and Services for the Aging** (*www.aahsa.org*).

- The **Continuing Care Accreditation Commission** (*www. carf.org*).

- **National Energy Assistance Referral (NEAR)** provides information about applying for the Low Income Home Energy Assistance Program (LIHEAP). Call its toll-free number, 1–866–674–6327, or visit *http://liheap.ncat.org/referral.htm.*

- The **National Aging in Place Council** (*www.naipc.org*) offers an online forum targeted at helping individuals continue to live in the housing of their choice. This includes support for health-care, financial, legal, design, and building concerns. Its website lists many resources for those who decide to age in place.

- **SeniorHousing.net** (*www.seniorhousing.net*) is a part of Realtor.com, a site that offers information about types of senior housing (ranging from independent living to continuing care, assisted living, and more), as well as an online tool to help you discern which housing option may be best for you or your loved one. The site also offers information about financing, and a "Health and Wellness" section.

- The **Home and Community Based Services Clearinghouse for the Community Living Exchange Collaborative** (*www.hcbs.org*) provides state-by-state information on community-based services and providers.
- Your state Long-Term Care Ombudsman Program will likely be a helpful advocate and resource for your parent and family if your parent resides in a long-term-care facility. To find your local office, visit *www.ltcombudsman.org*. This site also offers general information on residents' rights, and a library of resources and links.
- The **Multifamily Housing Clearinghouse (MFHC)** is a source of information on subsidized housing initiatives, programs, and policies of HUD's Office of Multifamily Housing Programs. It can be reached by visiting *http://www.hud.gov/offices/hsg/mfh/hc/mfhc.cfm* or by calling 1–800–685–8470.

DRIVING AND TRANSPORTATION RESOURCES

- For information on finding an occupational therapist in your area to help determine what changes could be made to your parent's car to facilitate driving, contact the **American Occupational Therapy Association** (*www.aota.org*).
- Organizations such as the **National Safety Council** (*www.nsc.org*) and the **American Automobile Association (AAA)** (*www.aaa.com*) offer driving-related courses. In many cases, upon completion of the course, your parent may receive a 10-percent discount on his or her auto insurance.
- For information on driving safety and alternative methods of transportation, visit *www.seniordrivers.org* or contact **Alzheimer's, Dementia & Driving** (*http://www.thehartford.com/*

alzheimers/), which provides specific resources for families confronting dementia and driving.

- The **American Medical Association** and the **National Highway Traffic Safety Association** have developed a guide to help doctors work with older drivers. It may be useful in preparing for any discussions and finding alternatives to driving (*http://www.ama-assn.org/ama/pub/category/10791.html*).

ELDER ABUSE

- The **National Center on Elder Abuse**, which is administered by the federal Administration on Aging, has a wealth of information and resources available on elder abuse (*www.ncea.aoa.gov*). Its website outlines various state-by-state resources and additional warning signs and preventative measures.
- If your parent has been the victim of consumer fraud, you and your parent should consider contacting the **Federal Trade Commission** (*www.ftc.gov*) and your state attorney general's office. You can find your state attorney general's contact information by visiting the website of the National Association of Attorneys General at *www.naag.org*.
- For general information on consumer protection and information on how to contact your state consumer protection agency, visit *http://consumeraction.gov*.
- The **National Fraud Information Center** can answer questions relating to consumer fraud and tell you where to report fraud and file complaints (*www.fraud.org*).
- The **Identity Theft Resource Center** (*www.idtheftcenter .org*) outlines the steps you can take to prevent identity theft and what to do if your parent is a victim.

APPENDIX B

Health-Care
Advance Directive

CAUTION

This health-care advance directive is a general form provided for your convenience. While it meets the legal requirements of most states, it may or may not fit the requirements of your particular state. Many states have special forms or special procedures for creating health-care advance directives. If your state's law does not clearly recognize this document, it may still provide an effective statement of your wishes if you cannot speak for yourself. The directions for filling out the form are provided first, followed by the form itself on page 282.

SECTION 1
Health-Care Agent

Print your full name in this spot as the principal or creator of the health-care advance directive.

Print the full name, address, and telephone number of the person (age eighteen or older) whom you appoint as your health-care agent. Appoint *only* a person with whom you have talked, and whom you trust to understand and carry out your values and wishes.

Many states limit the persons who can serve as your agent. If you want to meet all existing state restrictions, *do not* name any of the following as your agent, since some states will not allow them to act in this role:

- your health-care providers, including physicians;
- staff of health-care facilities or nursing care facilities providing you with care;
- guardians of your finances (also called conservators);

- employees of government agencies financially responsible for your care;
- any person serving as an agent for ten or more persons.

SECTION 2
Alternative Agents

It is a good idea to name alternate agents in case your first agent is not available. Of course, only appoint alternates if you fully trust them to act faithfully as your agent and if you have talked to them about serving as your agent. Print the appropriate information in this section. You can name as many alternate agents as you wish, but place them in the order in which you wish them to serve.

SECTION 3
Effective Date and Durability

This sample document is effective if and when you cannot make health-care decisions. Your agent and your doctor determine whether you are in this condition. Some state laws include specific procedures for determining your decision-making ability. If you wish, you can include other effective dates or other criteria for determining that you cannot make health-care decisions (such as requiring two physicians to evaluate your decision-making ability). You also can state that the power will end at some later date or upon some event before your death.

In any case, you have the *right to revoke* (i.e., take away) the agent's authority at any time. To revoke, notify your agent or health-care provider orally or in writing. If you revoke, it is best to notify in writing both your agent and physician and anyone else who has a copy of the directive. Also destroy the health-care advance directive document itself.

SECTION 4
Agent's Powers

This grant of power is intended to be as broad as possible. Unless you set limits, your agent will have authority to make any decision you could to consent to or stop any type of health care. Even under this broad grant of authority, your agent still must honor your wishes and directions, communicated by you in any manner now or in the future.

To specifically limit or direct your agent's power, you must complete Part II of the advance directive, section 6, on page 286.

SECTION 5
Instructions About End-of-Life Treatment

The subject of end-of-life treatment is particularly important to many people. In this section, you can give general or specific instructions on the subject. The four main paragraphs are alternative options—**choose only one.** Write your desires or instructions in your own words if you choose paragraph four. If you choose paragraph two, you have three additional options, from which you can choose one, two, or all three. If you are satisfied with your agent's knowledge of your values and wishes and you do not want to include instructions in the form, initial the first option and do not give instructions on the form.

Any instructions you give here will guide your agent. If you do appoint an agent, the agent will guide any health-care providers or surrogate decision makers who must make a decision for you if you cannot do so yourself.

DIRECTIVE IN YOUR OWN WORDS
If you would like to state your wishes about end-of-life treatment in your own words instead of choosing one of the options provided, you can do so in this section. Since people sometimes have different opinions about whether nutrition and hydration should be refused or stopped under certain circumstances, be sure to address this issue clearly in your directive. **Nutrition and hydration** means food and fluids administered through a nasogastric tube or a tube into your stomach, intestines, or veins, and does not include nonintrusive methods such as spoon-feeding or moistening of the lips and mouth.

Some states allow the stopping of nutrition and hydration only if you expressly authorize it. If you are creating your own directive and you do not want nutrition and hydration, state this clearly.

SECTION 6

Any Other Health-Care Instructions or Limitations or Modifications of the Agent's Power

In this section, you can provide instructions about other health-care issues that are not related to end-of-life treatment or nutrition and hydration. For example, you might want to include your wishes about issues such as nonemergency surgery, elective medical treatments, or admission to a nursing home. Again, be careful in these instructions not to place any limitation on your agent that you do not intend. For example, while you may not want to be admitted to a nursing home, imposing such a restriction may make things difficult for your agent if other options are not available.

You also may limit your agent's powers in any way you wish. For example, you can instruct your agent to refuse any specific types of treatment that are against your religious beliefs or unacceptable to you for any other reasons. These might include blood transfusions, electroconvulsive therapy, sterilization, abortion, amputation, psychosurgery, or admission to a mental institution. Some states limit your agent's authority to consent to or to refuse some of these procedures, regardless of your health-care advance directive.

Be very careful about stating limitations, because the specific circumstances surrounding future health-care decisions are impossible to predict. If you do not want limitations, simply write "No limitations."

SECTION 7

Protection of Third Parties Who Rely on the Agent

In most states, health-care providers cannot be forced to follow the directions of your agent if they object. However, most states also require providers to help transfer you to another provider who is willing to honor your instructions. To encourage compliance with the health-care advance directive, this paragraph states that providers who rely in good faith on the agent's statements and decisions will not be held civilly liable for their actions.

SECTION 8
Donation of Organs at Death

In this section, you can state your intention to donate bodily organs and tissues at death. If you do not wish to be an organ donor, initial the first option. The second option authorizes the donation of any or all organs and parts. The third option allows you to donate only those organs or tissues you specify. Consider mentioning the heart, liver, lungs, kidneys, pancreas, intestine, corneas, bones, skin, heart valves, tendons, ligaments, and saphenous vein. Finally, you may limit the use of your organs by *crossing out* any of the four listed purposes that you do not want to authorize (transplant, research, therapy, or education). If you do not cross out any of these options, your organs may be used for any of these purposes.

SECTION 9
Nomination of Guardian

Appointing a health-care agent helps to avoid the need for a court-appointed guardian for health-care decision making. However, if a court becomes involved for any reason, this paragraph expressly names your agent to serve as guardian. A court does not have to follow your nomination, but normally it will honor your wishes unless there is good reason to override your choice.

SECTION 10
Administrative Provisions

These items address miscellaneous matters that could affect the implementation of your health-care advance directive. Required state procedures for signing this kind of document vary. Some require only a signature, while others have very detailed witnessing requirements. Some states simply require notarization.

The procedure set forth in this book is likely to be far more complex than it would be in your state, because this book combines the formal requirements from virtually every state. Adhere to this book if you do not know your state's requirements and if you want to meet the signature requirements of virtually every state.

1. **Sign and date the document** in the presence of two witnesses and a notary. Your witnesses should know your identity personally and be able to declare that you appear to be of sound mind and under no duress or undue influence.

   In order to meet the different witnessing requirements of most states, do *not* have the following people witness your signature:

   - Anyone you have chosen to make health-care decisions on your behalf (e.g., an agent or alternative decision maker).
   - Your treating physician, health-care provider, health facility operator, or an employee of any of these.
   - Insurers or employees of your life/health insurance provider.
   - Anyone financially responsible for your health-care costs.
   - Anyone related to you by blood, marriage, or adoption.
   - Anyone entitled to any part of your estate under an existing will or by operation of law, or anyone who will benefit financially from your death. Your creditors should not serve as witnesses.

2. **Have your signature notarized.** Some states permit notarization as an alternative to witnessing. Doing both witnessing and notarization is more than most states require, but doing both will meet the execution requirements of most states. This form includes a typical notary statement, but it is wise to check state law in case your state requires a special form of notary acknowledgment.

HEALTH-CARE ADVANCE DIRECTIVE
Part i

APPOINTMENT OF HEALTH-CARE AGENT

1. HEALTH-CARE AGENT

I, _____ (Principal), hereby appoint

_____ (Agent's Name)

_____ (Address)

_____ (Home Phone #)

_____ (Work Phone #)

as my Agent to make health- and personal-care decisions for me
as authorized in this document.

2. ALTERNATE AGENT

If

- I revoke my Agent's authority; or
- My Agent becomes unwilling or unavailable to act; or
- My Agent is my spouse and I become legally separated or di-
  vorced,

I name the following (each to act alone and successively, in the
order named) as alternates to my Agent:

A. First Alternate Agent _____

Address _____

Telephone _____

B. Second Alternate Agent _____

Address _____

Telephone _____

3. Effective Date and Durability

By this document, I intend to create a health-care advance directive. It is effective upon, and only during, any period in which I cannot make or communicate a choice regarding a particular health-care decision. My Agent, attending physician, and any other necessary experts should determine that I am unable to make choices about health care.

4. Agent's Powers

I give my Agent full authority to make health-care decisions for me. My Agent shall follow my wishes as known to my Agent either through this document or through other means. In interpreting my wishes, I intend my Agent's authority to be as broad as possible, except for any limitations I state in this form. In making any decision, my Agent shall try to discuss the proposed decision with me to determine my desires if I am able to communicate in any way. If my Agent cannot determine the choice I would want, then my Agent shall make a choice for me based upon what my Agent believes to be in my best interests.

Unless specifically limited by Section 6, below, my Agent is authorized as follows:

A. To consent to, to refuse, or to withdraw consent to any and all types of health care. "Health care" means any care, treatment, service, or procedures to maintain, diagnose, or otherwise affect my physical or mental condition. It includes, but is not limited to, artificial respiration, nutritional support and hydration, medication, and cardiopulmonary resuscitation;

B. To have access to medical records and information to the same extent that I am entitled, including the right to disclose the contents to others as appropriate for my health care;

C. To authorize my admission to or discharge from (even against medical advice) any hospital, nursing home, residential care, assisted-living facility, or similar facility or service;

D. To contract on my behalf for any health-care-related service or facility, without incurring personal financial liability for such contracts;

E. To hire and fire medical, social service, and other support personnel responsible for my care;

F. To authorize or refuse to authorize any medication or procedure intended to relieve pain, even though such use may lead to physical damage or addiction or hasten the moment of (but not intentionally cause) my death.

G. To make anatomical gifts of part or all of my body for medical purposes, authorize an autopsy, and direct the disposition of my remains to the extent permitted by law;

H. To take any other action necessary to do what I authorize here, including (but not limited to) granting any waiver or release from liability required by any hospital, physician, or other health-care provider; signing any documents relating to refusals of treatment or the leaving of a facility against medical advice; and pursuing any legal action in my name at the expense of my estate to force compliance with my wishes as determined by my Agent, or to seek actual or punitive damages for the failure to comply.

Part II

INSTRUCTIONS ABOUT HEALTH CARE

5. MY INSTRUCTIONS ABOUT END-OF-LIFE TREATMENT

(Initial only ONE of the following FOUR main statements):

1. _____ NO SPECIFIC INSTRUCTIONS. My Agent knows my values and wishes, so I do not wish to include any specific instructions here.

2. _____ DIRECTIVE TO WITHHOLD OR WITHDRAW TREATMENT. Although I greatly value life, I also believe that at some point life has such diminished value that medical treatment should be stopped, and I should be allowed to die. Therefore, I do not want to receive treatment, including nutrition and hydration, when the treatment will not provide me with a meaningful quality of life.

(If you initialed this paragraph, also initial any or all of the following three statements with which you agree):

By this I mean that I do not want my life prolonged . . .

_____ . . . if the treatment will leave me in a condition of permanent unconsciousness, such as in an irreversible coma or a persistent vegetative state.

_____ . . . if the treatment will leave me with no more than some consciousness and in an irreversible condition of complete, or near complete, loss of ability to think or communicate with others.

_____ . . . if the treatment will leave me with no more than some ability to think or communicate with others, and the likely risks and burdens of treatment outweigh the expected benefits. Risks, burdens, and benefits include consideration of length of life, quality of life, financial costs, and my personal dignity and privacy.

3. _____ DIRECTIVE TO RECEIVE TREATMENT. I want my life to be prolonged as long as possible, no matter what my quality of life.

4. _____ DIRECTIVE ABOUT END-OF-LIFE TREATMENT IN MY OWN WORDS:

_____

_____

_____

_____

6. ANY OTHER HEALTH-CARE INSTRUCTIONS OR LIMITATIONS OR MODIFICATIONS OF MY AGENT'S POWERS

_____

_____

_____

_____

7. PROTECTION OF THIRD PARTIES WHO RELY ON MY AGENT

No person who relies in good faith on any representation by my Agent or Alternative Agent(s) shall be liable to me, my estate, or my heirs or assigns for recognizing the Agent's authority.

8. DONATIONS OF ORGANS AT DEATH

Upon my death:
(*Initial one*):

____ I do *not* wish to donate any organs, tissues, or parts, OR
____ I give *any* needed organs, tissues, or parts, OR
____ I give *only* the following organs, tissues, or parts: (*please specify*)

_____

_____

My gift (if any) is for the following purposes (*cross out any of the following you do not want*):
- Transplant
- Research
- Therapy
- Education

9. NOMINATION OF GUARDIAN

If a guardian of my person should for any reason need to be appointed, I nominate my Agent (or his or her alternate then authorized to act), named above.

10. ADMINISTRATIVE PROVISIONS

(*All apply*)
- I revoke any prior health-care advance directive.
- This health-care advance directive is intended to be valid in any jurisdiction in which it is presented.
- A copy of this advance directive is intended to have the same effect as the original.
- I intend for the person acting as my health-care agent pursuant to this document to be treated as I would be with respect to my rights regarding the use and disclosure of my individually identifiable health information or other medical records. This authority applies to any information governed by the Health Insurance Portability and Accountability Act of 1996 (aka HIPAA), 42 USC 1320d and 45 CFR 160–164.

SIGNING THE DOCUMENT

BY SIGNING HERE, I INDICATE THAT I UNDERSTAND THE CONTENTS OF THIS DOCUMENT AND THE EFFECT OF THIS GRANT OF POWERS TO MY AGENT.

I sign my name to this Health-Care Advance Directive on this _____ day of _____, 2___.

My Signature

_____

My Name

_____

My current home address

_____

_____

WITNESS STATEMENT

I declare that the person who signed or acknowledged this document is personally known to me, that he/she signed or acknowledged this health-care advance directive in my presence, and that he/she appears to be of sound mind and under no duress, fraud, or undue influence.

I am not:
- the person appointed as agent by this document;
- the patient's health-care provider;
- an employee of the patient's health-care provider;
- financially responsible for the person's health care;
- related to the principal by blood, marriage, or adoption; or
- to the best of my knowledge, a creditor of the principal or entitled to any part of his/her estate under a will or by operation of law.

Witness #1

Signature_____

Date_____

Print Name _____

Home Address _____

Telephone _____

Witness #2

Signature_____

Date_____

Print Name _____

Home Address _____

Telephone _____

Notarization

STATE of _____. My Commission Expires:

COUNTY OF _____.

On this _____ day of _____, 2_____,

the said _____, _____ (NOTARY PUBLIC)
known to me (or satisfactorily
proven to be the person named
in the foregoing instrument)
personally appeared before me,
a Notary Public, within or for
the State and County aforesaid,
and acknowledged that he or she
freely and voluntarily executed
the same for the purposes stated therein.

INDEX

401(k)s, 84–88
AARP, 266
ABA Commission on Law and
     Aging, 272
abuse. *See* elder abuse
activities of daily living (ADLs)
     assessment of, 2, 22–23
     assistance with, 113, 165, 167
     difficulty with, 2, 148
     long-term care insurance and,
          141, 143
     nursing home placement and,
          189
adult day care centers, 170–171
adult protective services, 224–225
advance directives, 34–50
     discussing with parents, 12–13
     for hospital visitors, 51
     resources, 270
agency services. *See* community-
     based services
age-restricted communities, 186
aging in place, 148–171
     adult day care centers, 170–171
     community-based services,
          156–171
     home equity conversion plans,
          151–156
     home-health-care services,
          164–167
     homemaker services, 166–167
     medication management
          services, 167–169

naturally occurring retirement
     communities (NORCs),
     149–150
     personal attendants, 166–167
     physical changes to home, 150
     resources, 150–151, 271
     respite care, 169–170
     reverse mortgages, 152–155
     sale-leasebacks, 154
     services required, 150
Alliance of Retired Americans, 268
Alzheimer's Association, 270
American Association of Homes
     and Services for the Aging,
     273
Americans for Better Care of the
     Dying, 270
America's Health Insurance Plans,
     272
annuities, 87, 94–95
anxiety, 248–249
area agencies on aging (AAAs),
     157, 267
assessment
     of activities of daily living, 2
     for care plans, 22–23
     of mental capacity, 1–2
assisted living communities, 173,
     175–180
     complaints, 179
     continuing care retirement
          communities compared to, 181
     contracts, 177–178

assisted living communities (*cont.*)
eviction from, 179–180
negotiated risk, 177
payment contracts, 174–175
payment options, 176
quality indicators, 178
regulations, 179, 180
attorneys
elder law, 31–34
estate planning, 33–34

board-and-care homes. *See* assisted
living communities
burnout of caregivers, 260–263

care plans, 21–30
assessment by professionals,
22–23
division of labor, 25–26
implementing, 25–26
parental input, 24, 25
caregivers
abusive, 218–219
burnout/compassion fatigue,
259–263
division of labor, 25–26
long-distance, 27–28
resources for, 261–263, 269
role of, 5–9
self-care, 259–263
Centers for Medicare and
Medicaid Services, 272
charity fraud, 242. *See also*
consumer fraud
cognitive decline
assessment of, 1–2, 22–23
capacity for decision making
and, 17–18, 105
lessening effects of, 19
medical evaluation of, 19
signs of, 1–5

communication with parents
about abuse, 220–221
about caregiver fatigue, 262–263
about driving, 12
about end-of-life issues, 12–13
about financial issues, 13–14
about health care, 12–13
about legal issues, 13
about living options, 11–12
barriers to communication,
15–17
events leading to discussions, 10
parental resistance to, 15–17
planning for future needs, 9–11
community-based services,
156–171
adult day care centers,
170–171
agency services compared to
non-agency, 158–161
home-health-care services,
164–167
homemaker services, 166–167
medication management
services, 167–169
personal attendants, 166–167
regulations and complaints,
161–163
resources, 274
respite care, 169–170
compassion fatigue, 260–263
competency
compared to capacity, 24
conservatorship and, 63
guardianship and, 70, 71
congregate-care homes. *See*
assisted living communities
conservatorship, 63. *See also*
guardianship
consumer fraud, 239–247
identity theft, 240, 241–242,
243, 245–246, 275
legal remedies, 244–245

prevention of, 243–244
resources, 246–247, 275
Continuing Care Accreditation
Commission, 273
continuing-care retirement
communities (CCRCs),
173–174, 180–185
assisted living communities
compared to, 181
complaints, 185
contracts, 181, 185
payment contracts, 174–175
regulations, 180
selection criteria, 182–184
credit freeze laws, 245–246
credit monitoring services, 246
credit reports, 245–246

daily activities. *See* activities of
daily living (ADLs)
decision makers, surrogate, 24. *See
also* powers of attorney;
surrogate decision-making
decision making, 21–26
best-interest, 98
capacity for, 17–18, 24
under health-care surrogacy
laws, 51–52, 57–58, 104–105
medical, 101–107
powers of attorney, 24, 43
state standards, 98
substituted-judgement, 98
defined-benefit plans, 83–88
Department of Labor, 271
Department of Veterens Affairs
(DVA), 82–83, 268
depression, 248–251
divorce
employee health insurance and,
138–139
pension benefits and, 87–88
Social Security and, 77

DNR (do not resuscitate) orders,
49–50
documents, finding, 44, 74–76
driving
discussions about, 12
legal interventions, 212–214
old age and, 207–214
resources, 274
driving courses for seniors,
209–210
durable powers of attorney, 35

elder abuse, 215–247
consumer fraud, 239–247
criminal prosecution of,
227–232
discussing with parents,
220–221
financial exploitation,
233–239
at home, 223
in institutions, 221–222
interventions for, 244–245
legal definitions, 222–223
legal interventions for, 223–232,
234–235
mandated and non-mandated
reporters, 231–232
motives for, 232
prevention of, 219–222,
238–239, 243–244
registry, 160
resources, 218, 275
signs of, 216–219, 221–222,
233–234
elder law attorneys, 31–34,
268–270
financial management and,
76–77
Eldercare Locator, 267
Employee Benefits Security
Administration, 85

employee stock ownership plans,
    84–88
end-of-life care, 12–13, 270
estate planning attorneys, 33–34

family members
    financial responsibilities, 7–9
    legal responsibilities, 7
Federal Long Term Care Insurance
    Program, 272
filial responsibility laws, 8–9
finances, 98. *See also* consumer
    fraud; financial exploitation
    assistance with, 76–77
    discussing with parents, 13–14
    home equity conversion plans,
        151–156
    liability fir mismanagement or
        exploitation, 98–99
    and representative payees,
        59–60
    responsibilities of family
        members, 7–9
    responsibility of family members,
        73–74
financial exploitation, 233–239
    by guardian or agent, 236
    legal interventions for, 233–235
    prevention of, 238–239
    by service providers, 236
    signs of, 233–239
financial services fraud, 242. *See
    also* consumer fraud
FirstGov for Seniors, 268
Folstein Mini Mental State
    Examination, 2
fraudulent conveyance laws,
    Medicaid and, 145–146
friends as caregivers, 50–54
funeral industry fraud, 242. *See
    also* consumer fraud

geriatric care managers
    fees of, 29
    locating, 29
    role of, 28–30
geriatric care plan, 21–26
granny cams, 170
guardian ad litem (GAL), 65, 68
guardians
    co-guardians, 70
    decision making, 69–70
    exploitation by, 236
    payment of, 70
    removal of, 71
    requirements of, 68, 70
guardianship
    compared to conservatorship,
        61–62, 63
    of the estate, 63
    legal assistance, 68
    legal expenses, 69
    length of, 70
    limited, 62
    and living wills, 48–49
    necessity of, 67–68, 105
    of the person, 63
    plenary, 62
    presumed competency, 64
    proceedings, 64–65
    professional, 52–54
    qualifications for, 61–62
    removal of, 236
    resources, 271
    response of family members, 66
    response of older persons, 66
    and revocation of powers of
        attorney, 43–44
    rights of older persons, 65
    standby, 64
    and state law, 71–72
    successor, 64
    temporary, 64
guardianship hearings, 69

Handbook for Mortals, 270
health care
    advance directives, 34–51, 270
    advance planning for, 272
    discussing with parents, 12–13
    government-sponsored
        insurance, 108–131
    Health Insurance Portability and
        Accountability Act, 102–103
    informed consent, 102
    medical appointments, 106
    Medicare, 109–125
    patient confidentiality,
        101–107
    privacy rights and, 101–107
health insurance fraud, 242. *See
    also* consumer fraud
Health Insurance Portability and
    Accountability Act, 102–103
Health Line, 270
Health-Care Advance Directive,
    276–289
health-care decisions, 101–107
health-care fraud, 242. *See also*
    consumer fraud
health-care insurance
    government-sponsored, 108–131
    long-term care insurance,
        139–145, 272
    Medicaid, 125–131, 272
    Medicare, 109–125
    Medigap insurance policies, 123,
        133–136, 272
    private supplemental,
        131–133
    retiree group health benefit
        plans, 136–139
health-care surrogacy, 57–58,
    104–105
hoarding, 255
home equity conversion plans,
    151–156

home equity loans, 154–155
home repair fraud, 241–242. *See
    also* consumer fraud
home sale plans, 155
home-health-care services,
    164–167
homemaker services, 166–167
hospice care, 115–117, 270
hospital discharge planners, 194
hospital insurance. *See* Medicare,
    Part A; Medicare, Part C
hospital visitors
    advance directives, 51
    restrictions, 106–107
housing options
    age-restricted communities,
        186
    aging in place, 148–156,
        273
    assisted living communities,
        173, 174–180
    continuing-care retirement
        communities, 173–175,
        180–185
    discussions about, 11–12
    homesharing, 156
    independent living communities,
        173, 174
    nursing homes, 188–204
    resources, 273–274
    subsidized housing, 185–188,
        274
housing with supportive services.
    See assisted living
    communities

identity theft, 240–243, 245–246,
    275
Identity Theft Resource Center,
    275
illness, serious and fatal, 270

incapacity. *See also* cognitive
    decline; mental capacity
  advance directives, 34–50
  legal preparedness for, 31–55
  with no surrogate, 57–58
  powers of attorney, 34–48
income, sources of
  accessing, 96–98
  annuities, 87, 94–95
  home equity conversion plans,
    151–156
  home equity loans, 154–155
  home sale plans, 154
  information and documentation
    retrieval, 74–76
  life insurance, 95–96
  pensions, 83–88, 269
  retirement plans, 83–88, 267
  reverse mortgages, 152–155
  sale-leasebacks, 154
  Social Security benefits, 77–79
  trusts, 88–94
  veteran's benefits, 82–83
incompetency. *See* mental capacity
independent living communities,
    173
individual retirement accounts
    (IRAs), 84–88
informed consent, 102
in-home assistance, 148–171
  agency services compared to
    non-agency, 158–161
  hiring, 158–161
  home-health-care services,
    164–167
  homemaker services, 166–167
  medication management
    services, 167–169
  regulations and complaints,
    161–163
  resources, 150–151
  respite care, 169–170

instrumental activities of daily
    living (IADLs), 2, 22–23
internet scams, 243
investment fraud, 242. *See also*
    consumer fraud
IRAs (individual retirement
    accounts), 84–88
irrevocable trusts, 91–93
isolation, 253–254

joint and survivor annuity, 87

Last Acts, 270
legal assistance
  appealing Medicare decisions,
    124–125
  filing petition for guardianship,
    68–69
  managing income and assets,
    76–77
  planning for incapacity, 31–34
  planning for long-term care, 76
  resources, 268–269
Legal Guide for Americans Over 50,
    268
legal responsibilities
  of family members, 7
  od caregivers, 9
life insurance, 95–96
limited guardianship, 62
living wills
  compared to "do not resuscitate"
    orders, 49–50
  and guardianship, 48–49
  and powers of attorney, 48–49
long-term care. *See also* assisted
    living communities;
    continuing-care retirement
    communities (CCRCs);
    nursing homes

Medicare and, 113
  planning for, 76
  resources, 272
long-term care insurance,
  139–145, 272
long-term care ombudsman,
  200–201, 202, 222
lottery fraud, 241. *See also*
  consumer fraud

Medicaid, 125–131
  annuities and, 94
  appeals, 131
  asset transfer limitations, 130
  assistance with Medicare costs,
    123
  claims, 131
  compared to Medicare, 125
  estate recovery program, 129
  fraudulent conveyance laws,
    145–146
  home care, 129–130
  irrevocable trusts and, 90–91, 93
  nursing home care and,
    128–129
  nursing homes and, 189
  qualifications for, 125–127
  resources, 272
  special needs trusts and, 92–93
medical appointments, 106
Medicare, 109–125
  appeals, 124–125
  claims, 123–124
  compared to Medicaid, 125
  custodial care, 113–114
  enrollment, 121–122
  home health-care, 114–115
  hospice care, 115–117
  inpatient care, 110, 111–117
  medical equipment, 117–120
  Medicare Advantage Plan, 110

Medicare Savings Programs, 123
  outpatient care, 110
  outpatient services, 117–120
  Part A, 110, 111–117, 122
  Part B, 110, 117–120, 122
  Part C, 110, 120, 122
  Part D, 110, 120–121, 122
  physician's services, 110
  prescription drug coverage,
    110–111
  resources, 272
  respite care, 116–117
  skilled nursing care, 111–117
  Supplemental Medical
    Insurance, 117–120
Medicare Advantage Plan, 110
Medicare Savings Programs, 123
medication management services,
  167–169
Medigap insurance policies, 123,
  133–136, 272
mental capacity. *See also* cognitive
  decline; incapacity
  assessment of, 2, 22–23
  and decision making, 17–18
  signs of decline, 1–5
mental health issues, 248–258
  anxiety, 248–249
  depression, 248–251
  legal remedies, 251
  self neglect, 252–258
mental health resources, 270
mortgage fraud, 242. *See also*
  consumer fraud
Multifamily Housing Clearing
  House, 187

National Academy of Certified
  Care Managers, 270–271
National Academy of Elder Law
  Attorneys, 268

National Aging in Place Council, 150–151, 273
National Alliance for Caregiving, 261, 269
National Alliance for the Mentally Ill (NAMI), 270
National Association of Professional Geriatric Care Managers, 270
National Center on Elder Abuse, 218
National Citizen's Coalition for Nursing Home Reform, 273
National Clearinghouse for Long-Term Care Information, 272
National Council on Aging, 268
National Family Caregivers Association, 261, 269
National Fraud Information Center, 275
National Guardianship Association, 271
National Hospice and Palliative Care Organization, 270
National Institute on Aging, 270
National Organization of Social Security Claims Representatives (NOSSCR), 271–272
naturally occurring retirement communities (NORCS), 149–150
negotiated risk, 177
neighbors as caregivers, 50–54
Nolo.com, 268
North American Securities Administration, 271
Nursing Home Compare, 190
nursing homes, 188–204, 273
  adjustment issues for all concerned, 193–198
  admission criteria, 189–190
  bed policies, 201
  complaints, 200–201
  contracts, 198–200
  expectations, 197
  fees of, 198–199
  inspection reports, 190
  medicaid and, 189
  patients' rights, 273
  pet rules, 196
  regulations, 198
  relocation stress, 194–195
  restraints used in, 201–203
  role of children, 197–198
  selection of, 190–192
  sexual assaults in, 204
  visitations, 197–198
Nursing Homes: Getting Good Care There, 273

Older Women's League, 268
orders of protection, 225–227

Partnership in Dying, 270
Patient Self-Determination Act, 45
Pension Benefits Guarantee Corporation, 271
Pension Rights Center, 86, 271
pensions, 83–88, 271
  defined-benefit plans, 83–84
  defined-contribution plans, 84–88
personal attendants, 166–167
personal-care homes. See assisted living communities
pets, 196
phishing scams, 243
planning for future needs, 9–11, 269
plenary guardianship, 62

poverty, compared to self neglect, 254
powers of attorney, 10, 24, 34–48
  co-agents, 37–38
  compared to durable powers of attorney, 35
  distribution of documents, 46
  duties of agent, 42–43
  finding documents, 44
  for health care, 36, 51–52, 104
  legal interventions in lieu of, 56–72
  and living wills, 48–49
  modification of, 41
  payment of agent, 44
  personal liability of agents, 48
  for property, 36–37
  revocation of, 41, 43
  selection of agent, 37–40
  springing clause, 44
  state requirements, 47
  statutory forms for, 35–36
  termination of, 236
predatory lending, 242. See also consumer fraud
privacy rights, health care, 101–107
profit sharing plans, 84–88
Public Housing Agency (PHA), 187

qualified domestic relations order (QDRO), 88

relocation stress, 194–195
representative payees, 59–60
respite care, 169–170
restraints used in nursing homes, 201–203
retirement benefits. See income, sources of

retirement planners, 269
retirement plans, 83–88
reverse mortgages, 152–155
revocable trusts, 91–92
routines, 22

sale-leasebacks, 154
self neglect, 252–258
  causes of, 252–253
  compared to poverty, 254
  environment and, 252–253
  interventions for, 255–258
  legal remedies, 256–258
  signs of, 254
SeniorHousing.net, 273
sexual assault, 204
Social Security Administration, 77–78, 79, 271
  and representative payees, 59–60
Social Security benefits, 77–79
  accessing, 97–98
  amount of, 78–79
  citizenship and, 78
  resources, 271–272
  Social Security Disability Insurance (SSDI), 79–80
  Supplemental Security Income (SSI), 81–82
Social Security Disability Insurance (SSDI), 79–80
Social Security Statements form, 78–79
special-needs trusts, 92–93
stay-away orders, 225–227
subsidized housing
  appeal of denial, 187
  complaints, 187–188
  cost of, 187
  eligibility requirements, 185–188
  resources, 274

Supplemental Security Income
    (SSI), 81–82
  annuities and, 94
surrogate decision-making, 24, 43,
    51–52, 57–58, 104–105
sweepstakes fraud, 241. *See also*
  consumer fraud

transportation, 274–275. *See also*
  driving
  alternatives to driving,
    211–212
trusts, 88–94
  advantages of, 89–90

disadvantages of, 90–91
types of, 91–93

U.S. Administration on Aging
    (AoA), 268

Values History Form, 38, 104,
    270
veteran's benefits, 82–83
viatical settlements, 95–96

wellness checks, 28

ABOUT THE AUTHORS

MARGUERITE ANGELARI is the Goedert Elder Law Professor & Director of the Elder Law Initiative and Elder Law Clinic at Loyola University Chicago. Professor Angelari's academic and advocacy efforts focus on adult guardianship, advance directives, elder abuse and neglect, long-term care, gender and aging, and disability law. She is the chair of the Aging and the Law Section of the Association of American Law Schools and a past president of the Illinois Chapter of the National Academy of Elder Law Attorneys. She recently received the Leonard Jay Schrager Award of Excellence from the Chicago Bar Association and Foundation for her efforts to improve access to justice for the less fortunate.

MARCIA SPIRA earned a PhD in clinical social work from the University of Chicago in 1982. She worked in hospitals and health care for many years, providing mental health services to individuals and families. She is currently an associate professor at the School of Social Work at Loyola University. Dr. Spira has published many articles on social work and health, and has received grants to conduct research on work with older adults and their families. She serves on the advisory board of the Elder Law Clinic at Loyola University and the board of the Gabe Miller Foundation, and directs the Institute for Intergenerational Study and Practice in the School of Social Work. Dr. Spira also has a private practice in which she works with individuals and couples.

For life's legal issues, turn to the experts at

THE AMERICAN BAR ASSOCIATION

THE AMERICAN BAR ASSOCIATION
Guide to Wills and Estates, Third Edition

On Sale 5/12/09
978-0-375-72299-8
$16.95/ $19.95 Can.

- Comprehensive guide to planning an estate, preparing a will or trust, and minimizing inheritance taxes

THE AMERICAN BAR ASSOCIATION
Complete Personal Legal Guide

978-0-375-72302-5
$22.95/ $25.95 Can.

- Advice on real estate, health care, home ownernship, retirement, wills & estates, and much more

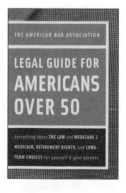

THE AMERICAN BAR ASSOCIATION
Legal Guide for Americans Over 50

978-0-375-72139-7
$16.95/ $22.95 Can.

- Everything from Social Security, Medicare and Medicaid benefits, and age discrimination, to retirement, estate planning, elder care, and disability rights

Available everywhere books are sold or at www.RandomHouse.com

Walla Walla
County Libraries